the coming out stories

the coming out stories

EDITORS:

SUSAN J. WOLFE
JULIA PENELOPE STANLEY

FOREWORD:
ADRIENNE RICH

PERSEPHONE PRESS
WATERTOWN, MASSACHUSETTS

The editors gratefully acknowledge permission to reprint from the following:

Cowrie for "Dragon Lady Speaks" by Liza Cowan; and "Peanut Butter Meets the Dragon Lady" by Alix Dobkin.

Focus for "Is This The Reward Of A Catholic Girlhood?" by Margaret Cruikshank; and "The Other Shoe" by Diane Stein.

Lesbian Connection and *Rubyfruit Readher* for "Dear Mom and Dad" by Wendy Judith Cutler.

Sinister Wisdom for "The Question She Put To Herself" by Maureen Brady.

"La Güera" by Cherrie Moraga Lawrence was originally written for, and will appear in, *A Woman To Woman Dialogue*, an anthology of essays by Third World feminists on their perspectives of the feminist movement. Co-edited by Gloria Anzaldua and Cherrie Moraga Lawrence. For more information, write: *A Woman To Woman Dialogue*, 2435 Jefferson Avenue, Apt. H, Berkeley, CA 94703.

"The Garden Variety Lesbian" by Barbara Grier also appears in *The Lesbian Path*, edited by Margaret Cruikshank. Angel Press, Monterey, CA, 1979.

Cover design by Maria von Brincken.
Text design by Pat McGloin.

First Edition. First Printing.

Library of Congress Cataloging in Publication Data

The Coming out stories.
    1. Lesbians—United States—Biography. I. Wolfe, Susan J., 1946-
II. Stanley, Julia Penelope, 1941-
HQ75.3.C65   306.7'6'0922   79-27073
ISBN 0-930436-03-2 pbk.

Acknowledgements

This is, conventionally, the place in a book where the authors/editors have an opportunity to acknowledge publicly all the individuals who contributed their ideas, resources, energies, and creativity to the book's existence. Traditionally, too, it is impossible to name everyone who has made a contribution. In this case, we are definitely in the "mainstream"! But, like everyone else, we're going to try to thank those wimmin who made this book a reality: First, Stephanie, Sandy, Cathy, Sarah, and Deidre, whose lively and intense conversation one Sunday morning made us understand the importance of our "coming out" stories; second, all of our writers, whose willingness to share their lives and to work closely with us throughout the preparation of the manuscript nurtured the vision and kept it alive for almost three years; third, the woman in California who wrote to us and said, "I wish I could write my coming out story for you, but I've only just now gotten up the courage to whisper the word *Lesbian* to myself in the mirror"; fourth, the secretaries in the Department of English at the University of Nebraska-Lincoln, Jo Garner, Carolyn Einspahr, and LeAnn Messing, who carefully typed the final manuscript version for us; fifth, the wimmin at Persephone Press who believed in the book enough to publish it; and, finally, Cynthia McGowan, who lived through the last-minute revisions with us, helpfully, quickly, and thoroughly, but not always cheerfully. There is, of course, the larger context of the Lesbian/Feminist movement, the growing community of wimmin whose names we don't always know and who we may never meet, but whose commitment to loving other wimmin and struggling to survive called this book forth. In every tangible sense, this is a womon-made book. It is dedicated to *all* of us.

Contents

Foreword

Adrienne Rich

The women gather their old flesh into sacks and carry it along the road. Under bridges in the middle of the night, they tell stories to each other. Each secret told gains a year.

"Why are you telling me this?" one asks.

"So I won't die."

They gather the secrets up like stones and put them in a rag bag, in a soup, under the house. The sack is as heavy as that which drowned the witch. It is with these very rocks that they were stoned once upon a time.

Once upon a time...

And no more.

Deena Metzger
from *The Book of Hags*[1]

As you open this book and begin to read, I would like you to hold an image in your mind. I would like to conjure this image before you like an immense wall-painting or an endless filmstrip: millions of letters and diaries of women, famous or obscure, going up in flames, sifting to ash; library stacks of biographies which do not tell the truths we most need to know; hundreds of the private papers of women acclaimed for their public contributions, sealed and placed under lock and key, or doled out by literary executors to those scholars who will accept censorship; dissertations, the work of years, which are forbidden to be published, read or quoted. As you read the stories in this book I would like you to think of those piles of ash, those cages behind which women's words,

[1] As excerpted in *Sinister Wisdom*, Vol I, 2.

lesbian words, lie imprisoned, those shelves of life-histories gutted of
their central and informing theme.

This is poverty. This is starvation. This is cultural imperialism—the
decision made by one group of people that another group shall be cut
off from their past, shall be kept from the power of memory, context,
continuity. This is why lesbians, meeting, need to tell and retell stories
like the ones in this book. In the absence of the books we needed, the
knowledge of women whose lives were like our own, an oral tradition—
here set down on paper—has sustained us. These stories, which bring us
together and which also confirm for each of us the path and meaning of
her individual journey, are like the oldest tribal legends: tales of birth
and rebirth, of death and rebirth; sometimes—too often—of death
without rebirth.

In the simplest telling profound questions are embedded: What
does it mean to *know,* or *not to know?* What does it mean to feel
passionately yet withhold the name of passion from those feelings? Why
did some of us assume from the first what it took others of us half a
lifetime to claim for our own? How does the outsiderhood, the
boundary-dwelling, of lesbians fuse with other outsiderhoods—of
poverty, of color, of physical difference—to forge a political vision? How
do these other outsiderhoods keep us apart, stranded on unexamined
shoals of difference?

And why is our common, "moral and ordinary"[2] love of women
not enough to create of us a mǣdenhēap—a band of female warriors, a
movement?[3] Why are we still so rent among ourselves? Why does the
vision tremble, fade, re-illume, blur, so that even committed friends,
seeking shared transformations, can do violence to each other?

Is it simply that the powerless, the disempowered, act out their
anger on each other instead of on their oppressors? Are women like all
other oppressed peoples (which of course include women) or is our
violence toward each other of a different order, stemming from
different sources?

I keep thinking about power. The intuitive flash of power that
"coming-out" can give: I have an indestructible memory of walking
along a particular block in New York City, the hour after I had
acknowledged to myself that I loved a woman, feeling invincible. For the
first time in my life I experienced sexuality as clarifying my mind instead
of hazing it over; that passion, once named, flung a long, imperative
beam of light into my future. I knew my life was decisively and forever
different; and that change felt to me like power. "Coming-out" over

[2]See Blanche Cook's pamphlet, *Women and Support Networks* (Out & Out Books, 476 Second
Street, Brooklyn, N.Y. 11215, 1979) p. 18.

[3]I am indebted to Julia Penelope and Cynthia McGowan for this Old English word. See their
paper, *"Woman* and *Wife*: Social/Semantic Shifts in English" (Department of English, University of
Nebraska, Lincoln, NE 68588) 1979.(To appear in *Papers in Linguistics* 12, 3-4.)

and over to others—to old friends, in the classroom, in print, at a poetry reading in the study hall of the girls' school I had long ago attended—each time, both fear and the renewal of that sense of power. And I ask myself, what is the fear about? that I can no longer "pass"? that I will see expressions alter, walls go up between my students and me, my old friends and me, some audience and me—that I will be dismissed, discredited, seen as monster?—or is it the fear of that old/new power, perhaps even some genetic imprinting of what was done to us of old, when we acted on our power?

I don't know. But I think "coming-out"—that first permission we give ourselves to name our love for women as love, to say, *I am a lesbian*, but also the successive "comings-out" to the world described in this book by so many writers—is connected with power, connects us with power, and until we believe that we have the right not merely to our love but to our power, we will continue to do harm among ourselves, fearing that power in each other and in ourselves.

The deprivation of our history is also a deprivation of power. The absence of names for our feelings is a deprivation of power. The desperate longing for mutuality, which leads us to try to bury our differences, is a deprivation of power, the power derived from difference, the twisting together of many strands into a stronger cable.

These stories both repeat and contradict each other, like other tribal tellings. They are incomplete; some of the truths we need are not here. The telling must go on. But here are raw materials for thinking more seriously about our lives, about what our life/work, as lesbians, is to be.

Adrienne Rich
November 1979

Introduction

Julia Penelope Stanley
and Susan J. Wolfe

This book exists because wimmin love wimmin. In spite of persistent denials from our culture that Lesbianism is real, each of us has found her way to the love of self and other wimmin. Claiming a Lesbian identity has been easy for some, a long and tortured journey for others; some wimmin have loved a womon and only years later decided that they are Lesbians, while others have discovered their Lesbianism and then set out to seek other Lesbians. However we have arrived at our Lesbian identity, whatever labels we have donned and shed in the process, we have eventually discovered ourselves in a society that denies our existence. We have made this book because we believe it should no longer be necessary for other wimmin to live so much of their lives in painful silence, thinking either that they are "the only one in the world" or that their love for wimmin is an abominable perversion.

Adrienne Rich, in her Introduction to *The Other Voice*, has spoken of the "unearthing [which] begins as much today or yesterday as somewhere in history." Her analogy to archeology is apt, because Lesbian culture has been concealed as effectively by the silence of the patriarchy as buried cities have been hidden beneath the earth. We, the wimmin who have participated in the creating of this book, offer it in the hope of unearthing our individual pasts and our common pasts, in the hope of bringing our lives to light at last. Our anthology represents that ongoing process of rediscovery of ourselves, our continuing reclamation of our lives and our strengths.

We have been silent for too long; we have been silenced for too long. For the first time in centuries, we can now hear the music of other Lesbian voices. As Susan Griffin has said in *Sinister Wisdom*:

We are a community of those coming to speech from silence. This is an elementary fact we share—a history of illiteracy, suffocations, spiritual and literal, burnings of body and work, the weight of the unutterable surrounding all of our lives. And in no way can this shared history be separated from what we write today, nor from our love of each others' voices.

As we emerge from the centuries of silence, it is the need to hear one another's voices and to share our pasts that motivates us to recount our individual "coming out" stories to each other.

For years, the coming out story has been among the first of the stories exchanged among wimmin, whether in the early morning intimacy of new lovers, the late night conversations that happen when everyone else has left a party, or in small groups of wimmin who are just beginning to know each other. Whatever the situation, exchanging coming out stories has been, and continues to be, a way of sharing oneself with other wimmin and getting to know something about their/our lives. In sharing our stories we open ourselves up to other wimmin and we make ourselves vulnerable. We tell our pasts to intensify the bonds between us and to tear away "the veil of silence" which separates us. Sharing our stories is a way of coming to know ourselves.

In March, 1976, Joan Larkin published her coming out story in Ms. In July, 1976, Ms. published letters responding to her narrative. Although most of the letters from readers were favorable, one reader criticized Larkin's coming out story, calling it a "confession" and asserting that becoming a Lesbian was the same as integrating one's sexuality is for any woman. She went on to claim that coming out is "more importantly a male homosexual phenomenon" because male homosexuals have experienced more "societal censure" than Lesbians. Her reason for objecting to a Lesbian coming out story was that she thought Lesbians should concentrate on the problems they share with all wimmin, rather than talking about their coming out processes. As attractive as her argument might be to some of us, however, the fact remains that we live in a heterosexist society that denies the existence of Lesbians, an atmosphere of such severe oppression (silence can be as oppressive as lies) that for many of us the *thought* of being a Lesbian was an impossibility. The barriers to self-realization for the Lesbian are so thoroughly entrenched in and supported by contemporary social values that the conceptual leap from heterosexually-oriented definitions to woman-identified relationships requires a highly creative imagination and a will to self-determinism that many wimmin cannot yet conceive of.

We are not implying that heterosexual wimmin *as* wimmin have not been silenced. Wimmin in general have been kept from audible, satisfying self-expression. Heterosexual wimmin, however, *are validated* by our culture. One may denounce the *roles* that define the limits of appropriate behaviors for heterosexual wimmin, but the fact remains that heterosexual wimmin get strokes from our society for their male orientation, while Lesbians are *not* rewarded for being womon-identified. One might argue, and others have, that heterosexuality is *learned*, socially-conditioned behavior. If heterosexuality were "natural," why would any society have to sell it so blatantly and persistently to the exclusion of other options? Many of our stories mention again and again the frustrations, the doubts, the feeling that "I am the only one in the world." If a womon likes males, she is not only assured that "there are others" like her, she is told that liking males is the only, the "natural," way to be. In contrast, Lesbians are told that they're "going through a phase" and "practicing for the 'real thing'," i.e., males.

> coming out at thirteen
> into the young arms of another woman
> ...
> the lies
> we didn't mean anything
> we were only practicing for the real thing
> [Constance Faye]

> Needless to say, Lesbianism was never presented to me as an alternative lifestyle. This, I believe, explains why I loved wimmin for such a long time without realizing the implications of my feelings.
> [Beverly J. Toll]

> I told my young fiancé I was a 'latent homosexual' but I was *sure* I would never do anything about it. (I didn't know how and who was there to do it with?) And then I tried to forget it.
> [C. J. Martin]

> No one told me I had a choice in terms of my sexuality. The only respectable and acceptable thing to be was a heterosexual.
> [Elana]

> I had fallen in love with my best friend ... It was seven more years before I managed to keep my vow to have a love affair with a woman.
> [C. J. Martin]

So strong is the pressure to relate to males that many wimmin, even those who have the courage to admit to themselves that their feelings for wimmin exist, even those who have a "label" for their feelings, continue to deny them, some for years.

> At 15, I decided I was just a *repressed* homo—I know this now because I
> documented the observation in my journal. It took me another 10 years to
> touch a woman!
> [Jean Carr]

And there are the other wimmin, mentioned only in passing in the
stories here, who have one or even several Lesbian experiences, but
then retreat into heterosexuality because the social pressures prove to
be too much for them to fight.

> I used to begin with my conscious recognition, at age twenty, that I could
> be sexually attracted to another woman. Since then I have realized that my
> lesbian herstory starts much earlier than that, although I did not recognize
> it as such at the time. In this way even our own personal herstories are
> denied us, because we do not have the information to identify them for
> what they are.
> [Anonymous]

As Sally Gearhart and Susan Leigh Star have each observed: "Lesbianism
is a miracle!" So many of us do find our way to each other, in spite of the
silence, in spite of the denial. We are each a miracle of self-creation and
self-validation! These are the stories of our survivors, the wimmin who
are coming home.

In our society, the becoming of a Lesbian is a leap into the void of
the inconceivable, that which is unutterable, that which has no name.
We are "coming to speech from silence." Our stories must be told, and
they must be heard.

> 'I began to write,' the dancer said, 'to allow the words which had
> accumulated in my throat to spill onto the page. They came in strange
> grunts, shapes, grimaces, at first, which I am just coming to recognize. The
> important thing,' she hoarsely whispered, 'is to speak. Don't be afraid to
> speak. Silence is death,' she said.
> [Deena Metzger, *Sinister Wisdom*, I, 2]

Adrienne Rich made the following comments in a letter to us
about the anthology:

> Living in the void of namelessness, as so many lesbians do, living in the
> silence, we must all have had intense experiences of immense significance
> which became unavailable to us because we had no names for them.
> When I think of the 'coming out process' I think of it as the beginning of
> naming, of memory, of making the connections between past and present
> and future that enable human beings to have an identity ('yesterday I was a
> woman, today I am a woman, tomorrow also I will be a woman';
> 'Yesterday I was ignorant, today I am learning a great deal, tomorrow I may
> be a teacher' etc.). A woman can say, to begin with, 'Yesterday I slept with
> a woman; today I am sleeping only with men; tomorrow I will definitely

be heterosexual' or, she may say, 'Yesterday I slept with men, and called myself heterosexual; today I am interested only in women; tomorrow I will be a lesbian.' But much depends on how she names her own past, how she remembers it, how she has been permitted to name and remember it given the limitations of language. There is still the possible denial that one is a lesbian even when deeply involved with women; the refusal to use the term, for all kinds of reasons.

Recognition of our feelings for other wimmin forces us to reevaluate and reinterpret our pasts. Acceptance of our Lesbianism, at whatever level, with whatever term is at hand, significantly alters our understanding of events in our lives up to that moment. Many of us lacked words to describe our experiences. Like other wimmin, we have "had the power of naming taken from us" (Mary Daly, *Beyond God the Father*). Because the words *Lesbian, Dyke,* describe what is an unimaginable reality in a patriarchal culture, some of us lacked even the word itself to describe our lives and feelings. Others attached it to stereotypical role-playing and could not assign it to ourselves. Still others among us refused to assign words to our actions and ideas. Silence takes many forms.

> I did not have the word for lesbian when I was nine years old in 1951 ... I did not know that I was coming out.
> [Janet Cooper]

> The day I accepted my label I still didn't know the word lesbian. The label I accepted was homosexual.
> [C. J. Martin]

> Gay-Lesbian-Dyke. These terms represent the changing self-image I experienced in the process of coming out.
> [Patricia E. Hand]

In fact, because the relationship between naming oneself and the processes involved in "coming out" is so clear, we have organized the stories in the anthology (very roughly) on the basis of whether or not the womon had a name for her feelings and, if she did, whether or not she accepted it; these stories are followed by those which tell of a process of self-recognition and acceptance that extended over years, even decades; finally, the stories toward the end of the book describe the many ways in which wimmin understand "coming out," in terms of their sexuality, their political beliefs, and their relationships with other people. For many, becoming a Lesbian is the beginning of wholeness, of feeling good about one's self, not a "coming out" but a "coming together" of oneself.

Judging from the experience of writing their coming out stories as the writers have shared their processes with us, telling their stories became both a recreation of their pasts and a validation of their present self-understanding. Many of the stories are narrations of pain, suffering and denial; yet the process of writing, expressing and affirming their identities, became a contemporary expression of the coming out process itself. With the telling of each of these stories, the silence is shattered, and the words themselves create a new reality past and present. The writing itself has caused many to realize that they have "always been coming out," that coming out is not a single, isolated act but an on-going process of self-definition and self-clarification.

> JUDITH: When did you come out?
> BW: It's hard to know.
> [Judith Katz]

> ... I've been 'coming out' to myself since age sixteen, 1963.
> [Ellen Anthony]

> Now, at age thirty-seven, I've been conscious of my lesbianism for twenty-two years. I've been coming out all that time, creating myself, and I'm not finished yet.
> [Caryl Bentley]

> Coming out as a Lesbian is a process that began when I was a child and was mostly unaware of what homosexuality meant ... 'Queer' was a name my sister got spanked for calling me. I knew why, but didn't know that such people really existed ...
> [Jane Sipe]

> My life, then and since, has been a continual process of 'coming out.'
> [Julia Penelope Stanley]

> I am always coming out,
> endlessly unfolding on an infinite number of levels
> [Constance Faye]

For Lesbians, our lives become a continual process of self-declaration in a society that denies our existence.

> First, there was the woman I was born from.
> [Diane Stein]

> In retrospect, I can clearly see my entire life as composed of steps leading to my eventual discovery of the joy of loving wimmin.
> [Beverly J. Toll]

> For many years, too many, I remained alone. Neither accepting men (who I hated desperately to touch me in any way), nor recognizing any attachment beyond 'friendship' with a woman. Too many years and too alone. When through feminism and through women's books I discovered

a word that meant who I am, a lesbian, I became afraid.
[Diane Stein]

I believe that it is very important for dykes to be out ... In the first place it proves to the straight world that we do exist (gay men exist but most people don't believe in lesbians). Secondly, it shows that we're regular people just like everybody else; and finally, that ignoring us won't make us go away.
[Patricia E. Hand]

You understand this has to be a kaleidoscope: layered, multiple, alternately foggy and clear. Coming out. And going back in. And peeking through the keyhole. Different parts bubble up from time to time. There's no such thing as a linear Lesbian.
[Susan Leigh Star]

As Adrienne Rich spoke of coming out: "When I think of the 'coming out process' I think of it as the beginning of naming, of memory, of making the connections between past and present and future ... "

... in writing this, I found that all of the above *count*. When I count the Lesbian in me at age seven, or ten, or fifteen, I count the part of me that was free, self-loving, identifying (however unconsciously) with female-ness. I begin to see my life as a whole: the places I held out, refused to settle; what they did and tried to do to me/us; and the reclaiming, the creating of my woman strength.
[Susan Leigh Star]

The stories themselves become part of every woman's coming out process, building a network of connections among wimmin. Many of the writers have since shared their coming out stories with wimmin who were involved in events in their past, and the letters move back and forth among them, a dialogue of each woman's understanding. Once on paper, each story has at least two realities: it exists as an artifact, as words on paper, and as oral culture, as a recounting of past experiences. Thus, it enters the world again on two levels, continuing the process of recreating reality and creating a continuum of wimmin's culture and community; connections are made among wimmin in the present, and a record of the past becomes available to wimmin of the future. These coming out stories are the foundation of our lives as Lesbians, as real to ourselves; as such, our sharing of them defines us as participants in Lesbian culture, as members of a community.

Some might feel that speaking of ourselves as a "Lesbian community" is misleading or premature, for we are as yet not a community in some senses. We are a cultural and spiritual network of wimmin whose only common herstory is that of oppression. The coming out processes and the creation of a bonding situation through the telling of the coming out story have been made necessary by the hostility of patriarchal culture. Because we have begun to speak of ourselves as a community, because communities are based on *shared* experiences, we believe that this book will give us one way of establishing our community in spite of our geographical and social isolation. These stories are our literature. If, as we believe, coming out is one of the most important events in a Lesbian's life, even her *entire* life, it is an experience that we should share with each other and with wimmin who have yet to label themselves as woman-identified. So many of us have come out in isolation from other Lesbians, struggling alone with our identity, or, even in the midst of local Lesbian groups, too many wimmin still feel alone because they don't know how to ask for the support they need and we aren't sure of how to give them support. A collection of coming out stories is one way of assuring other wimmin that they are not alone in their struggles, and perhaps it will make those struggles less painful, less frightening.

That is our hope. Too often, much of a woman's energy goes into the coming out process, and, instead of it being a joyous celebration of her freedom, it becomes a harrowing, terrifying journey toward an unknown, undocumented identity. Perhaps, if enough of us share our coming out experiences as the wimmin in this book have shared them, we can free our energies for the constructive enterprise of defining and strengthening our community of wimmin. So many wimmin have written to us saying, "I wish I'd had this book five years ago," or twenty, or thirty years ago. In writing their stories for all of us, they have created the world they (and all of us) have needed in order to survive. In preserving our herstories for all wimmin to read and share, we make it possible to come out into a new world, speaking a language which comprehends our lives.

October 1977

Two Years Later

As we look back over the history of this book, it is clearer and clearer to us that we have been working to bring it out almost as long as we have been working together—since October, 1976. For both of us, it has represented a commitment to each other and the community of wimmin who have contributed directly and indirectly to our lives.

Although we, as well as our contributors and supporters, have remained convinced that these stories would fill a critical need for other wimmin struggling to come out, to undertake a process that sets in motion radical changes in our lives, it hasn't been easy to assemble the manuscript and get it into print. The coming out of this anthology has been as difficult a process as any other. In our initial request for coming out stories, back in November, 1976, we optimistically set a March 31, 1977 deadline; by March, we had extended the deadline to April 30 for the wimmin who had just read our ad in *Lesbian Connection*.

By July, 1977, we finally had what we considered to be the final versions of the stories ready to be typed, and by October we had the manuscript ready for submission. On October 26, we heard that Diana Press had been vandalized, and we had been counting on them to be our publisher. We decided to go ahead and send the manuscript to Coletta Reid at Diana Press, and, with the consent of a majority of our contributors, offered to give them our 50% of the royalties if they were able to publish the book. In May, 1978, Coletta returned the book to us, saying that Diana was unable to undertake such a large project. (The manuscript ran to 400 pages.)

Since that time, four other feminist publishers have considered the anthology; one even suggested that we should try publishing it with one of the large, male commercial publishing houses, but such a possibility was unthinkable to us. (These stories were not written for "mass" distribution and consumption—they were written for us.) By the spring of 1979, both of us had given up on the book. We rarely mentioned it; the anthology was dead to us.

Then, in May, 1979, we met Deborah Snow and Gloria Z. Greenfield of Persephone Press at the National Women's Studies Association Conference in Lawrence, Kansas. They talked to us about seeing the manuscript, they sounded serious about considering it, but neither of us took them seriously. Would they be willing to publish what everyone else didn't want in its present form? They were. Neither of us was prepared emotionally for their decision to publish the anthology. It is still an event that isn't quite "real" to us, something we haven't managed to integrate yet as a "fact" in our lives. It is clear to us that we both had a tremendous emotional investment in this book, in the idea of it, in the year it took us to prepare it, and in the two years we spent sending it out and waiting to hear from publishers. There is no way to express here the investment we have in the stories themselves, in the wimmin we corresponded with about the book, or to describe what their lives have come to mean to us.

It is now three years since we decided to edit an anthology of coming out stories together, two years since we thought we were "finished" with it. If we were starting today to edit such an anthology and to write our own coming out stories again, there are many things we would do differently. For one thing, we would keep better track of our contributors; we have lost two stories because the wimmin didn't send us change-of-address notices. We lost them. But, by advertising in

Lesbian Connection yet once more, we found two that we thought were lost. (All of us owe more than any individual can know to the Ambitious Amazons of *Lesbian Connection*. Because of our publication deadline, they accepted our ad for our "lost" wimmin over the telephone so that it could appear in the August issue of *LC*, and it was through them that we "found" most of our contributors.) Initially, we had also hoped to have a broader representation of Lesbians writing for us; for example, we wanted to have more stories from Black and third world Lesbians, but we didn't hear from them. Those we contacted wouldn't or couldn't take the time for a variety of reasons. And, although there is some geographical distribution, it is still not as diverse as we would've liked. (There *are* Lesbians in Idaho, New Mexico, and Illinois, but they aren't in here.) We may have achieved some diversity in terms of class, but again we can't be certain. We suspect that many of our contributors are those wimmin who feel some confidence in their ability to put words in writing, still a middle-class privilege, although we advertised that we would accept the coming out stories in any form, including tapes (which we would transcribe). And our contributors tell us that they have been tempted to rewrite their stories now, with two more years of process and change behind them. Fortunately, they have generously spared us the work that would have been involved in "beginning again" to tell our stories.

If begun two years later, it would all be different perhaps, different stories from different wimmin, but these stories have a validity of their own. They tell our stories as we saw them, as we remembered them, as we were living them, two years ago. If we have any apologies to make, they would be to all of the Lesbians whose stories are not here, whatever the reasons. Perhaps someday we will hear all of our stories. This book is, at least, one chapter in the book that all of us are writing.

Julia Penelope Stanley
Susan J. Wolfe
October 1979

the coming out stories

1 Untitled Poem

Susan Leigh Star

suggestions and points
myself sifts down, in

how are the inner changes created?
life, light
      the rose satin center of a shell
      a candle as lit, catches, gutters
      a poise
there is no strength elsewhere

I bow to you
struggling for words
alternately running and silent
and at peace
a star
the tiniest underside of a petal
a rage
jagged and in love
helpless, free:

to offer you an altar
to offer you an altar
fear
filter the infinity of yourself
with the sifting risks
of my words

it is not a linear opening
each word birthed from a
different secret

as a child I wrote messages
on birch bark, thin as breath,
and practiced soundless walking
barefoot, in the forest

the messages were for you.

2   Untitled Story

Martha Pillow

Coming out. How could you explain it to anyone else? Could anyone understand what the whole thing meant? There are so many pieces, so many different stories. A womon could write a book. There is so much, too much, to tell; and it all holds much feeling, much deep, personal hard to explain feeling. Everything seems so tender, so strong, so close to the very core, so integral to yourself. It is hard to know how to begin, at what point to begin telling the story. It is so important to tell the stories.

You stand in the phone booth and hesitate before you answer. The young man on the other end of the line has just asked you if you are gay. He is connected somehow with the Gay Student Union at the University only he is afraid to talk to you if you aren't gay, also. He is not sure he can trust anyone who is straight. They have had too much bad publicity, too many misunderstandings from heterosexuals. You stand in the grimy phone booth on the clear spring day and remember the womon waiting for you on the concrete sidewalk only a few feet from you. You look at her straight back, the hair brushing the stiff collar of her jacket and you say "yes," quite distinctly into the cold black receiver. There is no mistaking it. You definitely said yes.

Even as you listen to the soft, masculine voice on the telephone telling you about the GSU, as you watch the womon standing in front of you shift her feet, patiently, waiting, images flash through your mind. What have you said? Gay? You said you were gay, a Lesbian. You do not really comprehend what you have admitted although you know you have always loved womyn. A Lesbian is something else, however. A

Lesbian is a big, tough womon who really wants to be a man. That's not you. You don't seduce womyn and you aren't mean and rough in a leather jacket with chains. What have you admitted? What is the meaning of this simple "yes" you have just uttered?

The meaning. The meaning is far more complex and far-reaching than you realize. You have a lot to learn about being homosexual, about the consequence of that realization. Remember high school? Remember those supposedly halcyon days, like a dream to you now, when all the womyn you knew were worrying about nothing but attracting boys and you were mostly glad that boys generally ignored you? You had more important concerns even then. Weren't you a Lesbian all those months and years? You'd made love to womyn, hadn't you? You dreamed secret dreams about loving womyn, loving your friends. Wasn't that homosexual? Were you a Lesbian at that point in your life, too?

Could it be that you were always a Lesbian?

When did you decide that you were a Lesbian? What kind of decision was involved? You were already involved with a womon the day you decided to be honest over the telephone. Even so, after you hung up, you said casually to the womon waiting for you, "He asked if I was gay and I said yes. I wonder if I should have told him that?" Do you remember saying that? That was you once. It's sometimes hard to believe, but we all believe, we all painfully know, that we are capable of having once been that womon. We have all been unsure and more than a little afraid of who we suddenly see ourselves as. A homosexual. You aren't alone as you wonder if you said the right thing, but you think you are. That's one of the worse parts, one of the longest and hardest parts to believe. You aren't really alone.

Afterwards, after you identified yourself as homosexual (dis-covered yourself, as it were), do you remember how long it took you to feel at ease with the situation? Sometimes now you feel uncomfortable; you know too well what other people think and feel about you. It's hard now, it was harder then, to keep good feelings alive. Too much was against you. At times it was overwhelming. You thought you might drown in the negative, hating emotions laid out for you like traps set to snare innocent unsuspecting animals. Many times you were, you still are, unsuspecting and innocent. Even being fully aware doesn't always save you from the anti-homosexual, anti-womon society. That moment you remember, that moment coming to mind now with jolting keenness, is one on which nightmares are built. Only this moment actually happened. You actually lived through this scene and there are times you live through it again and again and again in reality or imagination. It is almost irrelevant which it is.

In the scene you are sitting in some crowded public place full of straight, well-dressed, well-behaved people. The womon you are with knows you are a Lesbian and you always thought she understood you. She sits across the table from you, eating a vegetable salad and talking casually about nothing in particular. Suddenly, out of the blue, she hits you with her lightning bolt. In a loud, angry voice, she accuses you of always talking about Lesbianism. You seldom discuss the subject with her, and yet here she is, screaming at you and everyone is turning. Twisting heads everywhere look at you. The womon is crying. Her eyes turn red and tears soak her face. "All you ever talk about is Lesbianism!" she yells. You know you'd better not make a motion to go toward her or the whole room will explode on top of you. You know this. You have learned to keep your hands to yourself. This is the stuff bad dreams are made of, except it is actually happening to you. You wish you could sink into the floor, away from those punishing stares—again? Will you learn not to feel the stares, not to let them sting and wound so easily? It will take a long time. The traps of socialization are set deep. Sometimes you still get tangled in them, tearing your bruised flesh, still aching with ancient memory close to the center of your being.

It's so hard to explain, hard to get all the questions answered. Maybe you have to have been through it to comprehend the whole meaning, everything. You know the expression on the faces of your friends when you tell them you are a Lesbian. They say they're not surprised (meaning you always were strange), but they are. Some of them draw away; some of them don't. You find out who your friends are. In a small town you find out what it means to be alone.

Maybe that's one of the most difficult aspects to deal with, this feeling so alone, this gut-level comprehension of society's censure. You, as a Lesbian, as a womon in a patriarchy, are being continually misunderstood, constantly feared. Where can you go, who can you turn to in a small town? Maybe it's different somewhere else. You don't know. All you know is that you are learning to survive on many, many levels. It is not easy, but you are learning.

Painful memories mix with tender, joyful ones, uncertain ones. You can clearly recall that green plastered room, the bed pushed against a radiator. That radiator always banged and clanged and heated the room to suffocating so that you always had the window open even in the dead of winter, snow covering the ground. Even the tile floor was warm in that room. How things stick in your mind, all the crowding, pushing memories: the ugly pale green walls, the crash of the incinerator in the hall in the middle of the night, the bright red bedspread, the posters and mobiles and windchimes you and she carefully put up everywhere, the curtain you two made by hooking beer can tab tops together. She almost moved in with you that spring.

It was spring, wasn't it? You acted like you were afraid of each other. "Rub my back," you would say as you stretched out on the bed beside her. She would rub under your shirt and you would push her hand lower and lower and wish you had enough nerve to roll over and kiss her lips, touch her breasts. It wasn't like you'd never kissed a womon before. It was just that you'd never been so conscious of its meaning. You'd heard it rumored that you were a Lesbian because you never dated men and all your friends were womyn and you were fully aware of what that meant. Remember the courage it took to finally touch this womon running rough fingertips up and down your spine? And when you finally overcame your fear, at first it seemed like all you ever did was make love. Maybe it was because that first conscious move was so hard to make. Freedom to touch went to your heads, to your bodies. You can see the room now from the perspective of the bed where you spent most of your time that spring. You learned to ignore unsubstantiated rumors.

Suddenly you aren't alone anymore. This closeness, this sharing with another womon amazes you. This could be a womon you've known all your life, you know each other so well. You can't believe that all this happiness has descended upon you in the form of this blue-jeaned, thick-shoed womon. Friendship had drifted into love and you hadn't noticed it flowing that way.

What happens when the pond dries up? What happens when society, which *has* been noticing, gathers its forces to destroy this monstrosity your life has become? You'd rather think about the over-heated putrid green room years ago or about today, about how far you've come rather than about how you got here. Is it important to share the shame, the inner tearing scaring pain of those intermediate years? You didn't know you were such a strong, enduring womon, did you? Think of what you lived through. Think.

How could something so precious and natural be persecuted for so long? You didn't realize it—did you?—until it happened to you. You never really thought about it before until you were struggling for your own sweet life. You do remember when you were in college and majoring in subjects which prepared you for nothing in reality. Remember a sociology class where you wiggled on the hard uncomfortable chair while someone said homosexuals should be locked away? What should you have said? You were afraid. You didn't say anything. You noticed it everywhere. In your major subject, English, womyn writers were only occasionally thrown in and then it was always emphasized that they were only minor influences. But it gets worse.

You stand in the dean's paneled office, fists clenched at your side. You are both frightened and angry. You know who has the power and it's not you. He sits behind his cluttered, important-looking desk and tells you you can sit down. He smiles patronizingly as you sit awkwardly in the plush chair. You don't know why you have been summoned here. You cross your ankle over your knee, trying to appear nonchalant, unafraid. He clears his throat and his smile vanishes. You realize how closely his dark, straight mustache resembles Hitler's. He shuffles papers a second and you know this isn't a friendly visit. You're in for a little healthy intimidation.

He begins speaking. He wants to know if you are gay. That is not what he asks, but it is what he wants to know. He wants you to deny it. He, too, must have heard the rumors. So, they spread to high places, these rumors. He tells you he could throw you out of school. Your heart pounds. He says he can keep your friend (he glances quickly into your eyes) off campus. She doesn't belong here. He has the power.

You don't say anything. You don't have to answer him. He pauses a minute, letting his words sink in. He thinks he can scare you. You only feel anger. You want to smash his face with your tense knuckles. He continues after a space of time in which you stare at him in disbelieving hatred. Is this really happening? For some reason, yet to be understood, everyone is suddenly extremely concerned about your sexuality. Can this really be happening to you, to anyone?

It did happen; it does happen. He is speaking again. This time it is a new approach. Threats did not produce the desired results, perhaps a little humor would. He concentrates on burning a hole through your eyes with his sharp, disapproving gaze. He asks why you only hang around with womyn, particularly this one womon. When he gets no response he offers his opinion. He says he thinks that is pretty weird. He laughs. "I think that's pretty weird," he repeats.

You've had enough. "Is that all you want?" you snap, standing up.

He is taken aback by your abrupt manner. He fumbles with words. "Yes," he says.

"Then I'm going." You walk quickly to the door as he regains enough composure to remind you that he can throw you out of school. He can find a reason.

You bang the door shut behind you.

He didn't bother you again, probably only because there wasn't much he could really do that wouldn't create a public scandal. He didn't like scenes other than private ones. Just because nothing else came out of the inquisition didn't mean you weren't affected by it. It didn't mean you just laughed it off and forgot about it. It wasn't something you could just forget about. It's always floating away somewhere in the back of your mind. Always your mind is able to capture again these scenes, these memories. Remember you're a Lesbian. Remember what that means.

It took a long time to gain a useful understanding of the way things are, to get over letting other people make you feel guilty, ashamed, and frightened. Years later you still have occasional twinges of fear and self-hatred. Can anyone who has not gone through this understand how long those feelings can hang on, how long they can keep you back, silent, in your place? You're really a tough womon, even though you don't always think you are, you don't always feel like it. Just look at what you've lived through.

The womon sitting across the table from you smiles and you smile in return, coming gently back into the present. She runs her hand over the wooden table she bought and fixed up. The grains of the wood stand out in the sunshine streaming in through the window. It is a different spring from the one five years ago. You reach out and capture her roaming hand in yours. Only a womon who has survived the years would understand the freedom in that movement, the release from isolation. How can you explain how the hurt and the trembling fear suddenly become memories with that positive action, that open feeling? There are so many stories to tell, so many fragile memories to share at last with womyn who understand. It's been a long time since you've felt any real understanding. Yet here it is at last, the chance to share the feelings, the all-too-common experiences. You really aren't as alone as they want you to believe you are.

There are more scenes, more ways to come out. The process is a long one, going on daily. Coming out: so many feelings around that phrase, twisting about memories in and around your being. Have you explained yourself adequately? Can anyone explain herself adequately? This writing is as difficult as any, but it is important to have written. It is important to begin to tell the stories.

3

she & i

Diane Stein

when she & i were 6
we chased each other
round & round an open lot.
declared ourselves wild
thoroughbreds no man could catch

no matter how he tried.

when she & i were 9
our 4th grade teacher
called on 1 of us in class
& always got us both.
we answered to

each others names.

when she & i were 12
she said i couldnt walk her home.
she said she had another girlfriend
& she didnt want to talk.
she said that she was growing up

& didnt need me anymore.

when she & i were 14
& were strangers
still i hadnt understood ...

4 At Nineteen

Deidre McCalla

I came out because of Sharon. There were no long, painful years of suffering in silence, nor any early adolescent fears of being sexually different. I never went to a summer camp and to the best of my recollection, never had a crush on any of my gym teachers. During my freshman year of college I was primarily concerned with peace activism, learning how to smoke dope and be cool about it, and keeping my head above academic water. I was a virgin, asexual, intuitively feminist, and benignly aware that most of the men on campus were not worth my time. In my sophomore year, at nineteen, there was Sharon.

Sharon Lane crashed upon the campus green wearing oversized electrician's boots, two Linda Jeness buttons, a white sweatshirt emblazoned with a flaming red-fisted women's symbol, and blue jeans so dirty they would have stood on their own if she someday fancied a notion to remove them from her person. She chain-smoked Marlboros, stared straight into your eyes when she asked for information, and, unlike the other incoming freshmen, she did not scream, giggle, or laugh; in fact, she rarely smiled. The only visible evidence that Sharon had ever been a typical american teenager was the extremely well-scrubbed face hidden beneath a mass of tangled light-brown split-ends, living testimony to her thorough embarrassment at contracting something so counter-revolutionary and bourgeois as acne.

Within a week of school's opening, the campus was literally flooded with anti-war/imperialism posters announcing not only the organizational meeting of a local chapter of the Young Socialist Alliance, but also the formation of an all-campus anti-war committee. Socialists do not believe in wasting time. Needless to say the members of the already functioning campus Committee to End the War did not take kindly to having their territorial rights so rudely violated.

"Aw shit! Another fucking trot!"

It's not that we didn't like Socialists, they were just a pain in the ass to work with and as the last campus trot had graduated the preceding June, we were looking forward to a pleasant, peaceful year of demonstrations, anti-war coffeehouses, medical aid to Indochina, fundraising, and local non-violent training encampments. With the appearance of the YSA posters we immediately realized that all of our well-oiled plans would be bogged down with Marxist rhetoric, *Militant* special-issue reports on international imperialism, and unending analysis of how the movement was a changing dialectic. Even this would have been tolerable if not for the overbearing smugness of most Socialists in their belief that pacifists are dumb.

Since I was 1) a woman, 2) a committee coordinator, and 3) in Sharon's dorm, it was decided by the chickenshit male elite that I was to be the one to officially welcome our new comrade to college.

Sharon's door was a study in late 1972 Socialist decor; Linda Jeness placards, *Militant* subscription forms, miscellaneous photographs of young revolutionaries at work, and other assorted YSA paraphernalia. Her stereo was blasting away inside the room so I had to pound heavily on the door in order to be heard. I swear she didn't open it more than two inches.

"Yeah."

"Uh, are you Sharon Lane?"

"Yeah."

"Hi! My name's Deidre. Uh, you're the one who's been putting up the anti-war meeting posters around campus right?"

"Yeah. What about them?"

Hmmm. This was not going to be easy. For a Socialist she wasn't much on conversation.

"Well, I was just wondering if you knew there was already a campus anti-war comm—hey you know, it's a little difficult to talk through a crack. Could you open the door a little more? I mean, can I come in or you come out or something?"

She paused to consider it a second. "Yeah," she said reluctantly, "Come in."

With the notable exception of a life-size Janis Joplin poster, Sharon's half of the two-room double was an extension of her door, the leaflets were simply increased in quantity. She was obviously set in for a long siege.

"What were you saying about the posters?"

"Oh yeah, I'm a coordinator of the Committee to End the War and when we saw your signs go up, we figured you didn't know there already is a campus anti-war group."

"No, I didn't know. Why haven't you called a meeting or put out any information?"

"Well, you know, it's only the first week of classes."

"It's the second," she corrected. "What's the political base of the committee?"

"Well, we're basically a pacifist organization. We've staged a few local actions—"

"You're a pacifist!"

Damn, I had hoped she would be different.

"Yeah, that's right. What's so funny?"

"I'm sorry. Hey, would you like some Southern Comfort? I'm really sorry, I thought you were a C.P.er, that's why I didn't let you in at first."

"I don't understand."

"I'm from Boston and members of the Communist Party have been forming vigilante groups and attacking YSA members. I thought you were here to kill me."

"Yeah, but what made you think I was a member of the Communist Party?"

"Well, you know ... " she attempted to explain as her face began to turn bright red, "Angela Davis is a Communist."

"Ahh, I see. All black women with fros inquiring about an anti-war meeting must belong to the Communist Party, right?"

She smiled. "I'm really sorry. You just look like you could beat me up if you wanted to. A pacifist huh?"

"Yeah. A pacifist."

I liked her; she was as politically imperfect as the rest of us.

We became friends. Since the Committee to End the War members were the only activists on campus, Sharon resigned herself to working in a coalition effort. It was convenient for the two of us to pick each other up on the way to meetings, leaflet buildings together late at night, argue political differences over two or three or four rum and cokes and Southern Comforts, or simply waste an afternoon together listening to Janis Joplin and Joan Baez records.

Very few people who knew Sharon were surprised when, a month into the semester, she called an all campus-meeting of women only for the purpose of forming a women's liberation group; we would have been surprised if she hadn't. What did surprise many though, was when, two months into the semester, Sharon called for the formation of an all-campus Gay Liberation Union.

I was not surprised. Possessor of a fine eye for detail, I had quietly noted the gay liberation lambda among her collection of movement buttons; however, lest I should be accused of jumping to conclusions, I had refrained from bringing up the subject. It was so hard to know in those days; Socialists seemed to have their fingers into just about everything.

I had never known a lesbian before, or rather, if I had, I certainly didn't know I did. For the major portion of my adolescence I attended an all girls' Catholic boarding school in a white middle-class New York suburb; if there were any lesbians there during my six year internment, their closets must have been forged out of cast iron. Homosexuality was not suppressed in my school, it just never came up. Life was not a total vacuum; I knew there was such a phenomenon as lesbianism but as far as my day-to-day living was concerned, it was a non-topic. Not forbidden, simply irrelevant. My relationships with the women around me, nuns and students alike, were deep, powerful, and oft-times affectionate, but in terms of my awareness at the time, those relationships never even bordered on being lesbian.

Independently of my environment, I had arrived at the intellectual conclusion that there was nothing wrong with women loving women or men loving men; it seemed a logical extension of the civil rights issue. I'm sure the good sisters would have fainted dead away if I had ever mentioned this to them—I had enough trouble talking to them about feminism—but as I said, the opportunity never presented itself.

Although Sharon's lesbianism didn't bother me, her method of coming out to those around her was nothing if not blunt, and the idea of her spearheading a gay union on campus blew me away completely. So while twenty-odd budding gay activists calmly gathered in the downstairs living room and outlined their first organized assault on the campus, above them upstairs there paced a black, asexual, female pacifist on the verge of tearing her hair out.

Didn't Sharon know what people were saying? Couldn't she see that kids from all over the campus had suddenly discovered that the most efficient short-cut to another building was through our living room where the meeting was taking place? I was outraged! People found every reason possible to parade through the meeting place and check out who was (or wasn't) there and subsequently tear up the stairway to collapse in giggles at what they had just seen. The building was seething with voyeurs and passers-by who thought the meeting was one big freak show. Upset that they were perceiving Sharon so incorrectly, I could have personally strangled half a dozen people that night.

Unaware of my anger, a friend made the mistake of approaching me as I patrolled the corridor.

"Hey, Di, that meeting, where is it?" she queried, to which I, now totally unglued, replied, "It! they're not 'its' Joellen, it's a goddamn gay liberation meeting! They're people, not its!"

Joellen stared at me dumbfounded. Embarrassed by my over-reaction to a somewhat innocuous little question, I stormed back into my room and fumed for the remainder of the evening.

The gay liberation meeting served to break much of the ice that remained between Sharon and me and we continued to grow closer. Sharon would rarely talk about herself, deftly diverting any such questions into a Marxist analysis of personal relationships in a capitalist society. After the meeting she began to open up a little and I soon realized that her reticence was not only out of fear of trusting a new friend and/or of being misunderstood, but also out of a great deal of pain.

Sharon had been a lesbian since she was fifteen, coming out publicly during her senior year in high school. That year she had had a relationship with a woman who, from the way in which Sharon spoke of her, must have been incredibly strong and beautiful. Together they read poetry while listening to medieval music, created their own special music on guitars, and drank lots of red wine and Southern Comfort. The bits and pieces of Gregan that Sharon would share made their relationship assume an air of mythical magic and wonder. The fairytale ended when Gregan killed herself. Sharon never really explained why it happened; I don't think she knew herself. Gregan announced one day that she was leaving to visit her parents in Europe. A few weeks later, Sharon received word that Gregan had hung herself in Belgium. The pain, the confusion, the unconscious but ever-present guilt always showed whenever Sharon spoke of her.

"Go the FUCK away!"

"Hey, Sharon, come on, open the door!"

It was December. We were fighting. Again.

"Would you please just go away!"

"Just tell me why you're mad?"

"Look, just leave me alone right now, okay!"

"Fuck you, bitch!"

I stormed down the hall furious. What the fuck did I care anyway. I didn't know what the hell had come over her but I sure as shit was not going to stand in the hallway at one o'clock in the morning for the third night in a row screaming at a locked door trying to find out.

It had long since gone past my point of comprehension. Of late, the slightest thing would have each of us lunging for the jugular. The list of my offenses kept growing; my pacifism was fucked, my feminism wasn't socialist enough, I was too bourgeois, I had voted for McGovern, I couldn't hang leaflets straight, my fro was on crooked, and—as a straight woman, not only did I not understand her, but I was also now relegated to the position of her oppressor.

Sharon had decided to retreat into herself and never one to let sleeping turtles lay, I kept trying to pull her out again. It was a cycle; we would fight, one of us would apologize, and life would be fine until two days later when we were at each other's throats again. What confused me the most was that I cared so much; I refused to let her not be my friend. It seemed that whenever I had free time I found a reason to spend it with Sharon. It didn't matter if it was to help make posters, sound off about some particularly obnoxious professor I had recently run up against, or to simply sit in her room late into the afternoon watching her pen move as she sketched bold portraits of proud, angry women. More than once I caught myself staring at her, warmed inside from some inner calm that just being with her produced. This woman mattered to me.

"Why are you playing all these mushy love songs!"

"What?"

"Every song you've played for the past two hours has been some stupid love song. I can't stand it anymore."

As usual for a Tuesday, Sharon had accompanied me to my late-night radio program. January vacation had mellowed her quite a bit; we weren't fighting as much as before the holidays.

"Have I been playing an over-abundance of love songs? I'm sorry, I hadn't noticed. It's late you know, people don't want to hear the hard stuff this time of night."

The show ended at two and we walked back across the snow-covered campus in silence. It was early February and by now I understood that I was in love with her.

To anyone else, it would have been fairly obvious. In fact, several close friends told me months later that to them it was. Nowadays I can recognize those tell-tale signs in nothing flat but when I was nineteen, a sophomore in college, a virgin, and sexually dormant, falling in love was the last thing on my mind.

January had proven to be a difficult month. Over Christmas vacation I resolved that if Sharon wanted to cut me out, fine, my life could continue on without her friendship; there was really no need for me to stand around asking for my teeth to be kicked in. This kick-ass attitude lasted only until I returned to school and she came rushing down the corridor to greet me. She had been granted a room change over the holidays and was now living next door to me in a private room. Upon seeing her, my forced bravado flew out the nearest window as my stomach slid quietly to the floor.

I still did not know the reason for my erratic behavior but I did know that it was getting worse. Most of the time I ambled the grounds on the absolute verge of tears. I did not sleep but instead would lie in bed at night with one light on talking to myself—and answering back as the joke goes—praying for daylight to come and rescue me from my thoughts and my solitude; and all the while I felt it had something to do with Sharon.

It was then that I realized I loved her. It was so simple. I was not going crazy, I was in love! I remember thinking "of course! How silly of me!" My behavior for the past two months suddenly made perfect sense.

I was not frightened by the idea that this meant I must be a lesbian. I saw it as a matter of choice; either I was going to admit to myself that I loved Sharon, or I was going to have to kill myself as I could not continue living in the emotional hell I had been in since December. The idea of loving Sharon made me feel sane and at peace with myself; being a lesbian is infinitely preferable to being dead.

What did frighten me was the possibility that I was making it all up; I had never been "in love" before. How did I know what "being in love" felt like? Sharon had often told me how straight women would fancy lesbian experiences just to experiment. Was I really only projecting my fantasies upon her? Perhaps I only *imagined* I loved her to legitimize some subsonscious ulterior desire. Love couldn't arise without being fed from somewhere and Sharon certainly showed no signs of being in love with me. Where was I getting all this in love shit anyway?

In my usual courageous fashion, I decided to keep my mouth shut. Judging from all outward appearances, exposition meant opening myself to the possibility of getting hurt (rejected). We were still friends and as long as I knew why I was acting like I was, I could deal with me. Besides, I had heard so many speeches on straight women ultimately deserting their lesbian sisters, I took some small satisfaction in continuing to support Sharon and her seeing that not all straight women were bad. (Why I found it necessary to carry the banner for all straight women can only be explained by the fact that in any given situation I will usually root for the underdog.)

This plan might have even worked if not for the appearance upon the scene of *Another Woman*. Though Sharon's mood had improved over vacation she was still depressed by not being involved in a supportive relationship and this need for a lover was picked up on by a woman who proceeded to move in on Sharon like the flashette cannonball express. Given the chivalrous state I was in, I might have gallantly stepped aside, foregone my feelings and let Sharon and this woman walk off into the sunset as the orchestra played the theme from *Elvira Madigan*. However, I did not get along with this particular woman and was convinced that if Sharon pursued a relationship with her it would lead to disaster.

I found myself in the awkward position of being Sharon's confidante. Sharon was also leery about K.'s reliability as a lover/friend and took to talking her feelings over with me. I was privy to K.'s roses, cutesie notes, gifts, poems, and conversations. My room also served as Sharon's haven when K.'s ardor became too intense and Sharon required sheltering. K. was nothing if not persistent, and as Sharon's sense of isolation grew, she slowly but surely began to succumb to K.'s insistence.

When we returned from the radio station there was a rose-wrapped note from K. attached to Sharon's door. She stared at it blankly for a second and then just sort of shook her head looking very, very tired. I invited her into my room for a drink or some tea before she went to sleep.

"What would you think if I started having a relationship with K.?"

Holy shit, fuck, goddammit! I couldn't believe it; she asked me that question point blank. We had been small talking until now but the conversation had eventually gotten around to K. As protocol dictated, I had been assuming my usual air of casual, indifferent objectivity but Sharon's sudden bluntness threw me completely off balance. How do you avoid a direct question? As a kid I was always lousy at dodge ball. I supposed it was now or never.

"Well, Sharon, I don't think I could take you having a relationship with her. I don't think I could deal with you having a relationship with anyone."

"Why not?"

My heart was pounding so hard I was temporarily paralyzed. Sharon immediately launched into sermon #437 on how some straight women, though seemingly liberal, are not really able to deal with a lesbian in an actual lesbian relationship. This was too much.

"It's not that, Sharon," I interrupted.

"What then?"

I will never win an award for bravery. "I'll tell you why in a little bit," I said, pouring myself another full glass of Southern Comfort.

Sharon sensed how genuinely upset I was and mercifully changed the subject. An hour and two more glasses of Southern Comfort later I abruptly brought us back to the matter at hand.

"Sharon."

"Yeah."

"Uh, the reason I said before that I couldn't take you having a relationship with anyone is ... is because I have grown very attached to the socialist living next door."

I waited. She did not move nor register any surprise at my statement. It seemed an eternity before she spoke again.

"Do you know what you're saying?" she asked without even looking up.

"Yes."

Tears began to fall from her eyes and drop silently to the carpet around her.

"I'm a horrible person, you know that."

"No you're not."

We sat in silence across the floor from each other. It was as if time had suspended herself for us. Finally Sharon collected her cigarettes and headed for the door.

"I'll see you in the morning."

"Yeah, sure, good-night."

She left. And despite the enormous amount of Southern Comfort I had consumed in the past few hours, my mind was suddenly clearer than it had been for weeks. A great weight had been miraculously lifted from my shoulders and vanished into an air that was suddenly crystal clear and fresh. For whatever she chose to do about the situation, at last Sharon *knew*; I no longer had to bear it all alone. *She knew*! Heady with relief and my new-found weightlessness, I got up, cleared away the dirty ashtrays and glasses and, for what felt like the first time in a long time, I slept.

Our friendship continued as usual for the next few days. Sharon needed time to sort out the situation between herself and K. and I saw no need to push. Eventually Sharon admitted that yes, she did love me and had been in love with me since the previous October; her strange behavior toward the end of the first semester was the result of her inability to reconcile her feelings with my apparent heterosexuality.

If Sharon and I had spent a great deal of time together before, from this point on we were inseparable. It read like a script from the 1959 teen angel movie; we held hands under tables, constantly appeared late for dinner—laughing—and stared eternally into each other's eyes over slowly dying milk shakes. Although at the time I was certain no one noticed, looking back I realize we were probably about as subtle as two rhinos in heat.

My sleeping sexuality was slowly and carefully nurtured under Sharon's love. At first I expected her, being the well-rounded, experienced lesbian, to show me how to make love to her and I was initially exasperated by the fact that she steadfastedly would not. She insisted that I take my own time to explore her body and my own and discover together what made us feel good. There was no hurry and absolutely no sense of doing something "the wrong way." Besides taking the emphasis off sex and placing it instead on sensuality, Sharon's method of guiding my coming out (or coming of age as it were) also placed the responsibility for my actions solely on my shoulders. There was no way I could ever turn around and claim I was led, trapped, or recruited into lesbianism; the initiative originated from within myself and was acted upon with conscious decisions.

A side effect of this independent study method, as we jokingly referred to it, was that I ended up sleeping with Sharon in my jeans for the first six weeks of our relationship. You see, I wasn't sure of the protocol of these situations and I didn't want to appear rude by immediately ripping off my clothes and diving into bed. I was afraid she'd think I was only in it for the sex. She was very patient.

Our immediate circle of friends was taken aback slightly once they realized what was happening but for the most part their adjustments were made quite gracefully. Unfortunately, some of their not-so-close friends stopped associating with them because they hung out with us. More than once Sharon and I found ourselves apologizing for other people's bigoted behavior.

Outside of our close friends, the people who caught on the quickest were the dorm receptionists. We noticed we were being treated as one and the same entity. If Sharon had a phone call they buzzed both our rooms simultaneously. If I had a message or special delivery letter, it was deemed sufficient to give it to Sharon. If A came home early from class looking a little under the weather, B would immediately be informed upon passing the front desk that A wasn't feeling well and should be looked into. We might as well have sent them invitations to the wedding.

Undoubtedly there must have been numerous tacky rumors circulating through the dorm but Sharon and I rarely heard them; no one dared confront us directly. On one occasion we learned that one particularly homophobic woman on our floor insisted she had heard us making love in a bathroom stall one night. In our typically tactful, sensitive, sisterly, and compassionate manner, Sharon and I proceeded to run into a stall and pant heavily whenever we saw this woman go into the bathroom. She eventually changed dorms.

Our relationship might have qualified as perfectly idyllic if not for the recurring arguments over the extent of my closet. Having been an outfront dyke since high school, Sharon found it difficult to relate to my refusal to be more open. I in turn felt no need for us to go tripping across campus hand-in-hand, make appearances at parties of known homosexuals, or for me to attend gay liberation meetings or dances. In my mind we were sufficiently discreet and unobstrusive; a general proclamation was not necessary.

At nineteen, I was still very vulnerable to people's opinion of me, and having gathered a reputation as a campus activist, I wanted nothing to tarnish that image. In retrospect, I perhaps had an overinflated picture of myself as a campus figure, but nonetheless at the time I kept my hands planted firmly inside my pockets when we walked together. In her more insecure moments, Sharon interpreted this as my lack of true commitment to the relationship. We reached a compromise wherein she could be as open with her person as she liked and I would be as open with my person as I liked.

The semester drew to a close with the campus rag publishing a special issue on sexuality with an article and photograph from Sharon Lane, "Lesbian and Proud." Guilt by association never occurred to me; I didn't think much about the fact that mere acquaintances were congratulating me on her "fine article." Nor did I blanch when liberal males sat down at our bar table and lectured: "Yes, homosexuals are people too." I mean, it's not like she and I were obvious or something; so what if the only black female peace activist on campus spent ninety-nine per cent of her day with the college's leading lesbian/feminist Socialist; that didn't mean anything.

At twenty-three, when I spy two women staring deeply into each other's eyes, striding proudly down the street ever so closely with a satisfied smile on their faces, or standing in line for a movie passing quick knowledgeable looks, I know that they are lovers. When one woman's name is always used in conjunction with another woman's name as if it were inconceivable that one would be mentioned without the other, I know that they are lovers. At nineteen, I thought nobody knew.

Our love endured through a summer of virtual separation on into the following semester when I took a leave of absence to attend another program. A relationship via Ma Bell is not easy but we were working it out. Blessed Be. We were working it out.

"Hey Di, remember how you were worried last year that people knew you were a lesbian?"

"Yeah."

"Well, I've only been back here three days and all these people we barely know have been coming up to me asking how you are and how we're getting along. Deidre, everybody knew!"

I could see her clearly, standing there at the other end of the line, brown hair shining in the sun, gentle laughing, gently loving me. I smiled.

"Yeah. I guess I kind of always knew they did."

Sometimes I wonder how many other lesbian closets are made of glass.

5 Strong and Free: The Awakening

Beverly J. Toll

It is difficult for me to write the story of my experience of coming out. In retrospect, I can clearly see my entire life as composed of steps leading to my eventual discovery of the joy of loving wimmin. Since I am not called upon to produce an autobiography, I must delineate those events providing the major impetus for my Lesbian lifestyle.

I grew up in a lower middle class, Southern Baptist family in Little Rock, Arkansas. From my mother I learned that in every situation there is one correct course of action, this being determined through diligent study of the Word of the Lord. In contrast, my father emphasized dissociation from all that emerges from emotion and almost total reliance upon the rational intellect. In response to these conflicting values, after a time of general confusion during adolescence, I have learned to temper emotion with reason and to be aware of my own feelings throughout any logical analysis I undertake.

Needless to say, Lesbianism was never presented to me as an alternative lifestyle. This, I believe, explains why I loved wimmin for such a long time without realizing the implications of my feelings.

My earliest memories are of my rebellion against the traditionally female activities I was encouraged to enjoy. I was what my parents and teachers referred to as a "tomboy," preferring baseball to dolls and imaginative outdoor games to the pretensions of "dressing up" and "playing house." I was indulged, my parents recognizing this period as a "phase" that would be outgrown in due time.

At the age of 12, I entered junior high school and adolescence. I still enjoyed baseball (and do now, 9 years later), but I began to be aware of myself, for the first time, as a sexual being. The young wimmin I knew at school began to be aware of their male contemporaries, dressing for them and playing flirtatious games. I imitated my peers, wearing makeup and shaving my legs (ugh!). I did my best to conform, but the true impetus of attraction to the boys was simply not there. My motivation was to belong, to be part of the group, to not stand out in any unnecessary way.

I dated young men for more years than I like to remember. The pretenses, the lies, the sometimes overt repulsion that I felt during the adolescent sexual games made me question myself. What was wrong with me?

At some point during this time my parents, innocently enough, took me to a local theater to see a movie, involving an actress portraying the role of a frigid womyn. My reaction was intense and immediate. There really was something wrong with me! There were other wimmin like myself, doomed to a life of frustration caused by their inability to respond to men! I was a freak, a cold, sick womyn.

From that point on the fear built in my mind. I became extremely self-conscious regarding my body, much more so than the shyest young wimmin in my gym classes. I hated my body for refusing to respond "normally," and paid as little attention to it as possible.

I masturbated frequently. It is difficult to explain how I thought myself frigid while spending hours in my darkened bedroom, orgasmically exploring my own body. I learned, at a very early age, that masturbation was something dirty little boys did in bathrooms. Later on I read, in books of questionable literary value (always written by men), accounts of wimmin masturbating with soft drink bottles, bananas, and one lurid tale involving a mayonnaise and bologna sandwich. Had anyone asked me if I masturbated, I could have said no without believing myself to be dishonest. All I was doing was touching myself, making myself feel good. This was in no way associated, in my mind, with what I had been taught was an evil, perverted, sinful action, indulged in only by a few pitiful but dangerous persons. To this day I cannot be comfortable with the word *masturbation;* I prefer to think of the act in terms of making love to myself. It is strange that two denotatively synonymous phrases can carry such different connotations.

Around the age of 14, I began to fantasize while touching myself. While trying diligently to picture myself in beautiful, romantic scenes with my "knight in shining armor," much to my dismay, my knight kept removing her armor and stepping out a womyn. I fantasized about my teachers (thank heaven for gym teachers!), my friends, and other wimmin with whom I came in contact. I didn't recognize my crushes on these wimmin for what they were until years later. After all, wimmin had crushes on men, not on other wimmin, didn't they? I tried, fairly successfully for some time, to ignore my dreams of wimmin. These thoughts did not fit into the pattern I had been told my life must follow.

I was still dating men, lying to my friends and frequently to myself, inventing lovers of incredible ability and tales describing hours of blissful lovemaking. The other side of this is a series of years and men and excuses. "I might get pregnant." "I don't feel that way about you." "It's the 'wrong' time of the month." I claimed more menstrual periods in five years than most wimmin endure in a lifetime. It usually worked.

When my excuses did not work, I laid back and waited for it to be over. Several men told me I was frigid, and one started some nasty rumors to that effect, so I learned, from books, how to fake sexual response. I got no more complaints; perhaps I should be an actress! I also found no more enjoyment and finally settled down to dating a young man who was equally uninterested in having a sexual relationship with me. We were close friends, and we managed to convince our peers that we were also ardent lovers. We were strangely attracted to establishments frequented by gay people. We told ourselves and other people that it was fun to go watch and laugh at "the queers."

About a year later my ideal asexual relationship was dissolved when this young man left me for a male lover. For the first time I was confronted, head on, with the issue of a gay friend.

I was familiar with the term homosexual and had been for several years. Now that I knew one gay man, everything seemed to begin at once. I learned that several of the young men I had asexually dated were gay. I discovered that several of the men for whom I felt real affection were also gay. Then it was young men in my neighborhood, then two men that owned a neighborhood antique store ... Suddenly over half the men I knew were gay. *Where were the dykes?*

I had heard the word Lesbian once and confronted it a few times in my insatiable desire for reading. There were, in particular, two pornographic books in my possession containing detailed accounts of wimmin making love. Suffice it to say, these pages were worn quite thin. But this just related to experiences in my mind, never to anything concrete in my life.

I was rapidly becoming involved in the drug sub-culture and I found much less sexual pressure within this group of people. Although most of them were sexually active, there was very little pressure on me to do anything I didn't want to do.

My closest friend within this group was a womyn my own age that had been in school with me for several years. We went out in the evenings together, studied together and spent most of our weekends with each other. She was sexually active with men, which made me a little jealous, and I had her convinced that I was also getting off on men, which, I found out years later, also made her a little jealous.

Remembering those nights we spent together is like reliving a wonderful dream and a frightening nightmare, simultaneously. It felt so good to be with her, to lie in bed with her, my body pressed as close to hers as I dared. The sensations were incredible, so close to her, feeling the heat from her body, smelling the sensuous womyn-fragrance emanating from her skin.

But I could only touch her accidentally or with excuses of keeping warm in an under-heated room on cold nights. It very seldom occurred to me to try to touch her; I didn't want that ... I couldn't want that ... I was not supposed to want that.

One spring night, a few months after my 16th birthday, my friend and I drank a couple of bottles of cheap strawberry wine and decided to camp on my parents' screened-in back porch in sleeping bags. (On the porch my parents could not hear us talking, or know that we drank and smoked, so we slept there frequently.) We were both pretty loaded, feeling uninhibited, but certainly in control of ourselves.

We were feeling very close and hugged each other several times, not unusual in friendships such as ours. That night we kept our arms around each other and looked into each other's eyes. I felt so many things, so much love and desire, such an intense physical and emotional feeling that it quite overwhelmed me.

But years of taught passivity refused to allow me to kiss this womyn looking into my eyes, this womyn I loved so much. My socialization and education had taught me not to do it, but to talk about it instead. I asked this womyn what she would do if I kissed her and received the unhelpful answer, "I don't know. What would you do?"

We continued holding each other, enjoying our nearness. I looked into her eyes, trying to see what was happening within her mind. Summoning all my courage, I touched and kissed a womyn for the first time. I cannot describe what I felt at that moment. Very seldom does one experience anything nearing that level of intensity.

I kissed her, and I wanted to touch her and make love to her; I didn't know exactly how, but it never occurred to me, at the time, that a womyn could not "know how" to make love to a womyn. It seemed the most natural instinct possible at that moment. I was a womyn; I knew what made wimmin feel good.

This womyn that would, less than two years later, become my lover, pulled away from me, frightened.

"I just can't do it. I love you, but I just can't do that," she told me.

For a moment I felt the hurt, the pain of sexual and emotional rejection; but almost instantly I was overwhelmed by what I had wanted, what I had almost done.

Good God! I had almost made love with a womyn! Something must be wrong with me. I'm not frigid, it must be worse than that, something is terribly wrong!

There was no one I could talk to, no one to discuss this with. I was terribly afraid that someone would find out what I had felt that cool spring night in the arms of a womyn.

Our friendship remained strong, possibly it grew stronger after that evening, but my friend and I became significantly less physical in our expression of our affection. At the time I thought she had found the whole idea repulsive. I tried to put it out of my mind, tried to convince myself that it was nothing but the result of alcoholic indulgence.

I increasingly withdrew into myself, spending my time in reading, writing fiction or walking in the woods, all solitary pursuits that I found most comfortable. I had friends, but I saw less of them. I would visit them occasionally, get high with them, and lose myself in music or books. I felt, overall, that I had very little to offer others, and that they had very little to offer me.

I still did not conceive of myself as a Lesbian or even as bisexual; I simply ignored my sexuality except for the evenings spent luxuriating to the rhythms of my own body. But these times grew less frequent. My intake of alcohol and other drugs increased during this period of my life. I seemed to feel more comfortable with passing out than with the idea of self-love.

I dropped out of high school at age 17 and went to work in a full-time position. My evenings and days off were spent getting high, reading and writing. I was usually alone, spending most of my free time in the woods.

One Sunday afternoon in early spring, I went to a local park, quite a distance from my home, to spend a chilly afternoon reading. It got quite cold and drizzled a little and I began to think I should head for the main road and hitch-hike home before I got any colder or wetter. A womyn was walking through the park and I remember seeing her and wondering why she would be out in that weather.

She came over and spoke to me. She was in her early twenties, and like myself and most of the other wimmin one met in the park, she was wearing boots, a sweatshirt and jeans. I did not consider her in terms of attractiveness, having long before discarded the traditional male standards of beauty in wimmin and not yet having replaced them with standards of my own.

After talking a few minutes and smoking a joint she invited me to come home with her, to dry out and have a hot cup of coffee. As she lived only a few blocks away and was very friendly and I was rather cold, I accepted her offer without hesitation.

We went to her home, a small but cozy apartment in the upstairs corner of a very old house. The house was probably fifty years old and had once been an elegant residence belonging to a moderately wealthy local family. Like all the large, ornate houses in the area, it had been divided into several small apartments as the city's wealth moved, gradually, to the west side of town.

It was warm inside the apartment and my clothes soon dried. We had coffee and the womyn warmed up some chili from the small refrigerator. After eating we got high and sat in the space constituting the living room and bedroom of the apartment, listening to music and talking at length about many subjects. I felt as comfortable with this womyn as if I had known her all my life.

She made love to me.

It is difficult for me to describe exactly how this came about. It started with nothing more than a gentle touch of her fingers upon my hand, emphasizing a point in the conversation. Later I touched her arm while handing her a cup of coffee; perhaps my hand rested there a moment longer than was necessary to simply call her attention to the coffee. She touched my hair ...

The best way I can describe it, is to say that this is the only time in my life when making love was completely spontaneous. I didn't think about it; if I had I would probably have pulled away from this kind, gentle womyn that was touching me. It didn't occur to me to question what was happening. There were no decisions to be made. I thought of nothing, but experienced, for the first time in my life, the tender, satisfying love of a womyn.

But my conditioning caught up with me rapidly. Within minutes of our lovemaking, the realization of what had just happened slammed into me like a bolt of lightning, illumination from above. To put it mildly, I freaked out. I jumped up, dressed and got out of that apartment with amazing alacrity, muttering something about having to get out of there, having to go home, not being what this womyn thought me to be.

(I never saw this womyn again, although I've thought of her many times. I hope that now, over three years later, she is reading this and maybe for the first time understanding the significance of what happened that day in her apartment. My life would never be the same. Lady, you have my eternal gratitude and love.)

Now I knew. I couldn't accept it, much less admit it even to myself, but deep inside, I knew.

There was still no one to talk with. I could share this experience with no one and I spent many agonizing hours wondering what it all meant, what I could do about what I saw myself being and becoming.

About a month later I was sitting in a downtown cafe eating dinner when a womyn came up and spoke to me. She remembered me from a chance encounter some time previously, although I had to admit I had no such recollection of meeting her. We ate together and talked and found that we had many things in common. We exchanged telephone numbers and agreed to meet again for lunch, which we did many times. We became quite good friends that summer and this womyn played a significant part in convincing me to get a high school equivalency certificate and enroll in some classes at the University of Arkansas at Little Rock.

After a time the subject of sex came up. She freely admitted to me that she was bisexual and later confided that she vastly preferred wimmin as sexual partners. I told her that I had had one sexual experience with a womyn, but that I was really heterosexual, of course. Had this womyn told me she was a Lesbian, I would probably have ended the friendship. For some reason I felt I could have bisexual wimmin as friends while remaining sexually uninvolved, still denying everything I felt inside myself.

We grew to love each other and in time, became lovers. It happened very gradually and I let it happen because it felt so good, so right. I began to feel good about myself; I admitted to myself and to a few other people that I was "bisexual." I wasn't seeing men, except in firmly asexual relationships, but I clung for months to that label of bisexuality, desperately holding on to that last shred of what I had been taught to think of as normality.

A young man I was spending time with became interested in me sexually, and the time had come when I had to make a decision. I tried to be his lover, I did everything I could to chain myself to the moral strictures with which I had lived and suffered all my life.

I had other lovers during this time, including the womyn with whom I had come so near to consummating my love when I was 16. I loved these wimmin so intensely, with so much spontaneous giving and sharing that to lie in bed and let a man fuck me became unbearable.

My decision was made. For the first time I said to myself, "I am a Lesbian and I will never again deny this to myself or to anyone else." I was 19 years old and for the first time I felt really in control of myself and my life. The idea that I would have to endure sexual relationships with men now seemed like a nightmare of the past. It was/is such a feeling of power to know that my destiny, my future is in my own hands and will be determined by my own abilities and qualities of determination and persistence. I will never, *never* have to bow down to the man in that way again. I can live my life, proud and free to love wimmin.

Reclaiming my true womynhood, learning to truly know and love myself and other wimmin has taken time. This process of coming out, coming to terms with sexuality and Lesbian lifestyle, dealing with the general homophobic world, is a challenging process for every womyn that must continue throughout her life if she is to continue to grow. Coming out was not for me and is never, in my opinion, an isolated event in the life of a womyn. My entire life has been a process leading me to loving wimmin, but that process is certainly not over. Every aspect of my present life is centered around wimmin. As an undergraduate at the University of Arkansas, I am majoring in Anthropology with an emphasis on Wimmin's Studies. I am making plans to attend an institution offering graduate degrees in Wimmin's Studies and I eventually intend to teach on a college level.

Through my teaching and my writing (hopefully), I will be able to reach out to wimmin, to help them become aware of their alternatives and the immense power of womyn-strength, so necessary in making those choices. And perhaps by living openly and proudly as a Lesbian, I can help some young wimmin come to terms with their sexual identity more easily than I did.

Is This the Reward of a Catholic Girlhood?[1]

6

Margaret Cruikshank

My coming out story is unexciting. If I were to fictionalize it, I would make it sexier and funnier, and assign myself a younger age than 26 and a less staid personality. The other woman, Marcia, could keep her real age of 23; that's a good age for coming out.

I met her a few months before her 23rd birthday in a literary criticism class at the midwestern Jesuit school where we were both graduate students who had National Defense Education Act grants to get Ph.D.'s. Our educations contributed nothing to the national defense, of course; and it was certainly not the intention of the male bureaucrats at H.E.W. to bring young lesbians out of the provinces and into big cities, where they could meet, fall in love, and oppose the Vietnam war together. Left in the small towns where we grew up and dependent only on private enterprise, Marcia and I might never have felt free enough to love each other, or any other woman. From my failures to care deeply about a man, I would have concluded that I was not a caring person or someone who belonged in an intimate relationship.

That at least was my suspicion after an experience with a man in 1965, several months before I met Marcia and got her to stop sitting in the front row of lit. crit. class like a pious Catholic schoolgirl and to sit with sloppy indifference next to me in the last row. A male friend from my hometown, whom I had met at the Graduate Record Exam (I hope young lesbians are finding each other these days at the GRE), called to announce that he had that day passed his doctoral comprehensives and

[1]Kate Millet, *Sita*.

could now attend to other business—would I marry him? Confused as I was about love, men, and my future, I saw at once that there was something ludicrous about putting emotional life second to intellectual life. But what to say? I didn't love him, but I knew women were supposed to want marriage. Why didn't I? Awkwardness was the main emotion I felt. As potential mates, Frank and I had lumbered along in a way that reminded me of the Herbert Spencer-George Eliot romance; and, ironically, his dissertation was to be on Spencer, mine on Eliot. I said on the phone that I would send my answer by mail. I remember going to the library to do the letter, probably because I felt safe in libraries and no doubt also because the letter would be like an assignment. With a directness and honesty I hardly ever attained in those days, I told Frank that I couldn't marry him because I was not physically attracted to him. Thinking of the letter today I feel frustrated because, although I had correctly diagnosed the problem with that relationship, I was blind to the implications of the letter, which seem so obvious now: 1) no man would be sexually attractive to me, except in a casual/temporary way; and 2) I was attracted to women.

Not understanding these crucial facts about myself in 1965, I had no expectation at all, when I began to spend time with Marcia, that I could love her. How could I have been so ignorant of this possibility, I wonder now, when two years before the call from Frank, one of my roommates had fallen in love with me. I obviously couldn't connect one experience with a woman to another. I was attracted to Kathi, the roommate, an Irish Catholic from Iowa with a background much like mine. I remember walking by myself one day and getting a thunderous message from my brain *she loves me* which made me stop suddenly as I was crossing the street. But my attention was focused so much on her dilemma (poor Kathi—what a rotten thing to happen to her) that I never asked myself what *my* response might be or thought in any general way about women loving women. Soon I had persuaded myself that I was crazed from studying too much—Kathi didn't love me. But one night she came to my room late at night, sat on my floor, and looking very embarrassed she said that Marge, the third woman in our apartment, had been making fun of her for loving me. She hoped I would not be angry with her. I wasn't, but I couldn't have been very sensitive, either. All I remember is that our conversation was short and awkward. In the days that followed, although I did not feel love for Kathi, I did want some physical contact with her, but I was too inhibited to touch her. One night we got a little drunk together and sat next to each other on the living room couch with our arms around each other. Marge, who was with us but sober, said: "Goddamned lesbians!" I remember thinking, smugly, No, absurd, if we were goddamned lesbians we would have to be doing this in some secret place; we couldn't be hugging right out here in the living room in the presence of another person. This spectacularly false assumption was one I suppose I had to accept: to question it would have led me to uncomfortable thoughts about the significance of all my attachments to women.

The early weeks of close friendship with Marcia gave me no clues about what was to follow. We tossed a football around in the park, hung upside down from the jungle gym, and studied hard. After our long talks late at night, I'd walk her back to her apartment and then she'd walk me back to mine. That pattern should have been a clue. The first Superbowl was also her birthday. We watched together in high spirits and then our friends came for a surprise party. I had never liked a woman well enough to plan a party for her, and no one had ever given a party for Marcia. Those clues were lost on us, too. Although she asked me to move in with her when her roommate left, we were so far from knowing what was happening between us that we invited a third woman to share the small apartment with us.

Within a month after the move, I realized I cared for Marcia very much, but had no idea that my feelings were the appropriate ones for the beginning of a love relationship. I took my two new roommates to a Clancy brothers' concert on St. Patrick's Day, and during the concert I held Marcia's hand in the dark. I had never had that experience before. The raucous Clancy's must have loosened me up. Later that evening as Marcia and I were taking off our coats in our big walk-in closet, we stood for a long time with our arms around each other. I felt scared and excited at the same time. Hugging a woman through her winter coat is not very satisfying, I now realize, but for someone like me who had hardly ever been able to touch another woman (or a man or a child), this closet cuddling was a great step forward. One night not long after St. Pat's I was sick in bed. Marcia sat for a long time on the edge of my bed and then kissed me on the neck (I think she was aiming for my cheek) and ran out of my bedroom. I was overwhelmed. This was even more exciting than holding her hand or feeling her coat. I wanted to be kissed again but was too shy to say so or to kiss her. But one night when she was reading I sat on the floor at her feet and leaned against the chair she was sitting in. She lifted me into the chair with her and we kissed and laughed for about four hours. That we both liked prolonged physical contact was a great discovery. We must have known vaguely that we were doing a forbidden thing, but whatever guilt we bore did not keep us from doing what felt good. We had both had such repulsively successful careers as Catholic schoolgirls and devout young women that we ought to have been guilt-ridden, but somehow we escaped the tortures of a bad conscience. In all their vivid descriptions of the sinful, secular, atheistical world into which they were reluctantly sending us, those of us not good enough to want to imitate them and become nuns, our teachers never mentioned that feeling sexual attraction for another woman was an abomination. At Marcia's college, the "mulier fortis" was much lauded (the valiant woman), and at my school, her counterpart was the "dynamic Christian woman." But we were never told that a mulier fortis must refrain from passionately kissing a dynamic Christian woman. Maybe that's why the *sin* button didn't flash red the night I sat in Marcia's lap kissing her and knowing that I loved her.

The rest came only gradually. Once when we were doing our Beowulf lesson together, while sitting on the floor not too close to each other, we began to kiss and somehow got wound around each other on the couch, neither of us sure what to do with our bodies. Marcia knew enough the next time to touch me with her hand, and I was amazed by the pleasure she could give me. But I was too frightened and self-conscious to touch her until two weeks later when she came home late one night and demanded that pleasure for herself. I was too surprised to refuse (she was not at all a demanding person). After that, our love-making was less inhibited, although often furtive, because of the third woman in our one-bedroom apartment. Luckily she taught an early morning class. As soon as she walked out the door, I would bounce on her bed on my way into Marcia's bed. Those were exuberant mornings, and it pleases me to recall that we got the highest grades on the Beowulf exam, too.

We lived together very happily for three years, the last two in our own apartment. During summer vacations we had wonderful times traveling in Marcia's Volkswagon. We saw the iron mines in northern Minnesota and walked around on Isle Royale, and watched the Little League world series in Pennsylvania. We got thrown out of a pet cemetery for laughing at the inscriptions on the tombstones, and another time we were stranded in a small town in Scotland and had to sleep in the local jail.

During the school terms we helped each other with teaching (we had the same classes) and with studying. I might not have been able to write a dissertation without Marcia's constant reassurances and good suggestions. And for six terrible weeks in 1969 when I was fighting with my department over my dissertation, she plotted my strategy with great cunning, helped me figure out the moves against me, and once when I cracked and decided to go right to the chairman's office and curse him, she literally barred the door and kept me home. She even stood at my side for 2-1/2 hours while I xeroxed the required number of copies of my dissertation for the slippery misogynists who were to sit in judgment of it.

Those days were idyllic. Neither of us pretended to be looking for men to fulfill us. And yet we did not see ourselves as lesbians—the word had vile connotations—as women who had made a conscious choice of a woman to love. I told myself that the person I loved happened to be a woman, and she must have said the same thing to herself. In any case, we had no conversations about lesbians or lesbianism. Perhaps in our happy state we felt no need to reflect on our coming together. As survivors of unhappy families, we must have been relieved and constantly delighted to find ourselves always happy. It would have seemed unnatural, surely, to live together for three years and never mention that we were English teachers or that we loved literature. But a far more basic fact about ourselves (or at least about me), emotional and sexual identity, went unmentioned.

I wish I could end this story on a good lesbian feminist note— perhaps this can't be a *real* coming out story without a good lesbian feminist conclusion. Such as: Peg and Marcia discover that they are lesbians, rejoice in the discovery, drive off into the setting sun in the little blue VW, certain to grow more deeply attached to each other, thanks to their raised consciousnesses, and to continue their relationship for many years. Before the discovery and the rejoicing, unfortunately, we separated, without pain, partly because we could not get jobs in the same town and partly because we were ready for a change. But I'm afraid that we separated not really knowing that a female couple could stay together indefinitely, or even that we had in fact been a couple. We had experienced something for which we had no room in our imaginations—an alternative to marriage, a way of living ideally suited to us.

7 Meeting Myself

Judith Niemi

I've been telling coming-out stories for years—lots of us have, and mine were usually wry and funny. About how I got to be twenty-four before discovering I had a body as well as a mind. How I managed to be in love two years before noticing it. How I quit a job, travelled a thousand miles, made myself learn to drive and almost died, all in a pilgrimage just to be able to touch the woman I loved. How she said "You mustn't ever feel guilty about this" (she had rubbed my back through a flannel shirt) and when we had actually made love said "This doesn't mean we're lesbians, you know."

Now I discover I've been lying, and selling my young self short. After twelve years I've at last re-read the journals I wrote back then (and hid in a locked file box, willing them to friends with instructions to throw them into Lake Superior). It confuses me now to find out that I wasn't nearly as naïve as I'd remembered, that I knew I was a lesbian two years earlier than I'd remembered. I was plenty perceptive, considering that all the appropriate facts had been kept hidden from me.

For a long time I've looked back at that part of my life and been pleased by the blind courage I had—that so many young lesbians have. Now I'm thinking we aren't so blind either. We know what we know, in spite of all the crazy myths about us, and often we act even more wisely than we know.

The part of my discovery of myself that's easiest to watch, since I was finally acting on my knowledge, is the spring of 1965, when I was twenty-four and made that cross-country pilgrimage. That's the time I used to call my first coming-out until I re-read my journals and found that for years before that the most consistent theme was loving women. I cringe sometimes at my pompous and stilted language, and the ways I tried to be abstract about it all, but it's real clear that what I was trying to learn to do is to love and not be afraid.

When I started college I started keeping a journal, and in between comments on my studies and philosophical ramblings there soon started to appear recorded moments that now bring back vividly women that I loved in many ways. Trudy, who made me laugh more than anyone else ever has; we shared long talks, private jokes, even a birthday, and finally after many months her music, when she kidnapped me one day and gave me a private recital in an empty classroom. I was hurt and confused when after two years the friendship cooled. Carrie, who went off to graduate school hoping for once to find a man smarter than she was, and married one of her professors. Annie, with whom I shared one giddy spring term writing and secretly posting sarcastic doggerel verse; then she joined the convent. The night before she left we drove around town trying not to be serious, and she leaned out the window into the breeze, looking, I thought, as sensuous and elegant as a silky Irish setter.

Gradually I became self-conscious about my friendships. I'd never bothered to wonder why I wasn't interested in boys, but I sensed that whatever was going on with women needed a closer look. One summer at camp I was teaching outdoor skills, but spent every moment away from the mountains and rivers hanging around the stage, struck with the drama counselor. I said to my journal that my friendship with Carroll was "innocent, I think." I was feeling left out by her friendship with the music counselor, "listening for her voice and Kathy's, constantly imagining I hear them—not a good sign." I recorded "a strangely worried moment about my relationship, or rather my feelings, for someone like Carroll. No physical attraction for her—or for 'General'— but such a strange way of wanting them around—looking for them in a crowd, almost unconsciously ... hoping she'll stop to talk and afraid she will. Perhaps it's only hoping for more from a friendship that I can justifiably ask." I then wandered into some metaphysical musings on human isolation, and concluded (explaining to whom?), "the hasty hand does not indicate emotion but rather the damnable canteen pens. The emotion—the slight apprehension—associated with this is less distinct than the abstract idea." (Who was I kidding? Myself, fairly successfully.)

That period of devoted tender friendships, of fear that friends could just disappear, of walking around filled with loving and longing while acting correct and stiff, started to close in on me, or open up, or something, the spring that I graduated from college.

My best friend "General" Gage and I were in love, and we sort of knew it. We didn't care that our teachers noted, indulgently, this Damon and Pythias attachment. I made her May baskets. We sat all day at our special table in the cafeteria, and cut a lot of classes, and planned the log house we were going to build in Maine, a mountain behind it, and a lake in front. I was supposed to look for the land that summer.

I remember having careful dreams—about *other* women being lesbians, about an unidentified woman's slim hand by candlelight. And I developed asthma, learned the panic, sleeplessness and tense irritability of it. Someone told me lately that in one of those studies they like to do the only difference between lesbians and the control group turned out to be that we have more asthma—it figures, considering all the repressing we're supposed to do. So what I was doing that spring was not bothering to study, and partying a lot, and being overwrought. And for years I called it Senior Syndrome and thought I hadn't really known what was going on.

Last week, when I read what I'd been writing to myself that spring, I was astounded. I'd remembered being wistful and tense about leaving General, and I remembered a flattering flirtation with an older woman—about twenty-four?—whom I thought terribly sensual and worldly—her ambition was to look jaded. What I had forgotten is that there was a real triangle, and that I was perfectly aware of it. Just before a trip out of town with the exotic Iris I had "a distinctly sensual, homosexual dream... the understanding that I would not repel an advance." Well, she never made one quite obvious enough for my timidity, but she did (how could I have forgotten?) ask me to live with her (and how could I have hesitated? Fool.). And understandably General got jealous and said, "The team of Niemi and Gage isn't what it used to be." I was so upset that I wrote that in my journal twice, and I quickly repaired the partnership "partly, I'm afraid, through my rather deliberately seeing less of Iris."

My own words catch me being a lot less oblivious and innocent than I'd thought. In fact, I was wondering if the worldly Iris was "aware of a certain sensual element in any relationship, possibly ours in particular." I lay around my house after a party "smoking General's Kents lit with Iris's Tareyton matches." I came home late from another of our goodbye parties, "changed into my levis and an old shirt" (I made a point of noting that) and lay sleepless all night, thinking about separation and isolation and secrecy. Of course I knew what was going on.

But I forgot. I guess because what I don't talk about loses some reality. I'd never read about lesbians, never even heard a lezzie joke. So we never got past teasing. Iris read my palms, and at the end of the year gave me a tattered copy of *Childe Harold* given to her "by my lesbian friend Darlene." General and I didn't find the land for our cabin because although we'd one sunny morning agreed that she had the money, honey, and I had the time, we didn't know that women could take each other that seriously. That fall she started teaching, and I went away to graduate school.

Months later, missing her a lot, but still excited to be living in the rarefied air of Massachusetts, I raced up the stairs to my genuine garret apartment to tear open the latest letter from my love a thousand miles away. I read "by the way, am definitely not teaching next year. Am getting married." Sock to the stomach. I dropped into the chair and said "I will have hard work with my heart about this." Those words that I'd remembered are exactly what I found in my journal. But what I forgot for twelve years are the less romantic words I wrote next. That I also felt relief. Free. I recognized an emotional demand I wasn't ready for then, and a potentially symbiotic relationship that I don't want. But in the early sixties, what other kind of love did we know about?

So I retreated to the safer role of devoted friend, and that summer stood by through the pre-wedding frazzle and terror. I learned she wasn't in love (it seemed like she was rescuing him from alcohol, doing something useful with her life, being taken care of) so I didn't feel pushed out. And all this time, as she told me much later, I was supposed to say to her no, don't do it. Of course I didn't. I hid my feelings, sat through the wedding, and went back east. Then, within a few months, we "came out."

It's like a puzzle, a game of inventing difficulties so you can solve them. Now that we had me in an exciting new job in Massachusetts and her married in Minnesota, we managed to get together. Our bodies were smarter than our minds—I was still asthmatic, and she found other physical translations for mental pain. With the help of a doctor's misdiagnosis we thought she was dying, or at least gravely ill. And then since her husband hadn't stopped drinking, and she was frightened, she needed love and support and was able to ask for it.

She needed me. At last, a simplicity that I could act on. It even fit my idealism. Who I most loved and admired were tough old Quaker ladies who spoke their piece and got thrown in southern jails. I badly wanted to be old. (I think now that while I could easily imagine myself a feisty old lady in tennis shoes I didn't see how I was going to get through the years in between.) Now, like them, I had a cause. And just in case my nerve failed, the fates wove me a second: the lab where I edited space-age stuff wanted me to get a security clearance, which I properly refused to do. So I even had a plausible excuse for leaving the job, and didn't need to explain myself too much. "To keep from upsetting the universe" (my parents, that is) I never told them that the lab later backed down and said OK keep your principles and the job.

I tried to be casual about moving with no job and no future plans, but it wasn't easy. My good friend and roommate Isabel didn't understand, and I didn't know how to talk about it. When I was already packing, a phone call sort of blew my cover. (I used to think of this as a very special, uncanny event—lately many lesbians have told me about their experiences with being recognized before they wished to be, or even before they recognized themselves.) A young woman called, very upset. She said she knew me, she was breaking up with her roommate, she needed someone to talk to. I wasn't home; I heard all this from Isabel who was frightened by the woman's need and the sexual tone of the conversation, but who tried to meet her and talk with her. I've never known who the woman was, where she had met me, how she recognized me. Isabel never asked out loud why the woman had called me. When we discussed, in our mutual ignorance, how to help the woman if she called again I felt that I had some secret awareness, and wished I had been there to get the call, but I didn't say so. And after all, at that time I wasn't really any more familiar than Isabel was with the world of that unknown sister.

Maybe remembering this incident and how indirect I was in talking about it has confused me about how much I really knew. As closely as I can guess, I packed up in February to go home to the woman I loved, not quite sure this had anything to do with sexuality, and in March or April I knew. I was living in Minneapolis, a discreet but manageable distance from General. I worked junk jobs, rescued old ladies I met on the street, and I did an intensely private coming-out to myself.

That spring, while working out in my head what being a lesbian was going to mean, and what I was going to do about it, I didn't keep up my journal. (Did I fear its being found, or did I just lack words for what was happening?) I have a few scratched notes and some letters to go by, and a few clear pictures in my memory.

There was a phone in a dark hallway or stairwell at the boarding house. I would stand there, in the dark, the phone lines connecting our silences, each of us too pained to speak, offering love and consolation.

There was crabgrass in the scrap of yard next to the driveway. I sat there in the sun, trying to find the wisdom I thought books had. I had degrees in literature and months in the library behind me, yet all I could find was *The Children's Hour*, to warn me how dangerous my secret was, and Frank Caprio's porno-sociology, *Female Homosexuality*. Prurience passing as science. I found my lover-to-be among Caprio's descriptions of the causes of deviance, but nothing seemed to apply to me. I concluded that my own causes were more subtle, not yet described. I read about women deciding whether to act on their lusts, and of what happened, and I thought, I must make this decision carefully, it will certainly complicate her marriage.

There were nighthawks buzzing softly in the evening sky when I went walking with my friend Bob. I guess I was trying to prove that I didn't *have* to become a lesbian, because I was also letting my hair grow long. I spent a lot of time with this new male friend, whom I liked because he was tweedy and smart and because he spoke so warmly of his male and female friends—almost as nice as a woman. But his city ears couldn't hear the nighthawks, and it seemed a part of me was always listening for something I didn't have with him.

Every weekend I drove north to visit General, proud of having at last learned to drive, pleased with my beat-up Ford, my new independence and courage. We sat up late holding hands, gradually realizing that we were intending to become lovers, although we never spoke of it. Upstairs her husband slept. Then, and for years to come, Harry and I liked each other a lot, and in rare glances acknowledged that we also hated each other's guts. It never occurred to me to feel guilty that we were starting to touch, shyly, but I did feel guilty thinking of the nice man upstairs.

Remembering those scenes I hear the music that surrounded them. Along with General and Harry, I joined the orchestra performing a requiem mass that Easter. The rehearsals were a good excuse for my weekly trips. The music that filled my head was Faure's lament for his dead brother, my lament for my friend and soul-sister that I thought would die soon. All the tenderness and fear that I couldn't put in words were in a dark baritone voice singing "libera me, domine, e morte aeternam." Sunday evenings I'd drive back to the city, long spring shadows crossing the farmlands. Singing in the car "libera me, domine" and "kyrie eleison" and "black is the color of my true love's hair."

Back in the city I'd think some more, in a dusty room I hardly remember except for a tiny window high above the bed where I had obscure dreams that I didn't write down. Knowing I could get sexually involved, I felt heavy with responsibility. I don't know how I could have resolved the momentous decision I thought I was making for both of us, with only the help of Faure, the misinformation of Frank Caprio, and my own earnestness.

I solved it an easier way. I got sick. With spring pollens in the air, my tension mounting, my breath became shorter and shorter. Uninsured, not eligible to get sick, I left it untreated. I slept less and less until finally I got someone like the landlady, or maybe another tenant, to drive me to the emergency ward. They put me in the hospital where I spent the next couple days fighting like hell—about time, too—for breath and for life, and the next eight days in a slow peaceful recovery. No responsibilities. No decisions that I was allowed to make. The fight with asthma had also solved my dilemma, and I knew it at the time. I wrote in my "Commonplace Book" (safer than a journal) lines from Jean Christophe about eternal friendship, and about the purifying effects of severe illness. Other questions pale next to the incredible fact of being alive.

When I got out of the hospital the air was clean and sweet with spring, my lungs were clear, my sense of smell acute, my whole body clean and fine. I walked down the streets with a child's or an animal's sheer joy in living. It was all simple.

A few weeks later my friend and I went off together to our long-planned Quaker conference. I conscientiously recorded that I didn't wish to be hypocritical, I knew just why we were going—a chance to be alone for a week, to camp together. It was also the perfect supportive atmosphere, and I think we knew that. Loving people who didn't pry, children who didn't whine, eccentric and lively old ladies. It was probably one of the few places on this continent where we could be our best selves, and our whole selves, without criticism.

It took a few days, but then we did come back to our tent, moved by the evening speaker, and sat holding each other, and slept together. I was so uninformed that when I woke up damp I thought my period had started. The next day we shyly agreed it was cold, and wise to zip our sleeping bags together, so that was settled. And the whole time the weather was beautiful—I have color slides to prove it—and we were spiritual and committed and we hunted fossils on the beach and lived on buckwheat cakes and hamburgers, and fed the chipmunks. We were children, buying ice cream with the nickels and dimes we'd been saving up in my old marbles bag.

After the idyll, how did we return to routine life? That too we seemed to arrange with intuitive wisdom. I went to live at our family cabin; by that time I'd happened into a job teaching at my old college, in the same town General lived in, so I said and probably thought that I was going off to write lesson plans. Of course I never spent ten minutes doing that. But I lived by myself in a place full of childhood memories, and spent long hours picking raspberries, letting my thoughts circle and hover. Reassembling my view of myself in the light of new experience. On weekends my lover and our mutual friends sometimes visited— probably we managed to sleep together at times.

Somehow my retreat worked, and by fall when I moved into town I was only slightly shocked to find myself living a tense unacknowledged triangle, to be arranging secret hours together, secret phone signals. I almost enjoyed the acting, the absurdity of meeting her for lunch in the park where we watched the Meadowgold milk truck rendezvous with the maroon Oldsmobile.

It was early that fall that she said, "This doesn't mean we're lesbians, you know," and I said "Of course it does." But I knew what she meant. We didn't have to wear ducktails and men's shoes and drink ourselves to death. But being able to say the word wasn't at all like accepting it. There wasn't any women's movement then, no gay movement, certainly no lesbian feminism, and I could hardly have imagined a time when I'd feel free and proud.

In fact I became, for quite a few years, one of those lesbians I often resent, and pity, and understand. Women who, having defied convention so boldly in their loving, grasp desperately for convention some other way as John Birchers, or Florence Nightingales, or respectable, timid, and isolated professional women.

The first stage of my coming out had probably taken all the wisdom and courage I had, and living a subversive love affair provided a lot more excitement than I was used to. So I happily settled for trying to be respectable and inconspicuous. I wore little knit suits, and graded compositions conscientiously, and somehow forgot that I hadn't wanted to be a teacher. I devoted myself to teaching freshmen good grammar and clear thinking. My rebellion was limited to opposing the growing war in Vietnam. I don't think I imagined my future, but I acted as though I thought her husband would magically and painlessly disappear before too long, and we two would live in a white cottage, beloved and respected by friends and neighbors.

Well, we recognize as much as we can afford to. I didn't want to know then, even if I could have, where my life was going. It would have scared the hell out of me to guess all the changes and redefinitions and comings-out that would happen. There's no way I could have foreseen how strong and happy I feel now in a lesbian identity and lesbian community. That lonely time feels like a very long time ago. I'm glad I kept some record then so I can now try to bridge those years.

I wonder why I haven't read my old journals and letters until now. Maybe I thought it would be self-indulgent, narcissistic, or I thought somebody else would think so. And I'm pretty sure I didn't want to remember all the pain. I had to let it wait until now, when I feel less self-conscious, when I've learned I can get angry, can put my experience to use for myself. Until I felt that, I had to ignore much of my past, or falsify it in my memory.

Because if I wasn't that self I've been telling funny stories about, an ingenue walking around in erotic tender innocence until obvious reality got big enough to knock me on my naïve head—then who was I? A young woman whose intelligence and energy got diverted into channels irrelevant to her own life. Whose love for her friends didn't get expressed. Who knew a lot, in an obscure way, and dared tell the truth only in a long series of the smallest size Woolworth's notebooks. Who wrote what she knew and felt in an incredibly tiny neat hand, except occasionally, when the pain was really intense and came out in an illegible scrawl of emotion or brandy. And when the gap between who I was supposed to be and who I really was got widest, I went silent.

There's another side of myself that I've been slow to recognize, another lie. When I've been telling about my distant or more recent past I've often heard my own voice, quiet and controlled, saying "But I can't regret it. I mean, if you like where you are now, it seems pointless to regret the road that got you there." And that's pretty true, but dammit there is a lot that I *do* mind, and it leaves some scars. In the time I've been telling about, the foolish or risky things I did I feel OK about, but I regret a lot that I didn't do, and ways that we failed each other through lack of courage or merely lack of information. I'm sorry I lost touch with Annie and Carroll, and that I didn't know how to ask Trudy what went wrong in our friendship. I regret I didn't risk living with Iris. And although I like the guts and dedication that General and I put into that first really intimate relationship, it's too bad we had to put so much energy into hiding or fighting with the outside world that we never got to learn how two people live together, when we got the chance, nor how to leave each other with clarity. Unnecessary hurts, and years of unnecessary silence.

The day I first opened my locked file box, throwing away the note that said, "Trudy, please destroy these," I was exhilarated. I spread the secret letters and notebooks all over the floor, sorting, reminiscing, delighted to find so much. Glad someone—me—had cared enough to write it all down.

Then I felt awful. Reading about the past all morning made it so vivid that I forgot for a while that I wasn't young and afraid. As if I really were twenty-two again, I got "unaccountably depressed"—until I went to the gym. One of the best things I did for myself when I thought *Well of Loneliness* was my guide was to learn to fence, just like Stephen Gordon. Now picking up my foils reminded me that my depression is usually energy and anger turned inside out. I told the women I fence with that if they felt unusual hostility it wasn't directed at them—I was just letting myself get mad a little late. Thirty-five-year-old me, armed, in defense of the old me. Parry, tactical retreat, parry—I've always been pretty good at that—and then I let myself concentrate, attack. As soon as my random aggression settled down into a centered calm power, I stopped being competitive. As always happens when any one of us is really up, my partners picked up the energy, and for a while I fantasized that the five of us could have taken on anyone.

When you expected a past self to seem hardly recognizable, it's uncomfortable to have her look awfully familiar. I still worry about the ways I keep distance from others, and think I'm not sensitive to them. I worry that I learned too well to be secretive and passive, that I won't trust myself or others. I was fussing about it one day, shocked and irritated to find that I hadn't become an entirely new woman; my friend nodded, "Still playing with the same old bag of marbles, hey?" And I grinned, suddenly noticing that I was saying all this to a woman I had just met, with whom I was being not at all afraid and passive. "Ya, but I play a whole lot better." It helps that we expect openness and courage of each other. At its best, a lesbian feminist community feels to me like the only place we can be whoever we are while we work out together some better ways of being.

One of the few present reminders of my early lesbian years is that I still wheeze and run out of breath occasionally. Asthma is familiar and tiresome, but since it didn't kill me when it had the chance, it's not going to get in my way now. I got asthma in 1963 out of separation-anxiety, had my big coming-out attack in 1965, and had a first-love-isn't-forever attack in 1970; I don't expect ever to be hospitalized with it again. I've quit seeing the male doctors who tried to fix it up with needles and with chemicals that kept me speeding and jittery. Being happy is a lot better remedy. That's much easier to do in 1977, and I have a second family in my support group, a feminist therapist, and a community of friends to help me know what I'm feeling, lose my temper, and do what I want to do with my life.

I'd still like to stick around to be a seventy-year-old hellraiser, but I don't think about it a lot any more. I like being thirty-five and learning to break rules that used to seem important. I like talking with friends my age, laughing and feeling the closeness of survivors of a bad time. Talking with a younger friend, wiser than her years but with so many impossible decisions still to make, I feel an old ache and tenderness. She isn't angry, but I can't help getting mad for her, especially over her years of silence.

What I don't feel, or hear from any of my lesbian friends, is nostalgia. We'll jitterbug or bump to old music, but that's about it for recapturing past years. I called up General, whom I haven't seen for several months, and it was great to hear her old Yankee style on the phone, but better to know how much she too has changed. I'm writing a coming-out story, I told her, do you want me to try to disguise your identity? "Oh, don't bother. If anyone around here doesn't know I'm a dyke, that's their problem." Maybe I'll send this story to Isabel too, my old Cambridge roommate who was in on part of the story at a great distance. She's faithfully written at Christmas, telling about her work, her children, her hopes. I've been a rotten correspondent, not being able to explain myself in Christmas-letter terms. But we did our best to understand each other in 1965, and I don't remember now why I thought I couldn't bring her up-to-date on my world.

8 The Other Shoe

Diane Stein

First there was the woman I was born from. I would climb up on her lap and say, "Mummy, hug me," and sometimes she would. Sometimes she would say, "I'm busy now." Or sometimes my little sister would have gotten up there first. Or sometimes my daddy was home and I would not exist at all. "When you go to school, you won't need me," she said.

The day I started kindergarten I met standing in the corner by the easels a beautiful five-year-old with a fine long ponytail, and she became my friend. With her I needed no one else, though, I still liked Mummy's lap. I started to grow a ponytail like hers. We played in the kindergarten dollhouse, and we learned to skate. It took a year and a lonely summer before I discovered where she lived—just a few blocks down from my house with no streets to cross. She had a pond of goldfish and a spotted dog. Inseparable we were, our birthdays only days apart. We loved each other, unafraid to say it at that age.

The grade school teachers called one name and both of us would come; they mixed us up. Together at age eight we became swift horses running the Derby every afternoon across the lawns. She always ran it faster, but I never seemed to mind. She had a two-wheeled bike and I a bright red scooter that we rode on side by side. We walked each other home again by five o'clock each night.

In the sixth grade she was gone and I was crushed. Another friend. Someone said she liked *her* better and I never understood. No one to walk home with or to talk to anymore. No one could take her place. We had not fought, so why? What had I done? My mother said, "The teachers think you're much too close and it's not good."

The new kids in the junior high were not my friends at all. They dressed so well and always seemed so smart. No one from the grade school group was in my class. One girl broke my glasses and she ripped my skirt. They laughed at me. I ran away from them. The boys were worse. The boys would call me Uglypie and say I stank. They dared each other now and then to ask me out. I went for them with nails and fists; they thought that that was great. They took turns at games like "grab my front," while cheering each other on. They followed me home through alleys, told my mother that they loved me and how beautiful I was. One of them threw a beer-can, and the cut bled down my face. I learned to cry from men that year, and fight them. And I learned to hate.

High school meant more trying, failing, being hurt, to "be a part." It took a newer friend six months to bridge withdrawal, and she really *was* a friend. "You have the loyalty to love someone for life," she said, "but who would ever see it through that shell?" She saw and had the love in her to free the love in me. Quietly and slowly she and I grew close. But after graduation came she went away.

Oh sure, I had my fill of loving all the teachers, but I scorned the high school boys. There was nothing there to chase. I never saw the women that I loved as more than "friends," but friendship meant much more to me than any date. I would not stoop to reach for any men—or be stooped on. I always thought that I would fall in love—but not with Sara in the senior grade; and not with Marcy who was older than I was by three years; and not with Clare in college who slept over one night and hugged me, and who refused to stay the weekend then because we were afraid.

I loved a man once. Only one. He showed me things I never knew were there. Records, poets, books. One day he said to me, "I don't want you anymore." I wanted him but he was cruel and gone. For a while to me he was a god. And for that while there was no me, just him and me as his. It lasted long after he had disappeared. It took a woman again to show me who I was and why, and that I had to find myself in me and not in someone else. Not even inside her who I had only touched that once, one shy kiss before she too was gone. And each of these who left, left something of themselves behind.

I don't know when it finally occurred to me that it was women and not men that I could love. It should have been so obvious by high school days, but love of women was never a possibility that I even realized could be. You loved your mother and your aunts, and you had girlfriends for a while. Someday, though, you would always meet a man. I resented it when girls broke arrangements we had made to go out with a guy instead. Our plans had been set, who was any man to take priority? But they did, of course, and I never told anyone that I was hurt. It didn't seem right to be. It was selfish. Men came first. My one male love came first for me: it made no difference that I would not be first for him.

For many years, too many, I remained alone. Neither accepting men (who I hated desperately to touch me in any way), nor recognizing any attachment beyond "friendship" with a woman. Too many years and too alone. When through feminism and through women's books I discovered a word that meant who I am, a lesbian, I became afraid. I recognized myself, but thought that I was something wrong, that I had to change myself fast or be hopelessly empty and lost. I thought that maybe I had not met the right man yet, but one day I still would. My mother, when I spoke of it, had said just that. On lesbianism? "Don't be ridiculous. I don't want to hear such dirty things."

I have since learned. I am not looking for a man. I want a woman to love. I want a marriage with that woman, someone to share a life with, and I visualize my partner now as someone much like me. A woman. I am proud to be a woman for the first time: I know what I want. I am proud to be a woman too who can love women. Who but women would be worthy of that love?

Fishing Poles, Ice Water Teas and Me

9

Dee Graham

The opportunity knocked on my door for the first time when I was 14. Unfortunately, I only peeked through the chain.

Her name was Joleen. Joleen McQuerry. I should have known.

"Stay over tonight and we can feel each other up," she asked me.

She was blunt, the way of all the southern Florida crackers who populate the innards of the state away from tourist traffic. It was natural for her, and I loved her in a cautious way, despite her red neck. She was pretty all right, and I knew damn well she'd seen more sex than I had, her being 15 and all, but I figure I must have been just plain scared. Besides, her boyfriend was a Seminole and the chief's son at that. No way I wanted to get mixed up with some girl out to be an Indian boy's squaw. No way I wanted to get mixed up with that Indian boy.

"I'm not allowed to spend the night away from home," I lied.

"Well," she suggested, "how about getting out your Barbie dolls and letting them do it."

Mattel would have been shocked. Our teenage plastic models became French lesbians and their boyfriends were tossed in the corner to find their own amusement. The back porch began to look like a lavender lair and I became absorbed in the sport until the neighbor boy came over and we had to hide the dolls. We were too old for that, you know.

Joleen and I had started our infamous friendship when my folks bought a cabin on the lake. We spent lots of weekends there fixing up the place, but the only other kids were the sons of my uncles who were, of course, boys and not much fun to be around (unless you like shooting beebees into wasps' nests and running away almost before they can sting you). Joleen and her sister Jean were more my style. They lived with their mother and step-father in one of those A-frames and they knew lots about living in the country. Especially fishing.

My friends' step-father was a catfisherman and the whole family helped. He taught us girls how to use soap to bait the lines by slipping tiny squares of Ivory onto tiny hooks tied into plastic thread. Then we piled the lines, having strung them across square wooden frames, on top of each other in stacks. When I was there I could become absorbed in the work, but it was the conversation that went on in that workshed that kept my interest.

Joleen knew all about sex. She knew the words of things and even dared to sneak off with a boy after school sometimes. I figured living in town I was just stuck with being behind the times as far as such things— maybe I thought I could put it off longer—but I always listened closely and saved up my best jokes for her. Of course, we always had to find ways to avoid Jean, 'cause she'd tell on us and then we'd all be in trouble, but Joleen and I usually would sneak off to swim in the muddy water and share our secrets. We'd find excuses to touch each other, ducking under the waves when a boat drove by. Sooner or later, though, Jean would show up and we'd have to pretend we were bored and talking about something run-of-the-mill like the neighbors.

As we both grew older and I spent more time at home working on the class play or the student newspaper, the memories of those days all but left me. I dated boys, selected one out of the possibilities and became engaged. I started college and moved away from home. And then, like a flash from Wonder Woman's lariat, the lavender light hit again.

Sorority life was a packaged deal at Florida Southern. Delayed rush put sweet young things into a post-Christmas rush of ice-water teas in a country club atmosphere. Smile. Be nice. Look pretty, but not too pretty. Be charming, but not charmed. I put my best foot forward and then almost tripped over it. You're not supposed to fall in love at a getting-to-know-you party.

She was obnoxious and plump, but it was the look in her eye and her off-the-cuff butch attitude that drew my attention to her. Although I was too naive to know she'd been drinking, I laughed with her as she halted the rotation from guest to guest by spending the entire time at my side. And while I fought my urge to join that particular sorority because my friends were joining another, my heart was sold over and she had a foot in my closet door. No bones about it, the skeleton was out.

You couldn't really say I came out myself when I moved into her room, nor when I found myself in the middle of a jealous fight between her and another "sister." And you couldn't say I came out when our names became linked and I slept with my head on her breasts. Up until then it wasn't real. We were affectionate, but we weren't making love. Like birthing, my coming out was violent and bloody, framed with anger but driven by the deepest love I had known.

She was my big sis, a standardized sorority role that was supposed to mean a special friend, a guide. She guided me all right, her eyes penetrated my shell of heterosexual anonymity and I struggled against her possession (or my own possession of myself). Maybe that's why it hurt so much when I found out that boy had trespassed her lips—those other, somehow more private lips—with his tongue. It only made it more maddening that he had been my lover-of-sorts up to then. Since she and I had only stumbled across our physical loving in a clumsy way, I guessed she thought it made her "okay" if she slept with a boy at the same time. I tried to forget she was a virgin when I met her.

Still, this was too much! To have him buried where I had not been—to have him share her flavor when I had not tasted her. I knew I hadn't been especially eager to go down on her, since confronting the Monster was confronting myself, my own mysteries. But at 18 a woman doesn't stop to think through such things, she simply acts on impulse.

We pulled the mattress off my bed into an empty dorm room, not stopping to worry that others might hear. Still shy, I laid her down gently and touched her all over to reclaim her body, to demand territory the only way I knew how. Her hair was black and curly except where it was still damp. So soft. I touched her and then glazed her whole body with my hands. She looked at me through questioning eyes. I understood.

"You don't have to," she told me. She didn't know there was no question left, no point of return.

Blood was flowing from her lips, her vagina warm with menstrual blood. It stopped me for a second, my mind flashing on lifetimes past when women's blood was feared or considered sacred, but my Amazon-self was moving forward. I was driven by jealousy or anger or just simple determination, and I dove into the fleshy river of blood. It was thick and warm, causing my throat to choke in response to my squeamish mind. My face was surrounded with moving, circular folds that wrinkled next to my cheeks and I let myself drool into my oral caressing.

When I closed my eyes, nervously afraid of her pleasure and not yet recognizing my own, I was smothered in smells. I could hardly breathe. My mind raced onward, forgetting the anger that had driven me into her and rushing on, instead, out of an inner longing far deeper than the charge of a moment's jealousy. No longer could I return—I was inside the forbidden catacombs of the pyramids, repeating the dance of birth, revolving, evolving, inward, outward. Swimming, shaking in rhythm, she grabbed my head and my hands reached to her thighs, her stomach, her breasts, smearing her with blood as I might a sister warrior in the heat of battle. She cried out as she let herself tense and relax, her vaginal lips pressing together in response to her orgasm.

Still, I waited.

Finally, she drew me upward where she cleaned my face with the corner of the pillowcase and held my head between the fullness of her breasts. We were calm in the eye of a hurricane.

10 Coming Out

Janet Cooper

Although I did not have the word for Lesbian when I was nine years óld in 1951, I certainly had the awareness of wanting certain other girls and women to desire to touch me as much as I desired to touch them. My fantasies included such scenes of yearning as holding hands and lying in the arms of these other girls and women as well as sharing confidences, sympathies, and adventures with them. I have never had such fantasies about boys or men.

I did not know that I was coming out.

But imagining situations in which I was able to give and to receive affection and tenderness from other females was quite another matter than actually having the courage to act on those feelings. For too long I had no confidence that any of the other girls and women I dreamed about might want to share time with me in the way I wanted to share time with them. Before we could describe our fantasies out loud, and instead of making love, the girl next door and I would beat each other up. We found confronting each other easier than giving and receiving comfort.

She did not know that she was going to come out.

I had no words for what I was. I had no models. I did not understand my parents' nasty allusions to most of my friends. Whenever I was about to leave my parents' house to see most of my friends, my mother would direct my father to beat me. At the time I did not realize that such beatings were my parents' way of forming a homophobic vigilante.

My parents never came out.

My parents could not watch me all the time. They could not be in my skin when I thrilled creating the strategy to brush against another girl's or to arrange to sit so close to her that some part of our bodies touched, or to exchange sparkling glances longer than we had any reason to look.

I did not know how to name these sensations coming out.

Most of us who were into the girl-gang fighting scenes on the high school lawn at dawn now call ourselves Lesbian. I was not the first on my block to be that honest with herself.

Some of these girls did come out while we were entering puberty.

I often reflect on the value of my schooling when I remember that the most precocious girl among us who found the word Lesbian first, who found the Lesbian bars first, and who was able to call herself Lesbian first, could not pass high school tests.

By naming herself Lesbian and by seeking out other women who could call themselves Lesbian, she came out first.

Being a Lesbian still was not something I was. For me, being a Lesbian was still a word apart from my identity. I was still unable to conceptualize what being a Lesbian meant and I thought the context in which I heard people whisper the words bull dagger, dyke, lesbian, and homoserous was slanderous.

I did not know that whether I had the word or not, that whether I could apply that word to myself or not, I had come out. Just because I could not be honest with myself did not mean that I was not a Lesbian. Whether or not I could acknowledge to myself that my intimate personal affectional fantasy life was exclusively Lesbian, I had come out.

And because I must have feared rejection more than I wanted a relationship, several more years passed before I tried to share my affections sexually with another girl. And because I was shy and lacked confidence, I did not understand that some other girls wanted me to receive their affections sexually during this same time.

Because of such self-conscious awkwardnesses, I missed coming out sexually as young as I would have welcomed and enjoyed sharing my sexuality.

But all that self-denial which I had cultivated with more vigor than I had created any atmosphere in which I could lie curling my body around another girl's broke down. She and I had been friends for a long time. I only remember now how gradually we both became aware of growing tenderness and affection between us. We had taken a bicycle ride and planned a picnic. As we walked around after lunch, we just seemed to walk closer to each other than usual. As our arms shared the rhythm of walking, the backs of our hands touched and we finished our walk holding palms. After we returned to our bicycles, we stood still and only then did we look with favor into each other's eyes. For a long time we shared a tender glance until she brushed her cheek against mine and we kissed.

I had come out, but to this day she would not say that she had come out. Nor would she describe all the subsequent afternoons of our lying in each others' arms as coming out.

Maybe the reason she does not perceive herself as a Lesbian even now is because we did not share clitoral fondling. In the 1950's, sexuality had as many divisions as the Hollywood film rating system.

So maybe I had come out but had not really come out yet.

Many women who would never be able to apply the term Lesbian to themselves have participated in such scenes with other girls and women without sharing my fantasies and without sharing my passions. Throughout the latter part of the 19th century and into the early 1920's, girls and their mothers read stories portraying female crushes, affections and friendships in children's literature with a loving devotion that would be similar to the way a contemporary Lesbian audience gives attention to a new release by a popular Lesbian singer. I was fortunate in having access to such stories when I was a child. As a result this literature which I found in attics and obscure small town libraries complemented and supported the way I felt.

I have often wondered how many readers who lived vicariously through scene upon scene of affection in girls' story after girls' story ever came out. Not every woman is able to say:"I came out!" "I am coming out!" "I come out!" "I will come out!" Some women will never be able to come out. And somewhere in the future, coming out will no longer be a relevant distinction and no one will come out.

I began to meet other women who enjoyed cuddling with me as much as I enjoyed cuddling with them. I began to meet others who anticipated our playful sensualness as much as I did. Undulating rhythms in response to each other's gentleness did not offer enough satisfaction. Neither she nor I wanted to continue to love on the edge of our senses without some shudder of relief. Our wetness in response to each other's presence did not need any more strokes.

As we rolled each other around on the end of our tongues, we came out.

11 Diary of a Queer Housewife

C.J. Martin

The day I accepted my label I still didn't know the word lesbian. The label I accepted was homosexual. Still, I had problems with even that since what little I could find in the literature that was available to me in 1950 was about men or about women in prison. Since neither of those categories included me I concluded that I had to be what I had suspected all along—I was alone in my affliction—so horribly deviant, there were no others like me.

My common sense told me this was an extremely unlikely state of affairs. Nevertheless, I had to assume that being a female homosexual was at least exceedingly rare and the possibility of my ever meeting anyone similarly emotionally and socially crippled was utterly out of the question. That seemed especially true for me because, 1) I was not willing to go to prison where I could meet women who were using sex with other women as a substitute for sex with men (which the books I read all made plain was the only reason women could possibly have for such a reprehensible practice), and 2) I lived in an admittedly middleclass, mid-western college town where surely such people would stand out like the proverbial sore thumbs if they did exist at all.

i searched myself for *the cause* or at the very least *the beginning*. When did I start to feel sexual about women? Was it because my mother was a dominating factor in our family? Was it because I admired and wanted to emulate my brother? Was it because I had always felt more than vaguely silly and resentful about attempting to fulfill the traditional passive, giggling, inactive, non-achieving feminine role? Was it because I was a "tomboy" and always liked sports? Why? Why me, lord? I never found the answer and gave up trying.

That discomfort with my feminine role however was to cause me to make an early and conscious decision about my sexual fantasy life. I simply could not imagine myself interacting sexually with any of the males I knew. I couldn't make it in my head either with even the most handsome male movie stars I knew of. My self-image simply could not accommodate the concept. I knew I was too fat, too ugly and undesirable for one thing and my pragmatic self rejected the whole thing as just too ridiculous to even attempt to deal with.

The other factor I had to consider was that men just didn't excite me, but women did. I had already faced the fact that I had crushes on a couple of actresses and at least three different girls at school. This was "normal for my age" I was told, though it did seem to me that my crushes seemed somewhat more intense and certainly more sexual in nature than those my peers experienced, if, indeed, they experienced them at all. I was also somewhat concerned about the fact that a girlfriend and I had practiced kissing techniques with each other and *I* really liked it. Her mother found out about it and, much to my consternation and very real puzzlement, forbade us to associate with each other.

I also could not deal with a fantasy life where I, as my female self, approached other women sexually. The same negative self-image feelings entered into that decision, but in addition, I had never heard of such a thing and I knew instinctively it was "bad." Of course *all* sex was "bad" and not to be talked about, let alone "doing it."

And so, I made one more adaptation and in my fantasies I became the most desirable male I could imagine. There were times when I wanted intensely to be male and I would pray when I went to sleep that I would awaken and find the miraculous transformation had taken place. I felt I could not bear one more day as a female.

No one ever knew of my fantasies. I knew better than to ever talk about them with even my closest friends. Allusions to "fairies" and "queers" kept me in line even though I wasn't sure what they were talking about and was afraid to ask.

Occasionally I would wonder what was wrong with me. Why wasn't I like the other girls? Somehow I cherished the belief that eventually I would get over liking girls and I would begin to like boys. Indeed, as I entered my late teens and began dating I did fall in love with a boy and was utterly devastated when he fell in love with my best friend and married her. Even in my heartbreak I acknowledged, with no little sense of relief, that now I must be "all right" and I entered into a period of normalcy where my dating and fantasy life were largely heterosexual. My expectations of the future were never anything but heterosexual because I was unaware of any other alternative.

Even during this period I was not totally free of my attraction to other women but I could rationalize it because I was also interested in men and I was anxious to get on with the more serious aspects of my life—marriage and a family.

As a freshman in college, where the men outnumbered the women three to one, I enjoyed an unprecedented popularity with men. I felt sexy and desirable but vaguely uncomfortable. I also had a continuing problem of being attracted to women. I no longer fantasied about them as much, but when I did I had a harder time explaining it to myself. I also experienced, for the first time, an attraction to my best friend that was so deep and exciting I had difficulty repressing the sexual elements of it in my mind. Finally I had a dream about her that stripped away any pretense I had about my true feelings and I had to face the existence of the thought that perhaps this was not a "stage" I was going through—but I could not name it, even to myself. I also took no little comfort in the fact that I could not begin to imagine being sexual with a woman. The emotional aspect was undeniable but the physical was literally unthinkable.

By then I had chosen my life mate and we were already through the "going steady" phase and well into the "pinned" or "engaged to be engaged" aspect of our relationship. My life was set—pre-planned—unchangeable! I received my diamond in the midst of this secret turmoil and I felt this was really the end of the matter once and for all. I was engaged to be married. Such things were immutable and I was saved from my unnamed and unnameable deviance forever by the proverbial "good man." Thus I rationalized it away one more time and avoided confrontation with myself and my destiny.

Then came fate in the form of a Ph.D. candidate in psychology (no, not a woman) who requested that the members of my sophomore psychology class take a test he was developing and attempting to validate. I volunteered since I loved to take tests. That day is branded into my memory and along with it the feelings I experienced.

"I am attracted to members of my own sex"—(Oh, my God!)—False! Of course not! "I have many friends of the same sex as myself"—well, of course I do, dummy—(whew!)—True! What could be more normal? "I am sometimes attracted to members of my own sex"—well—what does *attracted* mean? Aren't you supposed to be attracted to your friends? I mean, if they aren't attractive, why would you want to be with them—true? "Members of my own sex are attractive to me"—I just said they were, didn't I? So, I guess they are. True. "I am often sexually attracted to members of my own sex" ...

I was nineteen. I put the pencil down, gathered my books and left the classroom with my ears buzzing and my heart pounding. I went to a familiar campus hangout and had a cup of coffee in an attempt to re-orient myself to what passes for reality. There it was. Confusion. Almost elation. More confusion. Pain. I really *am* different (meaning deviant).

What does it all mean? Who can I turn to? Am I a homosexual? What *is* a homosexual? I went to the library and came away empty. I talked to a friend (not my best friend, whom I loved, but another one) and she knew nothing but accepted me and wasn't threatened. I told my young fiancé I was a "latent homosexual" but I was *sure* I would never do anything about it (I didn't know how and who was there to do it with?). And then I tried to forget it. It was my cross to bear.

The night before my wedding was the only other time I was tempted to face my "disease." I tried to do it alone, although I was surrounded by my best friends. I lay awake tortured by the thought that I was not being fair to my husband-to-be. I knew I was not in love with him, and yet, I assured myself, as I had assured him, that I would never do anything about my feelings. I wanted to run away, but I had no place to go and I couldn't justify all the pain I would leave in my wake or even imagine the consequences of such an act. Besides, there were no others like me and I knew I did not want to function alone and unloved.

And so I stayed for eighteen years and I bore and raised four children who filled my life with love and activity. I was the president of the P.T.A., the chairman of my church circle, sang in the choir and the P.T.A. Mothersingers and I lived with my awful secret. I was Mrs. Mid-West Suburbia with my bridge club, golf and bowling league and no one ever knew.

I learned the word lesbian when I was twenty-four, after I'd had my first child. At thirty, after the birth of my last child, I made another decision—that I was going to have a chance someday to know what it was to love a woman. I didn't have any idea of how or when, but I was no longer willing to consider the possibility of going through life without that experience. I had done all the "right" things for everyone for eleven years and my overwhelming feeling was that life was passing me by. I felt there had to be more to life than what was happening to me.

Something else had happened. I had fallen in love with my best friend and I had no trouble at all imagining myself making love to her. It never happened, but I realize now it was only my lack of experience that kept us from it. She and her family moved hundreds of miles away a short time after the birth of my youngest child, leaving me shattered and grieving. We went to visit them in the summer, and I knew then if we had become lovers it would have destroyed two families because I would have torn down mountains to get to her.

It was seven more years before I managed to keep my vow to have a love affair with a woman. I still had no knowledge of a community of gay women and men. I still didn't know what "gay" meant, other than "happy." I certainly had no conception of a gay sub-culture. The big question for me even past my first affair was how to find other women like myself.

I reasoned finally if *I* had those feelings toward women then surely *other* women might also have them. The only way to find out was to start asking, right? But how, without exposing myself to danger? Eventually I worked out a system whereby if I became attracted to someone I would use all of the normal means of gaining closeness and then I would share the fact that I had some curiosity about homosexual behavior but I knew nothing about it. The kinds of replies I received told me a lot about general attitudes toward the subject and sometimes gave me clues about things they might have read, heard, seen, etc. Obviously it was a long slow process.

Finally, between my thirty-sixth and thirty-seventh years I found two women who were also curious and discussions in time reached the stage where I felt it was worth the risk of saying that I was attracted to them (individually, not collectively) and had thought about asking them how they felt about it. More time went by and one admitted she too had thought about it, but she decided she wasn't strong enough to face all that it would mean. The other woman became my lover.

I had always had the idea I would be able to maintain my marriage virtually unchanged. I envisioned a light little pleasant affair "on the side." That was probably true for about the first week of our involvement. After that I was so deeply committed to her I literally could not think of anyone or anything else. I had been able to *imagine* making love to a woman, but what I left out was her responsiveness. I was enchanted, obsessed, utterly done in! I could never have imagined anything so glorious and fulfilling.

I was a part-time graduate student when I finally managed to have that first affair, and I was still a housewife. My friend was also married (to an alcoholic) and had two small sons and, in addition, she worked full time. She had given me every reason to believe she was open to an affair with me, although I was unbelievably dense about it. She found opportunities to sit close to me, give me shoulder rubs, passed by me so that we could not avoid touching, invited me over to fix my hair while announcing softly, "One of the most intimate things you can do is fix someone's hair" (all the while leaning against me with her breast in my ear). She invited herself along and included herself in every activity she could manage. She invited me to her home on nights when her husband was out drinking. She wore seductive, revealing outfits that had me so weak in the knees I all but became a babbling idiot. And, when I finally psyched myself up to make my big move (I kissed her on her shoulder) she withdrew rapidly saying she didn't think she was ready for that. Docile to the end, I accepted her judgement—and within minutes she resumed cuddling close and touching. I was puzzled and hurt. I demanded that she stop teasing if she felt she wasn't ready because I *was* ready! She didn't stop, and boldly (comparatively speaking) I kissed her cheek—and then her eyes, and her neck and her ears and at last, breathlessly, our mouths met—and then I decided I wasn't ready after all. Not only that—what do lesbians *do*?

The next Saturday I went back and we quickly discovered no instructions were necessary.

We were together for eighteen months. Then she couldn't stand the social isolation, the secrecy, my demands for total and constant involvement. She began dating a man and I nearly lost my mind with the grief of my loss. I waited for three years, hoping she would come back to me. I still didn't know any other lesbians and I still had no idea of how to make contact.

I joined N.O.W. because I believed in feminism and because I thought I might meet someone at one of the meetings. I didn't. If there were lesbians there they weren't any better at finding me than I was at finding them. My first contact with other lesbians did happen to be at a N.O.W. Regional Conference in Illinois. Besides being out of the state they were all young and I was not.

I took a post-graduate course at the local university and became infatuated with my professor, but I had no idea of how to approach her. Meantime I read in the newspaper that the Gay Freedom Alliance had formed a chapter in town and I wrote to a local box number with great trepidation. One of the women contacted me but affirmed my fears that everyone was much younger than I and she didn't have any suggestions and didn't I know *anybody* near my own age I *thought* might be gay. My despair was complete. The only person I could think of was my professor. I decided that I *had* to find a way to try to get acquainted with her.

I worked with a young woman who had told me she was bisexual. I asked her if there wasn't some way to let people know you were gay without endangering yourself. She suggested the phrase "I'd like to get to know you better" as one which was fairly universal recognition but at the same time is innocuous enough to avoid trouble. I steeled myself and laboriously wrote a note to Dr. X. saying how much I had enjoyed seeing her again at a recent conference and how I would really like to get to know her better. I received no reply and so continued my aimless and haphazard search, feeling more and more hopeless about the possibility of ever meeting anyone again.

Throughout the fall I made attempts to re-orient myself to men and heterosexuality. My former lover convinced me I had never really given men a chance since my husband was the only man I had ever had sexual relations with and he was, to put it as kindly as I know how, inept. I went into what I now refer to as my "Screw-the world" phase. The main thing I learned was I don't bond emotionally with men and no matter how handsome and/or skilled they might be, for me that is not enough. I was also still very much in love with my ex-lover and we never did quite manage to make the break totally. I dangled helplessly knowing I could never really have her and yet I was not able to break away to start again.

Christmas came and a friend from N.O.W. who was also a professor at the university casually mentioned to me that Dr. X. was having a cocktail party and she had asked my friend to convey an invitation to me. Elation! Panic! What do I do now? I tried to be casual in my acceptance and when the night finally arrived I changed my clothes four times trying to find something that didn't make me look too straight.

That evening resulted in the establishment of my second relationship, but my lover was exceedingly closeted and she had a continuing fear that something I would do or say would result in disaster for both of us. I was also the first married woman she had ever been involved with in the twenty years she had been a lesbian and it was difficult for her to accept the fact that I had to go home and sleep with my husband after she and I had made love. It was a stormy two-and-a-half year affair during which we made every attempt to adjust our divergent backgrounds, but the obstacles were too great. I learned this time that love is not enough. She also taught me another important lesson—before I could hope to have anything to give to a relationship I had to find out who I was and what I was all about.

I really had no identity of my own. I was somebody's wife, mother, lover, friend, daughter and so on, ad infinitum. I blended, I accommodated. My theme song was, "tell me what it is you want me to be and I'll be that."

During that two-and-a-half years I formally ended my long-since dead marriage, not because of my lover or for any other reason except that it was time.

It wasn't as easy as one might think to end a relationship of that duration. I could, however, no longer attempt to be what I wasn't—but I wasn't sure what I wanted to be. My marriage might have been dull and dead, but it was safe. My husband might have made me miserable and unhappy, but he made me respectable. I feared I might not be able to take care of myself. I had gone from my father's house to my husband and I never had been on my own a day in my life.

My lover didn't want me to openly live with her, so I got a small apartment. My husband vowed he would never pay a penny of child support and said he would never give up custody of the children to me. My oldest child was eighteen and the youngest was twelve. Because I had known other women who had successfully done it, I found the courage to do what was best for my own self-growth and I temporarily left them in custody of their father. I called them daily from work as I had done before and I saw them as often as their schedules would allow. The loneliness was bitter at first and the guilt was difficult to deal with. My old practicality carried me through it all. If I couldn't take care of myself how would I ever take care of anyone else? I was also absolutely certain I would have them back again. They did, indeed, come back to me, one by one. My husband remarried within days after the divorce became final and in doing so managed to throw doubt on all the evil rumors he had spread about me to our friends. His wife had an authoritarian approach to discipline and in the resulting conflict she both physically and mentally abused our children. As they were deposited, one by one, on my doorstep and I accepted them with open arms, the stigma I had borne of having abandoned my children disappeared.They, interestingly enough, never felt I had abandoned them at all.

After my first daughter came to live with me I moved into a feminist collective with one straight woman and her one child and one single woman who was gay. We shared expenses and parenting and gave each other sisterhood and support. It gave us all strength and time to grow and discover who we were.

As each child moved into our wild and crazy loving household I shared with them my "secret." Each accepted me and shared with me that they really had it figured out all along anyway and they were pleased to be trusted by me. I have had inevitable fears of unduly influencing them during critical formative years and of agonizing over fear of exposure by their friends. They, however, are firmly who they are and their friends are, thus far, either oblivious or trustworthy.

Many more women I knew during that period re-evaluated their lives as I had and came out. I discovered gradually the complexity and richness of the lesbian community and sub-culture. Whereas before I couldn't seem to meet lesbian women, now I moved in circles where there were many woman-identified-women. My life changed dramatically in a relatively short time from Mrs. Straight White Suburbia to Ms. Alternative Lifestyle.

I had previously thought of my sexual preference as a handicap, an emotionally crippling disease. Suddenly I realized that most lesbian women I knew were people I greatly admired. They were self-actualized, independent and interesting people.

In the eight years since I first started to come out I have grown and changed in ways that would never have been possible otherwise. My attitudes and values have undergone drastic shifts and I have become younger in both appearance and outlook. I can't afford to "act my age." I have too much to accomplish and too little time left in which to do it. I am still discovering who I am and where I am going.

My children all know and accept me as I am. I find I am less and less able to compromise my appearance and the way I live and the games become less acceptable to me daily. I have already come out in ways I thought I never could and to people I thought I never would. Perhaps someday I will not feel the necessity to "pass" at all.

12 "Coming Out" to Myself

Ellen Roe Anthony

Scrawling it into my journals, writing very fast, especially around Christmas Holidays, I've been "coming out" to myself since age sixteen, 1963. The entries about my sexuality read raw, upset and not always truthful even to myself! They seem, for that very reason, authentic to the moment...

(1967, age 20)

We would lie on the living room floors of either house and just laugh and laugh. I said about a thin person once, "He is probably inbred" and right off she said, "Oh no—he's out of bread!" And we'd do borrowed jokes like, "I used to know a fellow, had two heads—name was Harry Harry. I'd give him advice, but it would all go in one ear out the other, in one ear out the other." And names we'd make up for people—Ted String, Cheryl Gristle. And lots of doing foreign accents. Declaring "Fraternite, Fertilite, Egalite," out the car window and then when we'd get home we'd drift into our ballet routine—one of us would bend and pose while the other described it, "Plie... Arabesque... Scalopini... Masquera..."

And today we're both twenty and still we hug and kiss good-bye and are pretty sad to be serious and alone. I said today, "But then the whole point of friendship is that you can go out from it, right?" trying to make our good-bye easier. And she almost cried it was so wonderful an idea for us to have about each other.

I wrote that about my six-year-long best friend, Naomi. It was out of the goodness of our relationship that I began to know I loved women. But it was her mother who then taught me to fear that love.

(1965, age 17)

I kind of swaggered out of my neighbor's [Naomi's] house. I think maybe I felt like a big shot because the moon was special—it was soft orange against navy blue. But that's unimportant.

I just saw "Brief Encounter." My neighbor's mother, who has just gotten a divorce, said the really lovely thing about it was the woman in the movie had character—she would have liked to sleep with her lover but she didn't. "That's just it. You can't just go busting up a home when you're very attracted to another man." It seemed lovely the identification and admiration she has for morality. I wish I had some of that.

When I see that kind of film I can hardly swallow because I could love so much if I had the chance. I swear I'd give anything. But they all repulse me or overwhelm me, men. I don't know what I want. I don't know what I'm trying to do to myself. I had mentioned something about some people thinking I'm a lesbian to Naomi's mom and she became very silent. She scared me into believing that I am one. I don't get it. I read last night that both sexes have a little of each other in them. Why is it so awful. I don't know what I'm doing though. I swear to God I'm a girl— just no one will believe me. During one of the intermissions tonight I got up off the floor. My ankles were so stiff, it felt like I'd been bunched up there all day. But I made myself jump up and down and kick my legs up. Mostly I loved swinging my arms out because I'm so careful up top all day, self-conscious about my breasts. Oh dear I keep thinking of my English teacher who gave me an "A" for the year which I didn't deserve. I love her. Sometimes I wish I were like her, sometimes I wish she were my mother. But mostly I wish I was worth something to her.

I love Naomi—not at all physically. I just God damn it to hell love her. And I only wish I weren't so suspicious to her and anyone else.

So many elements of coming-out that have recurred since then are right here. Seeing heterosexual models of love on TV, wanting to love and be moral. Thinking I'm not moral, period. Saying I don't know what I want, if I don't want what's on TV. Seeing my lesbianism as something I'm doing to myself, punishing myself for it, but then not taking responsibility for it either by saying, "She scared me into it." Feeling confused. Reading the "experts." Wondering if I am a woman. Tension in my body. Diverting my attention to writing/teachers/excelling ... putting me down, her up ... my worth dependent on her. Scared that I do love Naomi physically. Projecting my own suspicion of myself as lesbian onto her.

(1966, age 18)

I don't know what I'm doing. I do know that it is foolish. I have been calling it indulgence and that's accurate. I have hated a girl here for a year. Her name is Laurel. But she is now in my poetry class and she recently left a note on my door, "I wanted to see you but I couldn't knock." So finally last night we got together and "presented" ourselves for four hours. In a way it lost momentum, but God some of it was great. She's not as willing to fly off with me as I would like, but God we had good long silences. Anyway she likes me, I think—or at least has written about me. It's crazy what a jackass I thought she was all along. I still do, but I've just levelled with her and now we both know we're jackasses so it's o.k.

(5 days later)

Last night I was at her apartment. The usual pauses and I just kept thinking I wanted to kiss her. We talked but I mostly slapped my thighs and said, "Oh, wow!" not able to tell her what I meant. So when it got late, I just kind of distractedly sighed and started out the door, when she caught my jacket. And God, I just lay back in her. I felt so tangled up though. I couldn't even cry. But I tried to and finally I did and said I loved her. And oh, God, she just held my head and cared. Oh. God. When I was composed again—she said it was all o.k.—I wanted just to turn and kiss her but I still couldn't and waited too long. I looked out the window to a street light and promised myself that when it changed, I'd kiss her. But it never changed. Then she said I was way off somewhere and where did she fit in when I said, "I want to kiss you but I don't want you to hate me for it." She asked was I really afraid she'd hate me—or that I'd hate her or hate me? That really got me. Scared me, how perceptive she was. Like she knows I'm fucked up or self-indulgent. But please, maybe this time I can get so I don't lie or fool myself, so I feel her there and want her there, so it isn't all just me tangled up inside. I do want that, to be good to her, as she is to me.

I do want her—I don't know why or what to assert or what to hide. But I want to lie next to her and talk a little—maybe just quiet talking. I can't hold her yet, but I want to. I guess now that she knows how I feel, I shouldn't be afraid.

(some days later)

I am sick—I can't swallow. Every day it gets messier. My dreams are wild and I'm doing some of them in real life now. I'm out of control. There isn't even a strange city or anywhere I want to go to. Just leave me out. No one knows, I don't know—it's too much.

Former friends I just thought of. They are each me and I hate them so much. And I'll never play the French horn right. [Some notes from King Lear start here]

"Thy truth, then, be thy dower!

... Let pride, which she calls plainness, marry her!"

So that was the first I'd actually touched a woman. She soon dropped out of school so she could see a shrink more regularly. I went to Scotland for my junior year, where I tried to forget all that by being with men.

(1968, age 20)

O.k. I have been crying. I went to Priya's. We gave back rubs. And he asked why I was so cold to him and that that is dangerous. And I came back and cried and all of the horror comes back. I do not want to be a lesbian—am I? I am alone now, that's the hardest. And I have consciously kept to skirts—watching these married people and wanting to be in love. Maybe I cannot—is that it?

I feel sick and dizzy—I can't go back and I can't go on. And I've been working so hard at not being a tragic figure and certainly don't want self-pity. What is it? I must speak to Amy [an understanding friend]. But if I am a lesbian or end up with no one, I don't think I want to live.

(months later)

I'm troubled by the sleeping business and spoke to Amy who said "No" three times and then Geoffrey was different—slept with him for a year before marrying. After the first time, she thought she didn't want to do it again! All encouraging. Maybe I should be an athlete. Something is not suiting me. Dunno.

I am just exhausted—with people like Robert who said, "I'm at your feet" or people like Bill who knows I won't screw him and then writes me a note, "I'm gonna do you, girl!" Oh, how foolish for all this to go on when there are things to be done. Real things—what are we doing—dreaming and drinking!

(months later)

More and more as I learn my turn-off points and my happy and sad and right places, I feel I am right. I don't so much worry about femininity for example, or rather, I worry about it and sleep off depressions but all like a routine—I just feel it coming and excuse myself.

Well, trying to be heterosexual didn't work. I returned to college in the States—started drinking and smoking cigarettes and grass. In this last entry I try once again to "come out" to myself.

(1969, age 21)

Sally hasn't talked to me in three days. We were stoned Friday night, went over to the pub to get something to eat. A girl named Marty was there with another girl. I said, "See that girl over there. Isn't she interesting." She soon got up to leave. Sally was facing her and was terrified at what she saw ...

Apparently Marty got up—swung her cape over her shoulder, slipped on her gloves and looked me up and down fiercely (I didn't see any of this), then strutted off. I did see her walk away—she had a particular walk. I said to Sally, "See the way she walks—like a princess. She seems like a lesbian, you know?"

"That's just what I was going to say but it isn't even necessary to say it."

"I'd kinda like to get to know her." At this moment Sally said I looked hard at her—like, wouldn't you, too?

We walked out a little later and I said, "I'm hungry. I hate to go to bed hungry, and unfulfilled."

Later on, after Sally had taken a bite out of another friend's hamburger, I said, "Wouldn't you rather have a bite out of her?" So Sally came in tonight to explain what had upset her so that night—why she hadn't talked to me in three days. It was because this time she was in it, part of it—not like other times we'd talked about whether I'm a lesbian, but actually she was in it. She thought I wanted her!

God I don't know. It all fits—why would I say I wanted to know Marty? Why am I attracted except for that? I feel it must be so alone though—I feel it already that I must watch myself. Who does know? How can they tell? Why don't I know? ... Well, it's real now.

There are more entries—many more comings out since then. But somehow these tentative disclosures to myself, a good two years before ever sleeping with a woman at age twenty-three, touch me to this day. I share them in the hopes of easing someone else's pain and isolation.

13 My Coming Out Herstory

Anonymous

I do not tell my coming out story now the way I told it when I first publicly "came out." I used to begin with my conscious recognition, at age twenty, that I could be sexually attracted to another woman. Since then I have realized that my Lesbian herstory starts much earlier than that, although I did not recognize it as such at the time. In this way even our own personal herstories are denied us, because we do not have the information to identify them for what they are. Thus reclaiming the Lesbian in my past is very important to me and very affirming of who I am now.

Never interested in being "feminine," I was very much a tomboy: strong, tough and athletic. My mother never discouraged this. I was also very academic, spent a lot of my time doing schoolwork and had little social life. However, I almost always had one "best friend," invariably a girl, who was extremely important in my life and to whom I was devoted.

My relationship with Cas was the culmination and last of such friendships. Cas and I were best friends from when we were twelve until we were fifteen. We spent all our free time at school together, visited each other's homes a lot (usually staying overnight), and wrote each other long and, I now realize, passionate letters during vacations. Much later I learned that my mother and Cas' mother had wondered if we were Lesbians or would become gay. The thought never occurred to me. I remember Cas and I pulled our beds together one night so that we could play cards in bed. When my mother asked next morning why we had moved the beds, I explained to her about playing cards and never realized that she was wondering about Lesbianism, nor even that our behavior could be interpreted that way, so far was it from my mind. I did understand the word *Lesbian*, but in a purely academic sense; the concept just did not connect to any perceived reality of mine. Actually I do remember being very interested in Cas' breasts as they developed (bigger and earlier than mine) and wanting to touch them, but I never even really admitted those thoughts to myself, let alone to anyone else. Those things were just not done—and I mean I really thought that people *didn't* do them, not that they ought not to.

Our relationship ended very painfully. Cas wrote me a couple of cruel, invalidating and hate-filled letters, very suddenly and unexpectedly. I am fairly sure that her mother—who was Catholic, and extremely disturbed by the thought Cas might be gay—had a lot to do with turning her against me. At the time, however, I had no idea what motivated Cas' action. I was shattered: my self-image and sense of confidence destroyed, my whole life turned around, and all my usual activities interrupted. The pain I suffered was the pain of the break-up of any three-year love relationship; but because I had never been encouraged to think of relationships with other wimmin as legitimate or valid, I did not think of my pain as legitimate either, and did not confide in anyone about my feelings, nor even tell anyone what had happened, until several months later. After about a year Cas indicated that she wanted to be friends again and we sort of made up. I was jubilant, feeling re-affirmed because one of the most important people in the world still loved me. Soon, however, I changed schools and Cas again withdrew from me, not wanting to write and seeming embarrassed and uncomfortable on the few occasions I went back to visit the school. We quickly lost contact.

From age eleven on I also had a series of what are known, in our patriarchal homophobic language, as *crushes* on wimmin older than myself. All but one of them were teachers of mine, and most of them were gym teachers. I loved, adored and idolized them; I hung around them and liked nothing better than to do something for them or to be otherwise singled out for their attention. I identify completely with Meg Christian's song "Ode to a Gym Teacher." Each time I hear it waves of nostalgia sweep over me. I actually got into bad trouble with one gym teacher, when I revealed the extent of my feelings for her by showing her the diary I had written about her; and I still resent the scolding I got for being unrealistic about who she really was, when I would very much have liked to spend time with her and to develop a real (rather than fantasy) relationship. Such relationships are, of course, precluded by the ageist, elitist hierarchy of teacher-pupil relationships, as well as by homophobia.

Finally, when I was about fifteen, I managed to develop genuine friendships with two such wimmin whom I had previously worshipped. In both cases I took the initiative and told them about my feelings for them. Chris was very matter-of-fact about my feelings for her and other teachers, and said it was "useful practice in loving," as long as I was realistic. At the time it was such a relief to have permission to feel what I was feeling that what she said was a big encouragement to me; only now do I see the put-down of same-sex relationships contained in the assumption that they are "practice" for the real thing, i.e., relating to men.

Jill was another kettle of fish. She was twice my age, married with children, physically and personally very beautiful, and a brilliant field hockey player. I quickly developed a strong passion for her. Just the sound of her voice gave me a funny feeling in my stomach. On the way to hockey matches, I always wanted to be in the same car with her and was forever trying to "accidentally" touch her. Once, in the changing room, when no one else was around, I buried my face in her clothes, loving the smell of her. At a time when I was relating very badly to my mother, Jill became very important to me and I grew to love her deeply. It never occurred to me to want a physical relationship with her; I felt vaguely ashamed and confused about the physical manifestations of my love for her and kept them secret, again not really admitting to myself what I was feeling. Jill and I did spend time together often, always doing frightfully "normal" things, like sitting and talking or doing some of her household chores together. After I moved away we saw very little of each other. Although she was still tremendously important to me, our relationship had little enough legitimacy and significance in her life to warrant efforts to keep it up, and I did not know enough then to realize that I had any right to challenge her perspective.

Apart from my unreciprocated love for Jill, my relationship with Cas was my last close relationship with a womon until my feminist consciousness dawned several years later. Instead I got very much into men, preferring their company to wimmin's. Once I had discovered sex (age seventeen), it became my major outlet for everything. My chief goal on a Saturday night was to find a man to have sex with. In retrospect, I suspect that my frantic desire for sex was a vain attempt to compensate for the lack of physical affection from my father, who left home when I was seven. Actually I remember enjoying the validation before sex and the cuddling afterwards much more than the sex itself, which was usually very bad, male-oriented and unsatisfying (although I never knew it at the time, having nothing better to compare it with). I often reflect that, if Cas and I had not broken up, our relationship would probably have developed into a full, sexual love relationship, as I believe it was meant to; and I would have slipped easily into womon-loving and a healthy Lesbian sexuality, instead of into the painful and devious route that I actually followed.

For four years sex with men was a major focus of my life. I was completely heterosexually-defined, and it never occurred to me that I could be anything else. I went to boarding school for two years, and sneaked off on weekends for sexual adventures at the nearby university. I remember two specific incidents which illustrate my complete lack of gay consciousness. One was a lecture given by the headmaster to the whole school. He was concerned about sexual activity between the girls and the boys in the school (which was, needless to say, strictly against the rules). He failed to recognize that you do not need boys and girls together for there to be sex, and so did I. On another occasion a male friend asked if the girls at my school masturbated each other. I said: "No, of course not. The girls here just do not do that sort of thing." !! How much I missed out on because of my ignorance ...

Yet, despite this complete lack of understanding at a conscious level, positive feelings about gayness were beginning to surface from my subconscious, for during this time I had two specifically gay experiences. They were, of course, quickly repressed, and I have only recently recognized and claimed them as gay. The first was a dream I had about making love with a womon at my boarding school—and the consuming sexual excitement stayed with me for days afterwards. The second occurred at summer school with a young womon, exceedingly lonely and very drunk, who was determined to go out and pick up the first man she could find. I persuaded her to go to bed instead and, given her drunken state, helped her undress. Not thinking about how sexually oriented she was at that moment, I undid her bra for her. Doing so turned me on, though I repressed the feeling instantly. ("A mistake," I thought.) However, she turned and reached for me sexually. I told her very calmly I was not interested in sex with her, as though it were the most normal request for me to refuse.

Jill Johnston wrote in *Lesbian Nation*: "Identity is what you can say you are according to what they say you can be." This applies strongly to me. I did not think that Lesbianism was wrong or bad; it just never occurred to me that it was a possibility for me. I heard no vehement statements about the wrongness of homosexuality; indeed, I grew up in a tolerant liberal family. Homosexuality was just never mentioned. Our culture of silence about gayness was the biggest obstacle to my coming out.

I turned nineteen, and all kinds of changes began. I left high school, declined to go to college, and began to develop a radical consciousness and lifestyle, though as yet not feminist in any depth. I became very close with Jim, also a political activist: my only longterm and serious relationship with a man. We were lovers for nearly two years, and are still good friends. Within the limitations of heterosexuality, it was a fine relationship, and I learned a lot and grew a lot, especially since Jim's feminist consciousness was much higher than mine when we met!

The next year, in the summer of 1974, I came to the U.S.A. (I am English.) I have been here three years, and never before have I changed so much so fast. The conscious part of my coming out story begins soon after my arrival in the U.S. Until that time I had never discussed Lesbianism nor knowingly met a Lesbian. Suddenly I found myself in a political training program with an outspoken feminist whom I later discovered was a Lesbian. Within a couple of months I discovered my own bisexual feelings when I became sexually aroused by hugging this same womon, in a wood sauna in the dark. That was the time she chose to come out to me, and I responded coolly: "Yes, I'm bisexual," although I had only realized it about a minute earlier!

Actually, for a few weeks after that realization it felt as if the whole world had been turned around, so many of my previous assumptions were now rendered invalid. Everything looked different when no longer viewed from the heterosexual perspective—especially the fact that everyone in the world was now a potential lover! But gradually the dust settled, and as I made no effort to act on my sexual feelings for wimmin (I was still comfortably in my primary relationship with Jim), the issue of gayness did not seem very important.

However, I was changing in many ways. That year, my first in the U.S., I became a feminist, absorbing the feminist consciousness of the political community around me and learning to love and appreciate wimmin, not yet sexually, but as interesting people with whom I could have meaningful and fulfilling relationships. This was a new idea to me. I was in my first wimmin's Consciousness Raising group, which changed me more than I realized at the time. My interest in sex with Jim declined rapidly. Instead, I got more and more into masturbating, discovering my own body and sexuality and learning to love myself. In the process, I began to realize how it would be to make love with another womon and got turned on to the idea ... as well as gaining some understanding of how it could be done! My hetero sex experiences had certainly not been very imaginative.

The next summer, when I was twenty-one, was the turning point for me in terms of gayness. I returned to England for six weeks and visited some gay friends there, who challenged my bisexuality as politically ineffective. As a result of that conversation, I determined to be aggressively political and feminist about my bisexuality, and not to allow people to assume that I was basically straight but indulging in some gay sex on the side. I made myself a button that said "free yourself be bisexual" to use as a conversation opener, learned a lot from the various heated arguments I got myself into and the differing reactions I received, and came back to the U.S. determined to really tackle this thing called "sexual politics."

Then everything happened at once. Hitchhiking back via Canada, I agreed to have sex with a trucker. It was very different from all my other sexual experiences with men. Firstly, he pushed me to take responsibility for it, i.e., to admit that I wanted to have sex, instead of indulging my habit of passively agreeing and thereby avoiding responsibility for my sexuality. Secondly, he was actively concerned about my sexual pleasure and intercourse was not the focus of our activity. Thirdly, he went down on me. These were enough to bring all kinds of feelings about sexuality and my previous sexual experiences to the surface, and I began methodically to work through them. This resulted in a lot of anger about men, a deeper feminist consciousness rooted in my own experience of oppression, a new definition of my sexuality and, by November, the first draft of my paper on "Liberating Sexuality."

That fall was really a crash course in consciousness. At the same time as exploring my sexuality, I began reading feminist books and articles. Most of them made sense to me and I quickly gained a radical feminist analysis. I was part of a wimmin's counseling group and saw first-hand wimmin dealing with their feelings about what sexism had done to them. In October, in order to be able to stay in the U.S., I went through a marriage of convenience. Having to go through the humiliation of the marriage ceremony brought up lots more feelings, lots more anger at the patriarchy and contributed further to my feminism. I attended various wimmin's gatherings. I co-convened a gay and bisexual caucus in my political community which gave me, for the first time, lots of space to explore and develop the gay side of myself and also support from others who were feeling similarly about gayness. I became part of a Gay Theory Work Group, whose task it was to produce a theory paper on gay oppression and liberation; this further motivated me to study and to form a coherent analysis of the system of hetero-sexism, as we began calling it.

All through that fall I was fast becoming very turned off to men, physically and instinctively. Jim and I were still in a primary relationship, as far as emotional support, but I was pulling away and he could no longer meet my needs. We ceased to relate to each other sexually. Once, soon after I got back from England, we began to make love, but I could not handle it and burst into tears. Soon after we explicitly agreed that we would no longer be sexual with each other (although for nearly a year we continued to cuddle and sleep together sometimes). I was becoming gay-identified, and in November began to define myself as "gay" rather than "bisexual," a change based on political and emotional identification with wimmin. Sexually I still considered myself bisexual.

Also, in early November, right around my twenty-second birthday, all the different threads that had been running through my life during the fall came together and I suddenly felt for myself what it was to be oppressed as a woman. Until then, my understanding of wimmin's oppression had been mainly intellectual, gained from reading; then all at once it hit me in the gut. Realizing how I (and my mother and little sister, both of whom I am very close to) are oppressed, in all its painful personal specificity, was a shattering experience. For about two months, I mainly cried and raged, and found it difficult to put my attention to anything else. Compounding my pain, I began to understand the depth and extent of Lesbian oppression, and I tried for the first time to act on my attraction for another womon and found some of my own internalized conditioning getting in the way. I found it incredibly hard to take the initiative in starting a sexual relationship; and a relationship with a woman, which should have felt beautiful and natural, instead felt awkward and uncomfortable. The anti-gay attitudes I had absorbed from society had not magically dissolved on a feelings level just because I had rejected them in my head.

I went away over the New Year, visiting a friend. This was an important experience. I was with people who did not have expectations about who I was, so I could begin to be different, away from the tangle of past habits and past relationships based on my old attitudes. Moreover, for the first time in my life, my needs were being met exclusively by wimmin; this was exhilarating and empowering and helped me develop a vision of how my life could be.

Once I got back to the city (January 1976), I found I had worked through enough of my feelings about being gay and a womon that I could start thinking about my oppression and how I was going to change it. Recognizing my need for support and affirmation from other gay wimmin, I began to reach out, with my characteristic thoroughness and determination, to Lesbian groups, classes and individual friends. Within a couple of weeks, I became clear that sexually I was no longer bisexual but a Lesbian. This was both a personal and a political decision. I no longer liked men personally, and my analysis of the patriarchy told me that, since it was the system that made men behave in objectionable ways, I was not going to find an exception, the individual solution. Even though I had not yet had sex with a womon, I was sure that it would be far superior to sex with men. Politically, I wanted my energy to be going to support wimmin and to building a feminist revolution together, not to struggling with individual men.

About six weeks later, in late February, I met Sally. We were both in the same Lesbian Awareness class. The first time we spent time together alone, we each shared our life stories. I was scared to tell her that I had never slept with a womon, afraid she would not be interested in me because I was so inexperienced. She was very surprised and taken aback by my hesitating admission of Lesbian virginity. A dyke of ten years, out long before there was any such thing as feminism, she could not understand how I could be so militantly Lesbian before I had even made love with a womon! It did not deter her interest, however, and we became lovers. Within a couple of weeks we were well on the way to developing an intense and committed relationship.

Our relationship has more than met my expectations of what loving wimmin would be like. Sally, just by being who she is and by relating to me, has given me much positive reinforcement and confirmation of all my thinking about Lesbianism. In fact, the first few months of our relationship provided continual consciousness raising for me. I began to discover all the ways in which I had been un-free in my heterosexual relationships, which I had never realized because I accepted them as fixed realities (even though by heterosexual standards I was an aware and liberated woman). As a Lesbian, I found out that many of those "fixed realities" could in fact be different. Gradually I discovered all the ways in which I had previously been passive, unassertive and indecisive. There were so many new areas in which I had to learn to take the initiative!

Once I had decided I was a Lesbian, coming out publicly was a lot easier and less painful than the consciousness raising process which led me to want to come out. My political community was largely supportive of gay liberation, although at a personal level many people were also threatened by it, and everyone was deeply concerned with personal growth. Although I got little concrete support for my Lesbianism, I got very little negative feedback either. As far as employment was concerned, I had been doing a private childcare job for eighteen months and I felt secure in it, so I did not remove my "dyke" buttons when I went to work, and suffered no more than my own initial feelings of nervousness.

I was more worried about my parents' reactions, but both of them responded well. (My parents are divorced.) When I wrote and told my mother I was bisexual, she replied: "Yes, we all are, aren't we?" That blew me away—she was taking it much more calmly than I was! My transition to Lesbianism did not surprise or unduly bother her, and last Christmas she welcomed Sally into her home for three weeks. Of course she has had to do some fast growing and information-gathering on the subject, but she has never hesitated in her support and love for me. I put off telling my father for over a year, scared that he would be angry or condemning; but when I finally wrote to him, he too was very accepting of me as who I am, although predictably he was not overjoyed at the news and was less understanding than my mother. However, Sally and I recently visited him for a week, and we all had a fine time together. With both parents, Sally and I are free to be completely ourselves. I know I have exceptional parents and that my relationships with both of them are unusual.

I have thus always felt good about my Lesbianism. I do not think I *chose* to have a Lesbian side to my nature; I think all human beings are naturally bisexual/pansexual. I did consciously choose to be exclusively Lesbian, to not relate sexually to men as long as we live under the patriarchy and men are taught to behave in such obnoxious ways. But my discovery of my Lesbianism has been a source of deep pleasure and has been a major factor in helping me grow into a strong, self-actualized womon, despite the added oppression. I would not be any other way.

My Third Coming Out at Last Has My Own Name

14

Caryl B. Bentley

Now, at age thirty-seven, I've been conscious of my Lesbianism for twenty-two years. I've been coming out all that time, creating myself, and I'm not finished yet. My favorite thing about myself is that I am a Lesbian; therefore, making connections between myself and my Lesbian past, between myself and other Lesbians, and between myself and the cultural heritage, politics, and institutions of Lesbian Nation is most importantly what my life is about.

I think coming out is a life-long process. It consists for me of connecting feelings, ideas, and experiences to my identity as a Lesbian through naming and perhaps acting on them. In the mid-1950's, when I, like other Lesbians my age, was alone, claiming my Lesbianism meant recognizing and owning my feelings of love for one other woman. Refusing to bury and deny my feelings was a matter of integrity to me; this stubborn claiming is something I still respect myself for. At the beginning, naming my Lesbianism was simple. Then, and for the next decade, the vocabulary of my Lesbian consciousness contained only one word: Biz. Although I was aware from the first that the feelings I had for Biz were termed "Lesbian," I could not recognize myself in Ann Aldrich or Radclyffe Hall, much less in the abnormal psychology textbooks I studied nervously in libraries or in the Lesbian passages of pornographic novels. I knew no other Lesbians, and I did not discuss my love for Biz with anyone but her.[1] I attributed my love for Biz to her rare and wonderful qualities, as though she were a goddess fallen into my Midwestern life whom I was compelled to adore. I had no experience or

[1]The only exception is that I warned my future husband in 1961 that I might be a Lesbian. He said that was all right. We never discussed it again.

conceptual tools to help me see that my feelings for her came from *my* identity rather than hers.

Biz loved me; we were best friends, kindred spirits, and sisters to each other: she was not a Lesbian, and we were never sexual partners. During my first ten years as a Lesbian, her name was the emblem of my unexamined but precious interior life. In later years, I've reclaimed as part of my Lesbian identity other feelings, events, and thoughts from this decade, but at the time I did not generalize. I loved Biz: if that made me what the world called a *Lesbian*, so be it, but my conscious Lesbianism was tied to Biz alone.

In my Biz period, between ages sixteen and twenty-five, I had a conventional outer life: I went to high school and college, dated and later slept with men, married, taught school, worked in a library, lived in different parts of the country, bought material possessions, worked for liberal causes, became a widow, and again entered the university. All that time Biz was the most important person to me. I never understood why we, who loved each other, shouldn't touch. At least once a year, including the four years I was with my husband, I asked Biz if she'd changed her mind. Eventually I got used to her refusals, but for the first five years, her no's were agonizing to me, partly because I worried that my base and unnatural physical desires would ruin our relationship.

Biz and I met at the beginning of tenth grade. The first weekend we spent together completely dazzled me. We drove out of town with Biz's mother and aunt for a lobster dinner and an evening of Bob Hope, stayed up all night talking and giggling, went to a university campus for our first debate tournament (at which both of us were nearly mute on the subject of free trade). I had never done any of those things before, and the combination of all of them at once was delirious. Biz taught me about classical music and Broadway shows; she read to me from the *New Yorker*, Dorothy Parker, and James Thurber; she showed me her own poetry. She was witty, shy, and extremely sensitive. She brought magic to my life.

Soon we began to tell each other confidences, most thrillingly about how much we liked each other but also about the secret burdens of our families. To tell Biz about my family was to break an explicit rule called "family loyalty." It emerged years later, in therapy, that for me to cope with the guilt I felt over breaking the taboo and also to bring Biz even closer to me, I put Biz into my family, as a sister far more like me than my blood sister. By making Biz my sister, she became an insider and could know the family secrets.

This pattern of identifying with my lovers as family members has been a major theme of my life. Since Biz, the other two women I've loved most, Susan and Barbara, I have also seen as sisters. Biz was a twin sister in my family constellation. When her mother died a year after we met, I gave her rights to my mother, so that we were daughters of the same mother. We both had fathers then, but they weren't important in mythologizing my kinship to Biz. Susan was my half-sister through the male line. My father had died, and I dreamed Susan's father was our father. Each of us has a strong, competent mother, and in my mythology we kept our own mothers. Barbara's and my relationship is a new one. We came together recently at a time when each of us was bruised and weary. Very early we had a sexual and spiritual rebirth experience together which made us feel like mothers and daughters to each other. Since then I've also come to see her as a sister, but Barbara and I are still so much in the process of learning what we are to each other that I'm not yet certain of her place in my personal mythology.

About a year after Biz and I had become inseparable, she stayed overnight with me one night. We were giggling and tickling each other in my twin bed when I realized I was feeling physical sensations I'd never felt before. I puzzled over this for a few days until I had a sexual dream about Biz. Over the next few weeks I realized I was in love with her, which did not seem peculiar to me; rather, it was a relief to have a name to put to my feelings. In the summer, at a lake, I told Biz I wanted us to touch. That first night she was not horrified. She said, "Well, I don't know why it should make any difference if a boy or a girl scratches your back." (Neither of us had much idea of the specific behaviors I was proposing, but we knew it was a big moment.) Later, though, the whole idea seemed strange and frightening to Biz, and she said her first no. I've often wished I'd been more physically courageous at the beginning and less verbal. In the other adolescent coming out stories I've heard from friends, the women involved were not so articulate and formal in their loving as Biz and I were.

The longest time Biz and I had together was in 1959-60 when we spent our junior year of college in France and Spain. One of my happiest memories is of the rainy autumn day and night we spent at Mont St. Michel. In the afternoon we escaped from a tour and roamed around the monastery by ourselves, pretending we lived there, two princesses in a castle. In the late afternoon, the tide went out, giving us the ecstatic feeling of being marooned forever in our fortress on the sand. We stayed that night in a small room at the base of the monastery and talked of living together for the rest of our lives in France, where no one would know us and we could be like Gertrude Stein and Alice B. Toklas.

One of my most agonizing memories is also of that year. In Paris we had rooms across the hall from each other in a Latin Quarter hotel. Biz's room had a double bed, which we both slept in every night. I again invited Biz to make love; she said no, and I left her room. As I lay sobbing on my single bed across the hall, I heard her lock her door, and I felt like a monster of perversion. I remember a sentence I wrote in a journal I later destroyed: "I'm shaking so hard, and I feel I'm shaking exactly against the rhythm of the universe."

My relationship with Biz is still a central one in my life. We've been close friends for almost a quarter of a century. Biz is the woman from whom I first learned how much two women can share. We were always loyal and loving to each other in a period of history when female friendships were not supposed to be important. We learned things together. We dreamed together. We helped each other to become who we each wanted to be. Although in a technical sense it is not true, there is no question in my mind that Biz was my first lover.

After my husband was killed in a car accident in 1965, I decided to go to graduate school at the University of Wisconsin. The only friend I had there was Susan, who had been in the same small group of close friends in high school as Biz and me. We were tied together in other ways: her mother and mine had been school and college friends; both families were members of a small Unitarian church; her brother and my sister were married to each other. I vaguely suspected that Susan and her friend, Leigh, who lived not far from Madison, were Lesbians, but by that time in my life I didn't really believe that anyone I knew *acted* on her love for another woman; after all, Biz and I never had. When I got to Madison, I found some male lovers, but my most important times were spent with Susan. Eventually she told me that she and Leigh were lovers. My first reaction was vast relief that I wasn't alone after all, and my first question was classic: What do you do? (Susan said they did what I'd think they did—which was exactly what I wanted to know.) I told her that same night about my long history of loving Biz. That was an important coming out experience for me, to find at last someone I cared for and respected who knew what it was to love a woman.

It wasn't long before I fell in love with Susan. In April of 1966 I finally came out sexually as a Lesbian, with Susan. Susan loved me, but she also loved Leigh. Our triangle, which of course I knew about but which Leigh did not, lasted six months. It was an anguishing time for all three of us, but it also provided a useful function for me: it gave me the necessary time and distance to struggle with and accept myself as a Lesbian. That six months is the most intense coming out experience of my life because there was so much to experience, connect with, and name all at once.

This second coming out period is so thoroughly documented that it took me a whole day to re-read my journals and Susan's and my letters. I had at the beginning two major worries: would Susan choose me or Leigh? if Susan and I chose each other, did I love her enough to face the troubles with family, friends, employers, and society in general I was certain lay ahead? Following are some journal entries and passages from my letters to Susan.

April, 1966

My loving you is clean in private, dirty if made public—dirty, not only unpleasant and impossible.

I think of marriage [to a man] as a giving in ... to the easy way out, to security, ... to complacency, to boredom. Love has nothing to do with it; it can be present or absent and the other things still sneak in....This is ... not to say I might not get married again—I think not now, because I feel so tough—but I might....I hope my present state continues. It's complicated, wild, extremely difficult, and heady beyond anything I've experienced. I have some idea now of what freedom is.

I talk about morality and ethics because I know I'm in some kind of sphere where what I've thought, felt, and done before is irrelevant—in a more basic way irrelevant than the mere fact that I'm sleeping with Susan—but I don't know yet where I am. I've wanted to say, in times of peace or joy, this can't be wrong, it's too lovely to be wrong. Yet I haven't said that, because I know that's irrelevant, too. That is the response I'd have made before, when I was more certain of the use of conventional morality but was violating it for some reason of my own. Something is different now about what I am, but I'm not sure what.

May, 1966

Part of what it is is that I feel degraded. To love a girl is hard enough, to be uncertain of my position with her is worse, to have to dissimulate constantly is most humiliating of all. I don't think it's very surprising at all I'm so intent on appealing to men at the moment. At least I feel I'm holding my own. Christ, I'm proud.

Susan says homosexual relationships are inherently unstable. I'm sure one of the reasons she is homosexual is that she wants the freedom she thinks it gives her....What we'd have together could be absolutely great, ... but it would start off just hideously because of the people we might hurt and the illusions I, especially, would be shattering.

There is a streak of absolutism in me which may possibly be one of the things about me that is scary and tough. I am now nearly positive I would, if I have my choice, pick Susan and stay with her. That both appeals to her and scares her to death.

June, 1966

I would hate to have people know I'm a Lesbian....(If Susan and I were together)... the secrecy, suspicions, fears, hypocrisy, feelings of deviance and displacement would all be there. They are all here now.... My greatest source of unhappiness is... loving Susan ....

As Biz says, I thrive on futures. ... A far-distant problem is being old and having been a Lesbian. No children—no family—no common experiences to talk about with other old people....But what do I do? Get married just for safety, children, status, a role, a place? I could do that, but I get nervous and unhappy thinking about it. The fact is that I'm in love with Susan....I've thought every day since the beginning about ending my relationship with Susan.... It's the only rational thing to do, and I used to, anyway, think that people should use their minds to help run their lives. ... I am so frequently depressed and helpless feeling now that I hardly know who I am. ... On the one hand, I feel weak-willed for not breaking things off; on the other hand, it seems weak to stop. ... My happiness is so much more engulfing than it ever has been before. ... Christ, I wonder how people ever dare think they solve problems. What happens is that you eventually do something and then it becomes retrospectively the "inevitable" choice. Big deal.

July, 1966

Being Lesbian may be a great thing for both of us. The situation itself demands discipline, giving-ness ... and courage. It's possible to be both deviant (making out in gay bars, which I can conceive of us doing), which answers a need for excitement, and self-sufficient (I'm taking the less comfortable way out). There's a tough-mindedness about loving a female. You know so much more about a girl than about a man (and about a friend-lover than a lover). There's a complicatedness, a necessity to plan, to preserve your cool all the time in public.

August, 1966

Why not a record of happiness? That should be possible.... Talking of Reed College and all we know of Oregon. Let's go there. Okay. Do you want to live in a frame house? Either that or a big stone mansion. Either one, just so it's big. Fine. There are mountains, beaches, friendly people, privacy, good teaching conditions, big cities nearby, snow, skiing, fresh salmon, gorgeous views. First time we'd talked like that. Happy.

Towards the end of September, Susan told Leigh about loving me. The day after Thanksgiving Susan and I moved into a farmhouse ten miles from the university. We expected to live together for the rest of our lives. The model for our relationship was the straight monogamous marriage model, which was the only one we knew. I liked it that we could not legally marry; I valued the faint aura of sinfulness I felt in living "out of wedlock." Also, having no legal ties meant I could freely choose Susan over and over again—and I did, for ten years, until we were hopelessly enmeshed in the very assumptions that had seemed so solid in the first place.

Susan's and my courtship phase was secret from all but Biz and two or three others, because of Leigh. I was no longer the *only* Lesbian in the world, but I still knew no others for certain but Susan and Leigh. My coming out with Susan was, at the beginning, still a private matter, although it was the idea of future public comings out that worried me most. I had learned a few basics from Susan about the rudimentary gay culture that existed at the time; I'd learned the words *gay, coming out, butch,* and *femme,* which I'd never heard before; I knew two gay men; I had one good friend whom I thought and hoped was a Lesbian (she was); and I had *seen* some other Lesbians through going alone and completely overdressed to gay bars in Illinois and Colorado.

The first gay bar I went to was on July 4, 1966, after a family picnic. I wore a white flowered summer dress with a big flounce on it and yellow shoes. I knew I was wearing the wrong thing, but I equated gay bars with orgies and wanted to pass as a straight, at which I brilliantly succeeded. A straight man bought me a drink and escorted me to my car. A journal entry describes another evening of gay bars in Denver with Biz and a gay male friend of hers:

> We went back to Cherry Creek bar .... There were more women than men. I was absolutely fascinated. We were in the back room, the place where the action was, but we were in a corner. I was wearing slacks and a white T-shirt, but I looked out of place. All of them were wearing blue jeans (not levis), which were sort of baggy, and tops like short-sleeved white gym blouses. There was one girl in a slacks outfit, but she danced with a man all the time. Biz was the only girl there with long hair. Three girls near us looked nice and intelligent. Two of them were together and they were making out some. They really liked each other. The third one was the only one there who appealed to me, but at first I didn't know which sex she was. I liked her later because of the way she moved and the way she talked. I sat in my corner saying absolutely nothing (Biz thought I was sick) and staring. I felt weird—revolted and sexy, both. Actually revolted is too strong a word. Fascinated nervousness is closer.

Clearly I had no sense of sisterhood in 1966, but many of us didn't, back then.

Once Susan and I had set up housekeeping, we tried to find some other Lesbians. We'd met one Lesbian who arranged a small party so that three newly-established Lesbian couples she knew could meet. Susan and I went to the bar on the first floor of the apartment building where the party was to be, to scout out the territory and to fortify ourselves for the ordeal ahead. Across the room was another female couple. We stared at each other nervously. They left. Susan and I wondered if we would see them upstairs and felt triumphant when they were there. One of these women was Barbara, the woman I'm involved with now; she reminds me that no one mentioned the fact we were all Lesbians until about three in the morning, although there was nothing else on anyone's mind. It turned out that only Susan among us had ever been to a gay party before, and she only to one. It was an important night; each of us was certain the other guests would be freakish, and it was the beginning of Lesbian pride for us to find out how much we liked each other.

The other big coming out tasks of Susan's and my new married Lesbian relationship were to tell our straight friends in Madison and all over the country and to tell our families. Our friends were no problem at all, to my relief. My brother and sister-in-law and Susan's parents also accepted the news with equanimity. My sister and Susan's brother (the two who are married), Susan's sister, and my mother found our relationship horrifying. The ugliness and sorrow of that period are still hard to talk about. Susan and I were defined as sick, and, as anyone to whom that has happened knows, once you are so defined, there is nothing you can say to deny it.

There is one piece of dialogue I remember which is both sad and funny.

MY SISTER: Mother, what will you do when your friends ask about Caryl's and Susan's relationship?
MOTHER: I trust they will have too much discretion to ask.
MY SISTER: Well, my friends will. I'm from a franker generation. What will I tell them about her?
ME: Don't talk about me in the third person. I'm right here.
MOTHER: I hope you don't still plan to teach. You would be a bad influence.
ME: I would not. That's ridiculous. What about Leonard Bernstein? He's rumored to be homosexual, and he's teaching millions of young people about classical music this very afternoon on television.
MOTHER: That's different. He's not in the classroom; he's on television.

And on it went, like this, off and on for two years, until things settled down and Susan and I won acceptance, if not respect, for our relationship.

In the years between 1967-71 Susan and I pretended to write our dissertations at a farm on a northern Wisconsin lake and then moved to Duluth where we got teaching jobs. We knew fewer and fewer men and spent more and more of our time with other Lesbians; we were excited and liberated by the women's and homophile movements, but our lives were still essentially private, Lesbian-tribal rather than Lesbian-feminist.

In 1972 I did my first public pro-gay activities. I was the administrator of a federal project designed to involve consumers more meaningfully in determining health care policies. We interpreted this mandate as radically as we dared. I hired a gay man to start the first gay switchboard in the area (the health issue at stake was mental health of gay people) and soon had an excruciatingly embarrassing TV interview to defend my decision to hire a "known homosexual" with tax dollars. By then I was in the closet only at work, but I stayed in it during the interview. The gay switchboard director later attempted to put an announcement of a meeting for gays in the classified section of the newspaper. The ad was refused because it contained the word "gay." We organized a demonstration, picketed, made signs saying things like "There are 10,000 gays in Duluth"—and won. Also that year I was elected to the national board of the Medical Committee for Human Rights at a convention in Chicago. When I talked about my qualifications, I included my Lesbianism, my first public coming out. Since then I've done other public things and will continue to do so—but it still isn't totally simple for me, and every time I must summon up my courage.

In 1974 Susan and I made the first really bad decision of our relationship. Without discussing it much, we moved to New Jersey, where neither of us wanted to go, because she got a good job there. There were a few benefits of living there for me, like attending the Gay Academic Union conference and visiting A Woman's Place in upstate New York, but mostly I felt purposeless and miserable, trapped in endless suburbs with no job and nothing I wanted to do. It was the beginning of a mid-life passage I'm not quite through yet. Susan and I decided I would come back to Duluth, in January, 1975, and try to find a job; she would finish her teaching year and follow me in June. We still loved each other, but there was a resigned, trapped quality to our relationship that had never been there before. We'd become too dependent; we gave away more of ourselves than we wanted to; we resented each other.

I came to Duluth and entered group therapy with a Lesbian therapist. I began to get myself back. I eventually became the coordinator of a new women's center. Susan, in New Jersey, wanted to get herself back through having an affair, which she told me about during a spring visit to Duluth. I could not accept the idea: monogamy was then of rock-bottom importance to me, the fundamental premise on which my commitment to Susan rested. She never did have that particular affair, but for the next twenty-two months we struggled with monogamy, how to become our own persons again, how to uncouple, how to redefine our relationship. The structure we'd borrowed at the beginning from middle-class heterosexuals was now too confining, but we could find no way to enlarge it that satisfied both of us. We talked to each other and to the friends in our Lesbian support group, many of whom were having similar problems; we read about new ways of leading Lesbian lives; we went to therapy, alone and together—but we found no way out. In August, 1976, we separated; and in October, 1976, we decided to make the separation permanent. We are, however, still good friends; so far we have been able to keep loving each other, despite the grief and anger each of us has felt.

In the months since Susan and I split, I have had another intense coming-out period, this third time as a single Lesbian, which I have never been before. Many of the questions my Lesbian sisters resolved for themselves long ago were new to me. For example, my sexual relationships with women had been limited to Susan. I again had a version of my original question to Susan: what do Lesbians do? I am free again to choose exactly what kind of life I want, but what is it that I *do* want? Not an imitation straight marriage again, certainly—but what? I probably do want a primary relationship because I always have before; but if I love someone, do we live together? with what assumptions? I'm less committed to monogamy than I was. I am in an experimental phase, trying different kinds of lovings and friendships with women. I love Barbara the most, but just how and to what end I do not know.

What I've been doing since October is asking myself and my friends lots of questions. I went to a wonderful workshop on Lesbian culture sponsored by Maiden Rock, a feminist education center in Minneapolis; I've attended various political meetings of Lesbians in several Midwestern cities; I've gone to my first Lesbian concerts; I've made new friends in other cities; I've read a lot, especially women's poetry, *Of Woman Born* (the best book I've ever read), and books suggested by Rich. I think I will move soon, back to Madison for awhile, although I will miss my support group in Duluth and am not sure what I will do in Madison. I am learning how to think in new ways about new subjects—just as we all are. My first coming out was named Biz; my second coming out was named Susan; my third coming out at last has my own name, Caryl. That's all I know so far, but it seems enough to be getting on with.

15 Coming Out: Ten Years of Change

Judith McDaniel

Fragments: At the Beginning

(1965, Exeter University, England ... Journal Notes)

3 May ... Carolyn and I were discussing my novel—she really takes it quite to heart—I suggested at one point that the 'slow, steady woman' should in reality be a Lesbian and I thought she was going to call out her lawyers. It helps me, though, to take my writing seriously because she does ... Tonight I remembered a moment from last fall at Stratford. Two Japanese girls—quite sophisticated looking, but young—holding lightly to each other's hand—one leading, one following—as they worked their way up the theatre steps. A longing pang—not allowed in Western culture.

5 May ... I want her respect—hers and others'—which is the only reason I'm trying to organize my life. It's not easy, but it's worth it. I don't love many people.

12 May ... We were talking about letters this afternoon and how to sign them, etc. Anyway she said there were only 3 possible ways to close ... Yours faithfully, yours sincerely and love from. I said which category was I in and she said, oh, you're different. Don't know what that meant, but in the future she said I'll get a love from.

17 May ... I had some funny ups and downs today. I guess it was from sitting at my desk and working ... then Carolyn was going out and I

wasn't, which still galls occasionally. I went in to see Carolyn for a few minutes this afternoon. She had 3 exams this week and I knew she'd be busy, but she said so too—something to the effect of, well, you'll be on your own the next 3 days, you know. Well, I did, but don't like to be reminded of it—nor of the fact that in 4 more weeks I'll be on my own for good. So I indulged in being depressed and went and had my bath and came back when who should come rapping on the door. I hadn't gone in to say goodnight to her because the light was off, so I knew she must have gotten out of bed to say goodnight ... and that made all the difference. I could have sung.

22 May ... Carolyn and I sat and talked all afternoon. She started out calling me names. I didn't really mind because it's gotten to the point now that for my own preservation I can't afford to believe she's serious. Anyway, at some point I told her how hard it had been for me to watch her and Geoff together. Which brought her up short. It's funny knowing someone so well you can say that and know the precise effect it will have. Then we talked about us and how chancey any sort of attempt to establish communication was ... but we seem to have been successful and, god, it's going to be hard to leave.

23 May ... We talked all day again today. I've never felt so close to anyone. At times I think—panic—exams—and then I think, but does it really matter? Obviously not that much ... We went flower picking tonight under the cover of dark—one of the lesser social sins—it was cold and raining. Brought back lily of the valley, lilac, straw flowers and some other sprays ... there seemed to be a marked predominance of white ... except for the first rose of summer Carolyn found on a vine and put in the small vase for me—it's pink.

Fragments: Denial

1971, on waking in Jon's bed, a dream: In a kind of girl's dorm. I am standing with my friend in our room. Across the hall from my room is a bathroom with several stalls. For a while I am inside one of them or else I know what is inside one of them, as I am still across the hall. I keep urging my friend to hurry. Just then someone discovers the girl's body—she is dead. They say she was murdered, but it's my dream and I know it was suicide. I won't go look at her, but I know what she looks like. Now I tell my friend I want to leave quick before the police come or we'll have to wait longer. But she says no, it wouldn't be right. So they come to get the body on a stretcher but there's not much left. She killed herself by chopping off pieces—a bit at a time—and putting them in the toilet.

1972, July, a self-conscious fantasy: Sometimes I think I would like to have an affair with a woman. I don't know why—it's not curiosity—but I think that something is lacking emotionally in all of my relationships.

1972, October, journal notes: Driving home alone from hearing Adrienne Rich read her poems. She is a force, an intensity and affects me profoundly. There are many dimensions to her poems. I want to read them over and over. Can you dig it baby on the radio. I feel a sense of loss when I hear poetry like that. Because she is writing for me and I understand her in a way I never have understood the 'great' poets—Yeats, Eliot, etc. Why loss? There must be men who read Yeats and to whom he means as much, perhaps more, than this tonight meant to me. And I'd never really thought about it, but—she exposes herself in her work and I feel I know her well, like I should be driving home with her. But no man in that audience should feel *just* the way I do—something, perhaps, because her clarity is good—but not exactly as I felt. She is totally honest, but you have to have been there to know the truth.

1973, August, journal notes: I told Phyllis how I felt about Sue, making it sound as though I was horrified and terrified—which part of me is—but her reaction was that of the other part of me—that it was normal and understandable under the circumstances—that it is there under any circumstances more than we allow—and that even if it had gone further it wouldn't be a problem unless I made it that way. I really think that, but somewhere else, I'm fighting awfully hard.

The Process: Saying *The Word*

(1975, January, one week during teaching a course in "The Woman's Voice in Modern Literature")

Monday: Lesbian—for two years—more perhaps—I have been unable to write honestly—write at all. My mind stops there, afraid. I have spoken truthfully to no one. But I may have stopped lying to myself—perhaps. To admit that I do love Sue, that I am physically attracted to many women, would make love to them, do dream of them, have always been more emotionally involved with women—without the ambivalence and fear I feel with a man. I wonder how I seem to the world. I am happier now than I have been for a long time, personally and professionally—many things are good. But things inside me are turbulent, agitated, sometimes I feel like I will crack open from pressure. Having no one to confide in is a problem, but only a small part. I have a need to know some things and no way to inquire. I am relieved to finally be knowing some of this consciously, but it threatens me constantly. (And then I wonder whether it's all a game I'm playing with myself—a thing I have made up and could just as easily make go away again if I chose. Would I want it to go away? I don't know. Is it real? Or does that matter?)... Introduced "Woman's Voice" today. Talked about the imposed schizophrenia of the woman intellectual. How I always read books about men and identified with men, "knowing" that maleness was the moral, social and cultural norm, but knowing too that I was female. Or thinking I was. But if Molly Bloom was a woman, I must be a mutant. Some of it was getting too close.

Tuesday: Tomorrow is women and madness—how women keep control, how they lose it, what images they use to imagine it. And other enormities. Phyllis says there are also novels of men who are mad, but I don't agree. Portnoy is not mad, just obnoxious. I am furious. Sue is unhappy. Phyllis says it will be better for me when I get away from here. I am mostly content but very lonely. Tired and lonely.

Wednesday: Val called today. She wants to do an independent creative writing project with me. I don't think the department will let me. I'm talking about creating order tomorrow. I don't need that nearly as badly as I need approval and love. Maybe they follow if or when a woman creates her own little ordered enclave? My mind is chaotic, but I'm comfortable with that.

Thursday: I lectured today for 1½ hours. Just once I wish somebody would say Wow or make a connection with this stuff for me. Inappropriate, I guess, since I was talking about the lack of cause/ effect relationships in women's lives today.

Friday: I'm going through ... Edwin Hawkins singers. Sue is here. She was at the Van Duyn lecture. I didn't think she'd come up. She sounded sick on the phone. When I first saw her, looking at her, she seemed strange, not familiar and not attractive—but at dinner all of a sudden there she was again. There. I wonder what she and Lisa say about me. They both know how I feel about Sue. And whenever we embrace I can feel Lisa watching—not jealous even, but very there—observing.

The Process: What it Means

1975, February: Having Blanche Boyd here was important, but more for me than the class. I hadn't planned on letting a radical Lesbian have the last word on "the woman's voice." The class responded much better to Linda Pastan who spoke about trying to put her family and poetry together. People had fewer questions for Blanche. The question I had was personal and I didn't even recognize it until last night. We sat in the kitchen drinking brandy until 4 a.m. talking about god knows what— I can't remember, but it was fantastic. But I never asked my question. What I want to know from Blanche is, so how did you know? When did you decide you were in fact a Lesbian, not bisexual, reacting to a bad marriage, etc. I'm not sure there is an answer, but whenever I have one of my imaginary dialogues with Phyllis, she doesn't believe me and all I have is internal evidence. She probably would believe me, of course. I have this image of announcing to the world (i.e., myself, then Phyllis) that I am a Lesbian and having the world pat me on the head, take my pulse, and tell me I'll get over it soon. Obviously I'm not sure yet that I won't. It creates incredible tension and I'm afraid if I did talk about it— what? I don't know—afraid it would be real, or it wouldn't? and I'd have to try again with a man.

... So many of my students know I'm vulnerable. Some of them will protect me, others see it as a challenge. Ellen came out to the house tonight. She said Pat was telling other students I had propositioned her. Part of me laughed and part didn't. I told her what had happened, how Pat did this seduction number on me for three weeks and finally I said, o.k., I want you, and she freaked. I'd never seen her nervous or disconcerted till that moment. It was almost worth the risk. Anyway, Ellen is furious with her.

1975, March: For several days now I've been picking up Jill Johnston's book *Lesbian Nation* and reading it when I should have been grading papers. I don't know what I would have thought of it last year, but I think now it is an important political statement. At the same time I doubt my own judgment.

Jane said the other day that she doesn't fall in love with people much older or younger than herself—something about experience, etc. I thought that was true for a while, but then I think of Sue. I know I'm afraid of Ellen's promiscuity, not her age—at the same time I wouldn't mind some casual sex. I ache just to hold another body. I got drunk at Hillary's last night. I was sitting next to her. It's dumb to let myself get so imaginatively caught up where there's no chance of involvement— when others may notice and she could get really pissed off—and I don't have that many friends.

1975, April: I want a child, but not a man. I want Hillary, but she is with Tom. I'm not sure I ever felt anything about a man. I wish I knew whether I were terrified of sexuality or heterosexuality. I commit myself to men who seem to be able to control me, and then withdraw emotionally. What an incredible thing it is to realize after all these years that I hated dating, that I was never at ease in social situations when I was expected to dance or date or pick up men or whatever. The thing with Dan was typical. I'd really look forward to the ballet or whatever we were going to do, but I never enjoyed spending time with him, even though we had so many interests in common. On paper, he's perfect, I kept telling myself. But I didn't even like him and I saw him nearly once a week for over a year. I finally went to bed with him just to see if he'd be more interesting. He wasn't. Just embarrassing. I can't think of anybody I was ever comfortable "dating." And the men I've lived with became a kind of torture after a while, each in his own way.

The Process: How it Happened

1975, June: I feel more comfortable with my own body and sexuality now than ever before in my life—whether it's the negative—knowing I never have to sleep with a man again—or the positive—finding a natural and spontaneous expression of my deepest, most intimate feelings. And I can see sources for this in what I was ten years ago, but this doesn't invalidate that ... I don't even have to reinterpret those events: if Carolyn had kissed me that night in the garden in England I couldn't have responded positively, even knowing those feelings were there.

When I first started imagining what it might be like to make love with another woman, the idea terrified and excited me. My story line was pretty vague, a lot of embracing and some movement, a little hi-fidelity inhalation, but no technicolor and the lens was comfortably out of focus. Usually I was not even a participant.

Fantasies progressed on three different levels as I became more accustomed to the setting. My waking fantasies were the most fun and moved most quickly. Usually in this scenario a strikingly attractive woman would find me irresistible and allow me to be a passive observer at my own seduction. It seemed an ideal solution at the time—I could learn a few new things without taking the risk of looking foolish or performing badly. I had no access to my sleeping dreams at that time. They were gone before I awoke like the orgasm I hovered on the edge of, but lost with consciousness. The imaginative level I had the most trouble with was the one that came in contact with my everyday life. In all the mundane details of classes and meetings and casual associations I looked at women with new eyes, but what I was imagining became unimaginable when it was connected with Susan's hands or Carol's hair or Peggy's breasts. I developed a pronounced stammer in certain highly charged emotional situations—like the time in the A & P when I was standing across a grocery cart from Hillary Martin and saw for the first time how incredibly blue her eyes were and felt them looking at the back of my brain.

Meanwhile my less conscious fantasies established a pace and direction of their own. From fullblown scenes of faintly developed seduction, I found myself rerunning fragments and details. The projector would run, stick, rewind, run, stick, rewind, ad nauseum, or at least ad emotional fatigue. In one of these scenes I was standing across from a tall woman with long blonde hair held back by a barrette. Our eyes would meet in a direct challenge and erotic exchange. I reached across to her hair, ran my hand down the nape of her neck and unfastened the clasp of the barrette. As her hair fell forward I would lean to kiss her mouth and the projector cut off. And cut off again and again.

Finally my real life began to follow my fantasy life. As I became more comfortable with the idea of loving a woman, I gave myself permission to act on those feelings. I stopped waiting for an aggressive woman to seduce me. I stopped asking women I knew would say no. I stopped worrying about how well I would perform. Last night I took Karen's hand and led her back to my bed. About half way through the final scenario I remembered to ask, "Is this all right?" "Yes," she said with some surprise, "Oh, yes."

16 Five Years of Coming Out

Susan Wood-Thompson

I liked Meg the first time I met her, in the office at the University library. I had come looking for part-time work to support myself while getting my M.A. She offered me a job, and coming into contact with each other in the routine course of work allowed us to make friends unselfconsciously. I helped her with a research project, and eventually started driving her home and to the grocery store.

I was in a happy, confident part of my life, having within the previous eighteen months been able to rely on myself as a steady, emotionally-dependable person, after the see-saw sensations of my first sexual involvements—these were with men. I had more going on in my academic career and in other areas of interest than I ever had before, was making all my own money and decisions, and was feeling breezy. I loved the Southwest, it was fall 1969, and life there was never boring.

Meg was at a good time in her life too, doing well in her career, part of a closely-knit group of colleagues, and in love (also with a man). She'd had a brief affair with a woman several years previous, been rejected and decided that she probably wasn't gay after all. Both our romantic involvements were, for one reason or another, secret, but as our friendship grew, we quickly trusted each other enough to compare reflections on the problems hidden relationships entail.

About six months after I met Meg, my lover died unexpectedly. During the weeks of grief, I stayed at Meg's and she helped me. Before long I moved in, and shortly she discovered she was in love with me. Her heterosexual relationship was fading, so she briefly mentioned to me her past gay experience. I knew little of gay life, and nervously (outwardly blithely) assured her I didn't think she had anything to "worry about"; lots of people had such experiences, but that didn't mean they were gay.

The following week she told me she was attracted to me, and then I really was nervous. But I was also ready for a new relationship, and able to try handling the added challenge of living with a partner. Our life together began.

Coming out fully to ourselves wasn't an instant thing: it took five years. Even as our relationship went into months, we still had reservations about each other and gay life. Our backgrounds were different: she was from a working-class family, I from the upper middle class. Her family was Methodist, mine Episcopalian. In her home, sports mattered; in mine, books and music. We were afraid the differences were too great.

As for identifying as a Lesbian, I kept expecting to see my parents, superiors at work, the state legislators and God jump out from behind some arras and yank me out of bed. In addition, it had always been important to me to be a certain kind of person: alive, interesting, warm, in tune with subtle patterns in nature and people—like the teachers I had admired, not like those who had seemed stagnant. Since I had never heard any middle-aged or older woman say she was a Lesbian, I was stuck with the stereotype of a cigar-chomping, heavybooted, slicked-back woman with little vision or depth. I didn't want my lifestyle to turn me into this person. In those first years one of the most helpful discoveries was *Lesbian/Woman* and finding Del Martin and Phyllis Lyon, the authors, as good images of Lesbians.

At first, because of Meg's job and my attachment to a department whose attitude toward Lesbianism I could not figure out, we stayed pretty hidden, and consequently met only a few Lesbians. These were wonderful women, and we all wanted to compare experiences in depth, create new ones, hear each other's insights and give appropriate support. However, we didn't know how to do so in ways that worked for everyone involved.

As the seasons passed we had all the problems of living a hidden life and none of the rewards that heterosexual couples enjoy. We more or less shed our old straight-life friends, unable to change a major direction of our lives in front of them, or to deal with their resistance to what changes they sensed. I got to know a different group at school and came out to them, as well as to new straight friends elsewhere. Our most enthusiastic acceptance came from Lucy, a witty, affectionate friend who early on told us she was a fag-hag, and defined that for us as a woman whose primary attachments are to gay men. Lucy showed her high value for gay life so well that for the first time we felt well understood and respected as Lesbians.

At home we were in a power struggle, disagreeing about almost everything. Learning to communicate about problems we had living with each other was, for the first five years, the central issue. The particulars ranged from what was appropriate behavior at parties to whether the person whose turn it was to fix dinner was obliged to preheat TV dinners. Neither of us having had models for non-punitive, solution-oriented argument in our homes, we read and reread Bach's *The Intimate Enemy: How to Fight Fair in Love and Marriage*, trying to apply the guidelines for equality in all phases of a relationship. Some days we'd come home at five, sit down on the couch to get out all the complaints, and argue so long that eventually we had to work out arrangements for supper break and to say that no argument could last later than 11:00 p.m.

Several factors converged to make our broader coming-out possible. I finished my Ph.D. and got a job in a much smaller, conservative town when Meg started on her doctorate. We met several colleagues who felt good about their gayness, and their example was contagious. Although they were men, they were the first gay role-models we knew in person. They helped sustain us as we went through a big blow-up, a very painful confrontation that took eight months. Meg moved out, finally, for about six weeks, and we found a value in each other that allowed us to make use of all the learning we'd struggled for since our relationship began. We fought fair, using Bach's rules, and found the willingness to control ourselves from within, instead of so often ignoring each other's rights until challenged.

Meg moved back in, and we continued respecting each other on the new level. A semi-retired shrink friend of mine corresponded with us from the Southwest about our relationship, giving us practical tips for kindness (like, do one nice thing for each other every day), as well as the first establishment approval we had felt. We joined a small, faltering woman's group, which was just right for us since there were no people in it who represented the one "right" way to think. Ironically, living in a little, more conservative town than before improved our ability to come out. It was in this tolerant circle that one night when several new people were there, we went around clockwise, everyone telling her name and what she wanted most out of the group. Sheryl mentioned that she was interested in gay rights. Meg and I made our first successful Lesbian friendship with Sheryl and her lover Caroline. In addition, we sent our names in to the *Lesbian Connection* as the contact dykes for our town, and people in our isolated community and surrounding towns began calling us, delighted to have suddenly a way to find other Lesbians. Lesley, a friendly, resourceful woman, introduced all of us to other Lesbians in town. We had enough for a baseball team, which gave us a way to relate to each other that cut across our diverse characteristics and philosophies. Later we discussed problems and successes involving income-sharing and budgeting, house-cleaning, relationships between couples and single Lesbians, political issues, conflict resolution and life goals.

I believe it was not until these things happened that Meg and I had fully come out to ourselves. As a Lesbian at a recent workshop said, being happy makes it a lot easier to accept your Lesbianism. I have since heard other gay couples talk about taking five years to get their relationships working well, and some have speculated that it takes that long to get over the fear of losing your identity, or perhaps to learn how not to lose it in a close relationship. I also believe in the reality of slow, underground growth that can become apparent suddenly, long after it began.

Almost all our friends know we're gay, and it's an open topic with them and us. Most, if not all, the people at my job know. Meg and I have become, when necessary, adept at signalling our Lesbianism to new friends in ways that Lesbians would catch, but no one else. Some of us are starting a NOW chapter in town, and I hope that with a Lesbianism and sexuality task force we can publicize as part of NOW, a lot more Lesbians in this town will have a less threatening context in which to come out more fully to themselves and each other.

17 Untitled Story

Jean Carr

I am white, 27 and a Virgo raised in a non-religious, intellectual upper-middle-class family. I work as an epidemiologist at a medical school, doing research in occupational lung diseases, and am half-way to a doctorate.

I always tend to do things after thinking about them for a long time and never jump into experiences I have not considered carefully. My adolescence was very lonely. I read a lot, never dated (even once), and spent my time mooning over one teacher or another. I knew I was supposed to be having crushes on boys so I went to the library and read everything I could find on "sexual deviance" (that's where the card catalog made you look if you looked under "homosexuality"). I decided that I was gay, though I called it being a "homo." My only doubt stemmed from my not feeling anything *sexual* exactly—I just wanted to live with a womyn forever and ever and be hugged. But at 15 I decided I was just a *repressed* homo—I know this now because I documented the observation in my journal. It took me another 10 years to touch a woman!

So I knew I was a homosexual. I went to college, kept falling in love with old women, reading the old Lesbiana and, in my senior year, joining Lesbian CR groups and becoming "active." I was not shy, verbally, and told all intimate friends, male and female, that I was gay. I could be marvelously open "coming out" to everybody, but was still just as petrified of being touched by anyone. The Lesbians I interacted with evidently sensed the fear and did not attempt to bring me out. When I went to graduate school it was more of the same, except that I didn't fall in love with any old women and became slightly more aware of sexual

feelings toward young women. I was also in therapy with a wonderful
woman who didn't try to change my orientation though she did help me
lose my fear of being touched.

At 25, I came to New Orleans and suddenly opened up. I came out,
I learned to dance and smoke pot, all for the first time in my life. It was
like the Great Thaw. I discovered that one can sometimes enjoy oneself
at parties, and suddenly there was no time for reading.

Peg was in my classes at school. She was Italian, with curly black
hair and bright, dark eyes. I thought she was wonderful and was very
attracted to her. I would sit in statistics class trying to watch the
blackboard instead of her cleavage. She told me she was bisexual; I told
her I was gay. Neither of us happened to mention our attraction to each
other. The night of November 15, 1975 (Do you think I will ever forget
that date?) there was a party, a straight party, but we were the last to
leave. We were smashed out of our minds, I sitting nervously on a rolled-
up rug and Peg dancing alone in the middle of the room. I finally said,
"Peg, why do we have to get so drunk to make love"—and she came
over and kissed me. We went to bed and she passed out after doing no
more than running her hand down my side. I must have lain there for ten
minutes in a state of intense anticipation, until I suddenly realized she
was sound asleep. In the morning she didn't remember anything from
the night before and asked me, sheepishly, " Did we make love?" I
didn't know, but I did know that I wanted more, and more, and more.

That was a hard, hard time. My sex drive had the full force of a river
dammed for 10 years. Once a day did not begin to stem the flood, and
Peg was understandably alarmed at such an overwhelming undertaking.
It seemed to me that Peg was my first and last chance to love a woman
and my failure with her seemed to predict that I would never be able to
love women.

But I am very dogged. To fight the despair (and the desire) I
decided I had to go to the bar, where I'd never been before. With
relentless logic I decided that that meant I had to learn to play pool, so I
could *do* something when I went to the bar. So I spent every evening at
pool halls and at a deserted gay bar trying to learn to play pool. Although
I learned to sink balls in holes, I never learned anything about the
etiquette of pool-playing, and remember one night when a woman put
a quarter down on the table. I finally realized that meant that she wanted
to play, and so I went and told her that she was welcome to use the
table—she looked at me (understandably) as if I were crazy. I was so
confused I went home immediately. But that time is now over. I don't
have to play pool anymore.

There is one more chapter. I had never told my parents that I was
gay all this time since I felt I would only know for sure if I was gay (and
what that *meant*) after I'd slept with women. So last June I told them, and

my mother got very, very upset. At first she thought that the cause was genetic and so was not too guilty, but then she went to the library and read a lot of shit that made her very upset. She burst into tears, crying, "I didn't treat you like a boy!" We went around and around, making each other such nervous wrecks that neither of us could eat or sleep for days. Finally my father (bless his soul!) convinced my mother that her continuing love for me was far more important than any theoretical opinions that she might have about my life-style. So she calmed down. It eventually emerged that her primary concern was with orgies and promiscuity and not so much with Lesbianism per se. In a recent letter she confessed that she can't quite remember why she was so upset—it all seemed rather trivial now. But I can't honestly say that now all is well, and I am "accepted" and so forth; all I can say is that the subject is before us for discussion now, and that is a big step.

One of the best aspects of telling my parents was the experience of coming to grips with our love for each other. People say that they can't tell their parents because they love them too much, but that's a lie. Their not telling keeps them separate from their parents. My mother and I worked very hard with each other to make the other understand: the side-effect was a surge of love. I discovered how very much I love her, and she me. Our love was larger than my anger with her rejection and her anger with my insistence on her acceptence—we know now how deeply we are bound, how much pain we will endure to make the other understand.

I told my boss I was gay at the same time. He said, "So?"

Oh, one more thing. I have never been conscious of feeling that being gay was either sick or sinful. I have always been an intellectual maverick and would probably have been involved in some other socially unacceptable behavior if I hadn't been gay. Being gay satisfies at one fell swoop all of my desires to be perverse.

I know that my story is unusual. Most women seem to sleep with women and then realize that there is a word for that, and it isn't nice ... I am much too cerebral for that, I guess.

18 Not For Years But For Decades

Joanna Russ

I. Fact

When I was twelve I fell in love with Danny Kaye. For almost a quarter of a century I have regarded that crush as the beginning of my sexual life. But "sexual" is a dangerous word precisely because it splits one part of experience off from the rest. It was only when I began to ask, not about "sex" or my "sex life" but (more vaguely) about my "feelings" and about "emotional attachments" that I began to recall other things, some earlier, that the official classifications of "sex" censored out and made unimportant. Perhaps that's the function of official classifications. Names are given to things by the privileged and their naming is (wouldn't you think?) to their own advantage, but in the area of sexuality women are emphatically not a privileged class. So let's ask about "friends."

At eleven I played erotic games with girl friends, acting out nominally heterosexual stories I (usually) had made up. One script (minus the kissing and touching we added to it) I showed my mother, who praised it but laughed until she cried at one stage direction, which has a lover climbing a rope ladder to his sweetheart's window, being discovered by her parents, and gloomily exiting by climbing back down the ladder. About this time I went on my First Date with a nice, plain, gentle, thoroughly dull little boy called Bill (we called him "Bill the Hill"). The necking he wanted to do bored me, but I was tremendously proud of having a First Date. At about that time, one winter's evening, one of my girl friends seductively and skittishly insisted on kissing us all good night; that night I dreamed I was being led further and further into a dark forest by an elf who was neither a girl nor a boy, rotting oranges as big as people hung on the trees, and when a storm began, I woke in terror, knowing perfectly well that I had dreamed about my friend and that I was feeling for her what ought to go on with Bill the Hill. I told my mother about it and she "handled it very well" (as my analyst said many years later).

She said it was "a stage."

That summer I was in summer camp and all the twelve-year-old girls in the bunk necked and petted secretly (with each other) but the next summer everybody seemed to have forgotten about it. Certainly nobody mentioned it. Everybody remembered the "dirty jokes" we had told every night for hours (grotesquely heterosexual or homophobic stories I thought the other children had invented) and none of my friends had forgotten the (heterosexual) serial stories I had made up and which several other little girls continued. But that whole summer of fumbling with your best friend had become invisible. Since nobody else mentioned it, I never did either.

My "best friend" was Carol-Ellen. I called her my "best friend," not my "lover." I had strong and sometimes painfully profound feelings about her and would have been miserably jealous if she'd preferred anyone else to me. Yet I never thought that I "loved" Carol-Ellen or that what we did was really "sex" (although it was somehow not only sex, but a far worse kind than the boys' panty-raids or girls staying out with boys after curfew). I never gave to what had happened between us the prestigious name of "love" (which might have led me to stand up for its importance) or the wicked-but-powerful name of "sex." What I had begun to learn (in "it's a stage") continued that summer, that my real experience, undefined and powerful as it was, didn't really exist. It was bad and it didn't exist. It was bad *because* it didn't exist.

Simultaneously with being mad about Carol-Ellen, I read Love Comics. I believed in them. (Everybody read them and everybody, I suspect, believed in them.) Like dating and movies and boys, they were about real love and real sex. I remember disliking them and at the same time not being able to stay away from them. They demanded things of me (looks, clothes, behavior) which I disliked, and they insisted on the superiority and importance of men in a way I detested (and couldn't connect with any of the little boys I knew at camp). But they offered a very great promise: that if only I would sacrifice my ambitions and most of my personality, I would be given a reward—they called it "love." I knew it was in some way "sexual." And yet I also knew that those hearts and flowers and flashing lights when the characters kissed didn't have anything to do with sex; they were supersex or ultrasex; they were some kind of transcendent ecstasy beyond ordinary life. They certainly didn't have anything to do with masturbation, or with what Carol-Ellen and I

were secretly doing together. I think now that the most attractive
rewards held out by the Love Comics (and later by the movies, the
books, and the psychoanalysts) was freedom from responsibility and
hence freedom from the burdens of being an individual. At twelve I
found that promise very attractive. I was a tall, overly-bright and overly-
self-assertive girl, too much so to fit anybody's notions of femininity (and
too bookish and odd to fit other children's ideas of an acceptable
human being). If anybody needed an escape from the guilt of
individuality, I certainly did. The Love Comics told me that when it came
right down to it, I wasn't any different from any other woman and that
once love came, I would no longer have to worry about being
imprisoned in my lonely, eccentric selfhood. The hearts and flowers and
the psychedelic flashing lights would sweep all that away. I would be "in
love" and I would never have to think again, never agonize over being
"unpopular," never follow my own judgment in the face of criticism,
never find things out for myself. This is the Grand Inquisitor's promise
and I think Germaine Greer is quite right to see in the cult of "romance"
a kind of self-obliterating religion. I didn't know that at twelve, of
course. Nor did I know enough to look at the comic books' copyright
pages to see which sex owned them, published them, and even wrote
them. But I believed. And if I hadn't gotten the message from comic
books, I would still have gotten it (as I did later) from movies, books, and
friends. Later on I would get the same message from several (not even
one!) psychiatrist and psychology books. Nor did the High Culture I met
at college carry a different message. The insistence on certain kinds of
looks and behavior, the overwhelming importance of men, and the
sacrifice of personality and individuality (as well as the promised
rewards) were always the same. (The only thing college added was
contempt for women—which didn't change the obligation to be
"feminine.")

Ti-Grace Atkinson calls this the heterosexual institution.

Time passed. Carol-Ellen went to another camp. At fourteen I felt
for a male counselor of nineteen the vulnerability, awkwardness, and
liking I've since learned to call "erotic tension." Somebody else asked
him to the Sadie Hawkins Dance and I cried in the bathroom for three
solid minutes. I didn't know him well and didn't feel for him with one-
quarter of the intensity I had for Carol-Ellen, but this time I had an
official name for what I was feeling; I called it "love." I think what drew
me to him was his kindness and his lack of good looks, which made him
seem, to me, like a fellow-refugee. He was embarrassed at the dance
(about me, I suspect) and roared about, clowning, which disillusioned
me. I don't believe Carol-Ellen could have disillusioned me; I knew her
too well and she was too important to me. I don't remember his face or
his name, although I remember Carol-Ellen's perfectly (possibly

because I took good care to get a snapshot of her). And Carol-Ellen, though of course a fellow-creature, was not a fellow-refugee; she always seemed to me far too good-looking and personally successful for that, so much so that I wondered why nobody else noticed her beauty. I always felt graced by Carol-Ellen's picking me for her best friend; after all, she could've been friends with anybody. But somewhere in my feelings about Bernie (Sidney? Joe? Scottie?) was the disheartening feeling I came to recognize later in my dealings with men: *He'll do.*

The year before that, in junior high, an older boy of fifteen (a popular person whose acquaintance I coveted) complimented me on a scarf I was wearing and I responded as we always did in my family: "Thanks, I got it at.…" He laughed, partly amused, partly critical. "I didn't ask you where you got it! After all, *I'm* not going to get one." I knew that I had made a social mistake, and yet my embarrassment and shame were mixed with violent resentment. I knew then that the manners I had been taught (they seemed to me perfectly good ones) were now wrong, and that I would have to learn a whole new set for "boys." It was unfair. It was just like the Love Comics. I knew also that somewhere deep down I didn't believe in the absolute duality of male and female behavior (in terms of which he'd criticized me) and that somewhere in the back of my mind, in a reserve of boundless arrogance, I was preparing revolutionary solutions for such people: *That's false and I know it. And just you wait.*

Yet all of this: revolution, Lesbianism, what-have-you, took place in profound mental darkness. I wrote moody Lesbian poems about Carol-Ellen, played with the idea of being a Lesbian, a tremendously attractive idea but strictly a literary one (I told myself). I wrote a Lesbian short story, which worried my high school teacher into asking me if I had any "problems you want to talk about." I knew the story had bothered him and felt wickedly pleased and very daring. The story itself was about a tall, strong, masculine, dark-haired girl (me) who falls in love with a short, slender, light-haired girl (?) and then kills herself by throwing herself off a bridge because the light-haired girl (although a Lesbian) will have nothing to do with her. I couldn't imagine anything else for the two of them to do. A few months later I began a novel (without connecting it with the story): here the dark-haired girl has become a dark-haired young man and the two lovers do get together (here I *could* imagine something for them to do) although light-hair eventually breaks the love affair off. On what grounds? That she's a Lesbian! The young man, by the way, does not kill himself.

At the same time I began to wonder what pregnancy felt like and to write poems about Being Female, which I thought meant having no mind and being immersed in some overwhelming, not necessarily pleasant experience which was much bigger than you were (no, I didn't yet even know that D.H. Lawrence existed; it was Love Comics again). I fell in love with a male gay friend and went with him and his sister to the Village, where they adjured me to pretend I was eighteen ("For God's sake, Joanna, put your hair up and wear earrings!") so that we could drink real liquor in a real bar. I had disturbing dreams about him in which he came to the door of my family's house in a dress and a babushka. (At the time I interpreted the dream as worry about his effeminate mannerisms. Now I'm not so sure.) Later, in my first year of college, he came to visit and I teased him into kissing me; it felt so good that the next day I insisted on going farther. The only place we could use was the dormitory lounge, and possibly because of the publicity of the location, things turned out badly; he got scared, I got nauseated, and after he left I spent a wretched hour surrounded by friends, who cheerfully told me that the first time was always rotten. The housemother, a youngish psychologist, told me the same thing, and when I told her about my feelings for women (I must've had them, although I can only remember telling her about them) she said I was "going through a stage."

Somehow, in a vague and confused way, I didn't believe that. I found *Mademoiselle de Maupin*, a nineteenth-century novel in which a woman disguises herself as a man and has a love affair with a woman and a man (I thought the man was a creep and was really only interested in the woman). I wore slacks and felt defiant and ashamed. I tried to find out about Lesbianism on campus and annoyed my friends ("This school is awful. Do you know there are Lesbians here." "Where! Where!" "Oh, Joanna, *really*."). I acquired a "best friend" for whom I had painful, protective, profound feelings &c. without ever recognizing &c. I found another "elf" and followed her around campus at a distance, feeling embarrassed. I went out on dates, which were even more crucial than they had been in high school, and got kissed by various men, which mildly excited and not-so-mildly disgusted me. My "best friend" told me stories about Lesbianism in her high school, in which everyone was a Lesbian except her, but when I wanted to go with her to a Lesbian bar in New York (over vacation) she wouldn't, and when I desperately asked her to pretend we were lovers in front of a third person, whom I said I wanted to shock (I didn't know myself at that point exactly what I was doing) she got very angry and upset.

So I gave up. It wasn't real. It didn't count, except in my own inner world in which I could not only love women but also fly, ride the lightning, be Alexander the Great, live forever, etc., all of which occurred in my poetry. I regarded this inner life as both crucially important and totally trivial, the source of all my vitality and yet something completely sealed off from "reality." By now I had learned to define the whole cluster of feelings as "wanting to be a man" (something I had not thought of before college) and saw it simultaneously as a shameful neurotic symptom and an indication of how much more talented and energetic I was than other women. Women with "penis envy" (another collegiate enlightenment) were inferior to men but were somehow superior to other women although they were also wickeder than other women. My best friend thought so. The psychology books my mother read thought so. The movies seemed to think so. Two years later the second elf turned up one summer (we had become distant friends) and the whole business started all over again. I now recognized it as a recurrent thing. I laughed at it and called it "penis envy." It was about at that time that I began the first of a long series of one-way infatuations with very macho men (these lasted into my thirties), agonizing experiences in which I suffered horribly but had the feeling that my life had become real and intense, even super-real, the feeling that I was being propelled into an experience bigger and more overwhelming than my own dreary life, a life I was beginning to detest. The first man I picked for this was my "best friend's" fiance. I kept the infatuation going, totally unreciprocated, for almost a year. He left school, they split up. I managed to go out with him once (we necked) and felt, in immense erotic excitement, that if only he would love me I could submerge my individuality in his, that he was a "real man," and that if I could only marry him I could give up "penis envy" and be a "real woman."

It sounds just like Love Comics.

In high school I believed (along with my few friends) that college would see an end to the dating game, to the belief that women were inferior to men, and that intellectual women were freaks. But it was in college that I first got lectures about "being a woman" from boys I knew, and heard other women getting them, heard that so-and-so knew "how to be a woman," and was surrounded by the new and ghastly paraphernalia of dress rules and curfews. (My parents had been extremely permissive about where I went and with whom.)

After my twelfth summer I had gone (very early) into a high school where I knew nobody; I became depressed. In college I became more depressed. I went to the school psychiatrist, who told me I had "penis envy" and was in love with my father. I was willing to agree but did not know what to do about it (he said, "Enjoy life. Go out on dates") and became even more depressed. By the end of graduate school I no longer had problems with "feelings about women"; I felt nothing about anybody. Occasionally I slept with a short, gentle, retiring man for whom I felt affection but no desire; puzzlingly, the sex didn't work. Later, when I got into my twenties and into psychoanalysis, and began to feel again, I "fell in love with" handsome macho men who didn't know I existed; I hated and envied them. The more intense and unreal these one-way "love affairs" were, the more dead and flat my life became in between. (When the man was not inaccessible, I made sure I was.) I got married to a short, gentle, retiring pleasant man (*He'll do*) and worked very hard at sex, which I loathed. I fell in love with a male homosexual friend because he was so beautiful and his life was beautiful and I wanted to be part of his life. I certainly didn't want to be part of my own life. I acquired a series of office jobs, none of which I could bear to keep ("Isn't there anything you like about your job?" "Yes, lunch hour."). I went into analysis because I was extremely depressed and very angry, and when my analyst asked (once) if I had homosexual feelings, I said "Oh, no, of course not," without even thinking. Even if it hadn't been nonsense, everybody knew that the real problem was men, so I thought endlessly about men, worried about men, worried (with the active help of my analyst) about the orgasms I wasn't having with men, worried about my childhood, worried about my parents, all in the service of worrying about my relation to men. Nothing else mattered. When my analyst asked me if I enjoyed sex, apart from ˙orgasm, I remember wondering mildly what on earth he meant. It's quite possible that analysis did help me with my "dependency problems," although for a man who urged me to be independent, he was remarkably little concerned at my being economically dependent on my husband; he thought that was O.K. I didn't; for one thing my husband hated his job as much as I hated mine. He told me that my relationship with my mother was bad (I agreed) but when I talked about my father I would get so enraged (about all men, not just about that one) that he would become tolerantly silent and then tell me I was showing resistance. He once said that if I'd been born a boy, I could've turned out much worse: "You would have been homosexual." He said that what had saved me from going really crazy in my childhood was my father's love. He once remarked that I had intense friendships, and I said, "Yeah, I guess," not at all interested. But apart from the two remarks I've noted we never talked about my homosexuality. We talked about my "frigidity."

I remember someone in the group (I was in group therapy for years) asking me if my husband was a good lover, and my absolute, blank helplessness before that question. I remember analytic remarks that enraged and baffled me: that getting married showed "ego strength"—I had done it partly because I was running out of money and couldn't stand working, a motive of which I was bitterly ashamed and which I never told anybody; that it was surprising that my husband could "function sexually"—I had an impulse of absolute rage, which I suppressed; that I was afraid I would be physically hurt in the sex act— "No, I'm afraid I'll turn into a 'real woman'," "But you are a real woman"; that I could be "active" by telling my husband what to do *to* me; and that men and women had different social functions but the same dignity—"Yeah, separate but equal" and that one I actually said out loud.

If analysis did any good, it certainly did not do it in the area of sex. Perhaps having some stories published helped. Being invited to writers' conferences and, for the first time in my life, meeting people like myself helped. (Question: why is it so hard making friends in group therapy and so easy making friends at writers' conferences? Answer: because writers are crazy.) Years later when I heard the phrase "the iron has entered your soul" I entirely misunderstood it. I thought that when you passed a certain point in misery you could really take the misery into you and turn it into strength. Perhaps I did that somehow. I made the first genuine decision of my adult life and left my husband—I was panic-stricken, clearly a matter of "dependency problems" but also a matter of getting out of the heterosexual institution. I got a job I liked, partly by accident ("You mean they'll pay me for *that*?"). I learned to drive. I got a job in another city and left analysis. I was desperately lonely. I kept "falling in love" with inaccessible men until it occurred to me that I wanted to be them, not love them, but by then feminism had burst over all of us. I stopped loving men ("It's just too difficult!") and in a burst of inspiration, dreamed up the absolutely novel idea of loving women. I thought at the time that my previous history had nothing to do with it.

Just before I left my husband I had a dream, which I still remember. (I had begun to have nightmares every night after we made love.)[1] I was alone in a city at night, walking round and round a deserted and abandoned schoolhouse, and I couldn't tell if I was frightened because I was alone or frightened because I wasn't alone. This dark schoolhouse was surrounded by uncut grass and grass was growing in the cracks of the sidewalk. I sat down on the front steps, in a world unutterably desolate and deserted, wishing very hard for someone to take me away from there. Then a car, containing the shadowy figures of a man and a woman in the front seat, pulled up, and I got inside, in the back seat. The car began to move and somehow I strained to keep it moving, for I suspected it wasn't going anywhere; and then I looked down and there, through the floorboards, grew the grass.

There was no car. I was back on the steps, alone. And I was terrified.

It was years before the phrase "grass growing in the streets" connected itself to the dream. (I knew from the first that it was about being alone.) I think now that the deserted schoolhouse is psychoanalysis (where I am to be "taught" what to be), and that the shadowy man and woman are what psychoanalysis is teaching me; that is, the heterosexual institution. But the schoolhouse is dark and deserted, grass grows in the streets (as was supposed to happen in the 1930's here if that radical, Roosevelt, won), the man and woman are only

---

[1] And only *if* we had made love.

shadows, and I'm totally alone in a solitary world. Marriage is an illusion. My "teacher" is nonexistent.

It seems to me now the only dream I've ever had, aside from (a possible) one in childhood, that's genuinely schizophrenic, with the changelessness of madness, the absolute desolation, and the complete lack of hope.

But it didn't happen. Instead I got out.

II. Fantasy

But now we reach problems. Am I a "real" Lesbian?

There is immense social pressure in our culture to imagine a Lesbian as someone who never under any circumstances feels any attraction to any man, in fantasy or otherwise. The popular model of homosexuality is simply the heterosexual institution reversed; since heterosexuality is (supposedly) exclusive, so must homosexuality be. It is this assumption, I think, that lies behind arguments about what a "real Lesbian" is or accusations that so-and-so isn't "really" a Lesbian. I have been attracted to men; therefore I'm not a Lesbian. I have few (or no) fantasies about women and do have fantasies about men;[2] therefore I'm not a Lesbian. This idea of what a Lesbian is is a wonderful way of preventing anyone from ever becoming one; and when we adopt it, we're simply doing the culture's dirty work for it. *There are no "real" Lesbians*—which is exactly what I heard for years, there are only neurotics, impostors, crazy virgins, and repressed heterosexuals. You aren't a Lesbian. You can't be a Lesbian. There aren't any Lesbians. Real Lesbians have horns.

Since we are outside the culture's definitions to begin with, most of us are not going to fit the culture's models of "sex," not even backwards. There is the Romantic Submission model for women. There is the Consumption Performance model for men. A few years ago *Playboy* came out with a cover made up of many small squares, each of which contained a picture of part of a naked woman: a single breast, a belly, a leg, two buttocks, &c. There were no faces. I had just come out at this time, and was very upset and confused because I couldn't respond to this model. Not only wasn't I relating to women that way; I hated the model itself because I had spent so much time on the other end of it and I knew what that detachable-parts business does to a woman's sense of self. Did this mean that I was not a Lesbian? Not by *Playboy's* standards, certainly. Mind you, I was not therefore a healthy or good woman. I was merely sick, criminal, or crazy. Oddly enough, I don't think I've ever felt guilty about sleeping with women per se; I always felt that my real crime was *not sleeping with men*. After the first euphoria of discovery

[2] Up to about a year ago.

("Joanna, for Heaven's sake will you lower your voice; do you want the whole restaurant to know?") what plagues me—and still does—is the nagging feeling that in not sleeping with men I am neglecting a terribly important obligation. I'm sometimes attracted to men I humanly like; when this happens I feel tremendously pressured to do something about it (whether I want to or not). When I don't act on it, I feel cowardly and selfish, just as I used to feel when I didn't have orgasms with my husband. Women, after all, *don't count*. What happens between women *isn't real*. That is, you can't be beaten up on for more than twenty-five years and not carry scar tissue.

Unfortunately there is something we all do that perpetuates the whole business, and that is treating fantasy as a direct guide to action. Suppression doesn't only affect behavior; it also affects the meaning and valuation we give behavior. And it affects fantasy. The popular view (which Molly Haskell attacked in her recent *Ms.* article) is that daydreams or other fantasies are fairly simple substitutes for behavior and that the two are related to each other in a simple one-to-one way, i.e. what you can't act out, you daydream. I don't believe this. For years I did, and was sure that my heterosexual fantasies indicated I was a heterosexual. (My Lesbian fantasies, however, could be dismissed as "wanting to be a man.") I think now that fantasy, like any other language, must be interpreted, that it does not "translate" simply into behavior, and that what is most important about it is the compromise it shows and the underlying subject-matter at work in it. For example, fantasies about "sex" may not be about sex at all, although the energy that feeds them is certainly sexual. I know that in growing up I had fantasies about rescuing Danny Kaye from pirates at the same time that I loved Carol-Ellen. I couldn't find my fantasy of a gentle, beautiful, non-masculine, rescuable man in any of the little boys I knew; there was only dull Bill (*He'll do*) and the creeps I hated and feared who grabbed me at parties or came up to me in assembly and said, "Baby, your pants are showing." By the age of fifteen I was having two kinds of fantasies: either I was an effeminate, beautiful, passive man being made love to by another man or I was a strong, independent, able, active, handsome woman disguised as a man (sometimes a knight in armor) who rescued another woman from misery or danger in a medieval world I could not picture very well. The first kind of daydream was full of explicit sex and secret contempt; the second was full of emotion and baffled yearning. Whenever it came time to go beyond the first kiss, I was stopped by my own ignorance. There was a third daydream, rarer than the other two, in which I was an independent, able, strong, woman disguised as a man and traveling with my lover, an able, strong man who alone knew the secret of my identity. This kind was not satisfying, either emotionally or sexually, and I think I tried it out of a sense of duty; the one virtue it had was a sort of hearty palship that I liked.

In a sexual situation there are at least two factors operating: who you want the other person to be and who you want to be yourself. If I try to analyze my own past fantasies, I come up with one theme over and over, and that is not who the Other is, but what kind of identity I can have within the confines of the heterosexual institution. What I'll call the Danny Kaye fantasy is William Steig's *Dreams of Glory* with the sexes changed: little boy saves beautiful adult woman from fate worse than something-or-other. (If you look at the early Kaye films, you find that something of the sort is indeed happening, although not nearly to the extent I thought when I was twelve.) I still think that if I had emerged at puberty into a female-dominant culture in which little girls could reasonably dream of rescuing handsome, gentle, sexually responsive (but non-initiating) men from peril, I could have made an uneasy peace with it. I would probably have ended up the way a good many men do within the heterosexual institution: homosexuality for them remains an area of profound uneasiness, although their outward behavior and what they allow themselves to feel matches the norm.[3] However, even the cultural artifacts that turned me on in my youth all took it back in the end, just as Mae West's wooing of Cary Grant in *She Done Him Wrong* is shown up as a fake in the end of the film; he's really a tough cop. In fact, though this model of sexuality is not totally inconceivable and unspeakable, it turns up rarely and is explicitly disallowed. The 'sixties produced it in grotesque form in Tiny Tim; it took the 'seventies to produce David Bowie. But the heterosexual institution is wary of this model; it's politically very dangerous. And heterosexual men are trained to avoid it like the plague. Even as a fantasy it disappeared early in my adolescence.

Fantasy Number Two was cued off at age fifteen or thereabouts by something I read, and later on there were movies about Oscar Wilde and so on. (I have never ceased to be amazed at the fact that works about male homosexuality can exist in libraries, quite respectably bound, some even minor classics. They're few enough but Lesbian works are far fewer.) The one film I hoped would be about Lesbianism (*Maedchen in Uniform*) wasn't and disappointed me very much. This fantasy got more and more important as I got older, more depressed, *and more outwardly conforming to the heterosexual institution.* There were years in my twenties when this was the only way I could daydream about sex at all. I had, by that time, put into this fantasy all the explicit fucking that never got into the others, I'll give you all the passivity and charm you want ... if only I'm not a woman.

[3] I don't mean that such men are "really" homosexual. That's going back to the model of the heterosexual institution again. They've suppressed a good deal of themselves, although what is allowed to exist isn't necessarily false.

Number Three (woman/woman) began early; it was modeled on a (totally sexless) parodic little story by Mark Twain about a woman disguised as a man, entitled "A Medieval Romance." At fifteen I added material from *Mademoiselle de Maupin*. For close to a decade my knowledge of Lesbianism was limited to these two fictions, one of them a parody (I was too naive to spot this at twelve), and although the emotional tenacity of this fantasy has been awesome, I never put much "sex" into it. I did not, after all, know what women did with each other.[4] And since the only way I could get near a woman was to disguise myself as a man, I had to protect my disguise (otherwise she wouldn't want me). So it was all impossible. Also, I was uneasy about wanting anybody else to "be the girl," since I knew what a rotten deal that was; I couldn't imagine anybody choosing it voluntarily. And how dull she was! But because I was a sort-of-a-man I couldn't very well love anybody else. Lesbianism modeled on the heterosexual institution didn't work and I had not the dimmest social clue that any other form of it could exist. And in my heart I think I would infinitely have preferred the reality of loving a woman to any fantasy; the very fact that it was a fantasy used to make me cry (in the fantasy). So this daydream also dies eventually.

The woman-disguised-as-a-man with a man was a pale one; it was too close to the reality of the heterosexual institution. Male attire is a flimsy protection for the culturally harassed female ego. I used this one rarely.

A fantasy that appeared sporadically through my 'teens and (like the male homosexual fantasy) got heavy in my twenties was explicit heterosexual masochism.[5] It was physically exciting, erotically dependable, and very upsetting emotionally. I never connected this one to Love Comics and never imagined that it might have social sources; I thought I had invented it, that it meant I was a "real woman" and "really passive," and also that I wanted to be hurt and that I was crazy.

There were two situations I never used in any of my fantasies: a woman loving a man and a man loving a woman. That is, I could never imagine myself in either role of the heterosexual institution. I think now that the heterosexual-masochistic fantasy was a way of sexualizing the situation I was in fact in, and that one of the things it "means" (in translation) is that I was being hurt and I knew that I was being hurt *because* I was a woman, that it was not sexual at all (as I had been promised) but that I wished to goodness it would be; then at least I

[4] I have only recently become aware of the extent of my own woman-hating and my own valuing of male bodies as more important, valuable, strong and hence "beautiful" than female bodies. Even a Lesbian wouldn't want an (ugh) *woman*! Even if she loved her. Feelings of inferiority climb into bed with you.

[5] I'm talking of "masochism" as most women I know understand it: i.e. humiliation, shame, embarrassment, impersonality, *emotional* misery. Physical pain was not part of it; oddly enough, physical pain is what most men I know assume to be "masochism."

would get something out of it. I also suspect that sadomasochism is a way of preventing genuine involvement; either he wasn't emotionally there and present or I wasn't, and anyhow *the only thing* I can get from all of this is an orgasm.

The one cultural cue I had in abundance was the Dominance/Submission model of the heterosexual institution. The one cultural cue I barely had at all was Lesbianism (there is no cultural vocabulary of words, images, or expectations in this area). Oddly enough, for someone who thought she "wanted to be a man," I never imagined myself a man at all; by what sheer cussedness I managed to resist that cue, I'll never know.

What do people do with their sexuality? Whatever they can, I think. I think fucking can "work" within a wide variety of physical conditions. And the head-trips may not be connected to what one responds to in real life at all. In a fine essay on female sexuality Linda Phelps says that female sexuality is "schizophrenic, relating not to ourselves as self-directed persons, not to our partners as sexual objects of our desire, but to a false world of symbols and fantasy. ... It is a world whose eroticism is defined in terms of female powerlessness, dependency, and submission. ... In a male world, female sexuality is from the beginning unable to get a clear picture of itself." She says also that many women "have no sexual fantasies at all" and those who do "often have the same sadomasochistic fantasies that men do."[6]

Yeah.

Looking back, I think my fantasies were desperate strategies to salvage something of my identity, even at the expense of any realistically possible sexuality. There was, of course, this behavior with women that I wanted but I couldn't talk about that; it was the most taboo of all. (My first incredulous words at thirty-three: "You mean that's *real?*" Yes, I knew it happened, but. ...) I recognized my Lesbian feelings at age eleven; less than a year later I could no longer even recognize *what I was actually doing*, let alone what I later wanted to do. The only remotely positive encouragement I got, as well as the only analysis or naming, was the "stage" business. So partly I hung on in a muddled way and partly I gave up; after sixteen I gave up completely. The non-verbal messages were too strong. I think that anyone trying to maintain behavior important to them in the face of massive social pressure can only do so in a crippled and compromised way (especially in isolation), whatever form the crippling takes, whether it's guilt or an inability to fantasy or an inability to act. Or perhaps a constant re-shuffling of the roles prescribed

---

[6]"Female Sexual Alienation" by Linda Phelps, reprinted in *The Lavendar Herring: Lesbian Essays from "The Ladder"*, eds. Grier and Reid, Diana Press, Baltimore, MD 1976, pp. 161-170. Ms. Phelps does not address herself exclusively to gay women. I think in this area she's probably right not to, as I suspect the mechanisms are the same for both, though one would suffer more symbolic distortion and the other more total obliteration.

by the heterosexual institution. As I got older things got worse; in my twenties I began to have occasional night dreams in which I was physically a man. I dreamed that a bunch of men was running after a bunch of women with felonious intent. I dreamed that I was being unmasked as "not really a man" and that everyone was laughing at me. As I had progressed from college to the less sheltered graduate school and from there to the not-at-all-sheltered job market my situation became worse and worse. I wasn't a man (let alone a homosexual man). I certainly couldn't love women, I was a *woman* and *women* loved *men* and dull, gentle men weren't "really" men and if I liked them I wasn't "really" a woman (and anyhow I didn't like them except as friends; sex with them was no good). I was out of college now, I had to earn my own living, I had to get married, I had to shape up and have orgasms, this was the *real world*, dammit.

So I read Genet and Gide (I scorned *The Well of Loneliness* which I came to much too late anyway) and believed the art and life were totally separate. By then I really did want to be a man (for one thing, men didn't have such horrible lives, or so the heterosexual institution informed me). I was married. I was frigid. I couldn't earn my own living. I wasn't sure I was a writer. Psychoanalysis seemed only to prove more and more that the impossibility of my ever being a "real" woman was my own fault. I was hopelessly crazy and a failure at everything. My analyst, in the kindest possible way, pointed out to me that my endless infatuations with inaccessible men were not realistic; I tried to tell him that for me nothing was realistic. My maneuvers for retaining some shred of autonomy within the iron-and-concrete prison of the heterosexual institution were getting desperate; they now involved wholesale transformations of identity or the direct translation of my real situation into "masochism," which terrified and disgusted me. (I only brought myself to write about these fantasies many years later, by which time they had lost much of their glamor.) I knew that I did not really want to sleep with men. But that was sick. I did want to sleep with men—but only in my head and only under very specialized circumstances. *That* was sick. In short I had—for close to twenty-five years—no clear sexual identity at all, no confidence in my own bodily experience, and no pleasure in lovemaking with any real person. I had to step out of the heterosexual institution before I could put myself back together and begin to recover my own bodily and emotional experience. When I did, it was only because the women's movement had thoroughly discredited the very idea of "real" women, thus enabling me to become a whole person who could then pay some attention to the gay liberation movement. (My most vivid feeling after my first Lesbian experience: that my body was well-put-together, graceful, healthy, fine-feeling, and above all, *female*—a thought that made me laugh until I cried.)

Whenever people talk about the difference between politics and personal life, I'm dumbfounded. Not only were these "political" movements intensely "personal" in their effect on me; I can't imagine a "political" stance that doesn't grow out of "personal" experience. On my own I would never have made it. I can still remember—and the institutional cruelty behind the incident still staggers me—telling my woman-disguised-as-man-with-man fantasy to my psychoanalyst, and this dreary piece of compromise (which did not, in fact, work erotically at all) met with his entire approval; he thought it was a real step forward that I should imagine myself to be a "real" woman being made love *to* by a "real" man. Then he said, smiling:

"But why do you have to be disguised as a man?"

There's a lot I haven't put in this story. For example, the years of limbo that followed my first Lesbian affair ("What do I do now?") the overwhelming doubts that it had happened, which attacked me when I had to live an isolated life again in a world in which there exists absolutely no public sign that such things happen, or the self-hatred and persisting taboos ("Women are ugly" "Vaginas are slimy and strong and have horrible little teeth") or the terror of telling anyone.

As I said, by the time I read *The Well of Loneliness* I had learned that the whole business was absurd and impossible. (The book's gender roles also put me off.) I never dared buy one of those sleazy paperbacks I saw in drugstores, although I wanted them desperately. I was terrified to let the cashier see them. (Mind you, this didn't mean I was a Lesbian. It only meant that if I read all of the arousing scenes I glimpsed in them, I might become so aroused that I might go to a bar and do something Lesbian, which would be awful, because I wasn't one.) I suppose not reading about all those car crashes and suicides was a mild sort of plus, but I don't think it's a good idea to reach one's thirties without any cultural imagery for one of the most important parts of one's identity and one's life. So I've made some up. I hope that in filling the fantasy gap for myself, I've helped fill it for others, too.

I would like to thank various literary women for existing. Some of them know me and some do not. This is not an exhaustive list. Among them are: June Arnold, Sally Gearhart, Barbara Grier, Susan Griffin, Marilyn Hacker, Joan Larkin, Audre Lorde, Jill Johnston, Marge Piercy, Adrienne Rich, and too many more to put down here.

Postscribbles

1. Overheard at a gay conference, Lesbian to gay man, nearby a woman minister in "minister suit" trying not to smile: "We're *all* in drag."

2. A common way to cloak one's hatred of and dismissal of an issue is to snot it, i.e., the outraged ignorance of the reviews of Marge Piercy's *Woman at the Edge of Time* and the more sophisticated (and more hateful) reviews of Adrienne Rich's *Of Woman Born*.

3. The paralysis of the "open secret," everyone reassured about their generosity and your safety ... *except you.* Or the (even worse) open secret which everybody knows *except you*, a closet so vanishingly small that it's collapsed into a one-dimensional point and extruded itself (possibly) into some other universe, where it may be of use but not in this one. A well-meaning woman friend, upon learning that I was a Lesbian, "That's all right. It's nobody's business but yours."

4. Some white male reviewer in the *New York Times* speaking slightingly of the *irredentism*[7] of minority groups in our time. The Boys never cease to amaze me.

5. That isn't an issue
   That isn't an issue *any more.*
   That isn't *really* an issue *any more.*
   Therefore why do you keep *bringing it up*?
   You keep *bringing it up* because you are crazy.
   You keep *bringing it up* because you are destructive.
   You keep *bringing it up* because you want to be annoying.
   You keep *bringing it up* because you are greedy and selfish.
   You keep *bringing it up* because you are full of hate.
   You keep *bringing it up* because you want to flaunt yourself.
   You keep *bringing it up* because you deliberately want to separate yourself from the rest of the community.
   How do you expect me to support a person as crazy/destructive/annoying/selfish/hateful/flaunting/separatist as you are?
   I really cannot support someone as *bad* as that.
   Especially since there is no really important issue involved.

6. Vaginas do *not* have sharp little teeth! Pass it on.

---

[7]Italian radicalism of the later 19th century, calling for a unification of all the Italian-speaking peoples. I.e., nationalism: by extension, fighting for the rights of a group which perceives itself to have common interests. How wicked.

19 The Question She Put to Herself

Maureen Brady

The question she put to herself every morning those days was—
Are you or are you not a dyke? She'd gotten to the point where the
question didn't titillate her any more, it badgered her. There wasn't any
place she could go, any thing she could do without it coming up,
demanding immediate resolution and yet just hanging there. She felt as
if her whole life were suspended on a question mark. Lena, the shrink,
told her this was not so, it was just one aspect of self-definition, and even
though Ginger found Lena a relief to talk to, she knew she was wrong.
She knew Lena was denying the truth of her every waking moment and
she minded but not much, partly because Lena was such a relief to talk to
and partly because she knew by then that most shrinks work that way,
whether they know it or not. They supply you with a denial of your
existence but a more straightforward one than you'll find most places.
Thus you can see more clearly what you have to fight against. Lena was
good that way.

Most Saturdays and Sundays Ginger didn't lift her head from the
pillow before noon. She knew it meant climbing out of bed and up onto
the tightrope again and another day of gradual inching along. She was at
that mid-point of maximum sag so that either way she went had to be
uphill. Sometimes when she left herself suspended on the mattress
those mornings, she had the dream fragments to fondle. In the dream
she lay full length beside the other woman who didn't know any more
about this business than she. They both had warm skin, smooth, no
perspiration. They gave each other long, light caresses, touched hair,
cupped faces, sighed, knew precisely the location and sensation of the
other's clitoris, didn't know—should we, will we touch there, softly

moaned. It would have made a good commercial if this was the sort of
thing Madison Avenue had wanted to sell. With any perspective at all,
Ginger would've attributed the imagery to Violette Leduc, but then, she
had none. She could only fondle the fragments and try to hold off her
coming for a while because that would mean bladder urgency and time
to rise and face real life—smack—in the mirror. Are You or Are You Not
A Dyke?

It certainly wasn't the newness of the question that made it so
difficult; it was the proximity. All her life it had been there but usually
across the road, over there on the other side of a barbed wire fence
where you didn't go because if you did the bull would charge you, Santa
Claus wouldn't come, mine fields were planted to blow you up, the
boogie man was up a tree and the shadow lurked and knew. It was by
learning the primer lessons of feminism that she had come to
understand that her life was already heavily engaged with all those
spooks. She had been charged and rammed by plenty of bulls and who
gave a damn if Santa Claus never came again—that was his problem.

She had a kind of rollcall list that flipped up before her mind's eye
every time she tried to solve this problem by going back to her
beginnings. Lesbians I Have Known.

First there were Bernie and Marilyn, who as far as she knew had
always been lesbians and had always been part of her town. Bernie and
Marilyn, that's how the town folks referred to them, just like they called
her parents Dan and Mildred, never Mildred and Dan. Bernie wore the
pants. Actually Marilyn wore pants too, men's pants with pleats and
knee creases and owned the town store and was very strict about not
letting kids charge candy on the family tab. It was Bernie who had short,
straight hair and combed it back behind her ears. Ginger figured that
was the factor that made them put her name first. She was sure it wasn't
the inclination to alphabetize.

She had done a good deal of historical research—not the library
kind but in her mind, some of it with Lena, the shrink. For instance when
Lena had asked her about these women, she had said, "Oh, they were
just wonderful."

"Did you know them well?" Lena asked.

Ginger had a picture in her mind of Bernie pushing the lawn
mower, graceful and intense. She could remember Marilyn holding the
door open for her when she had groceries to carry home, then staying in
the doorway until she was sure you had a good hold on the bag.

"They lived in my town," she said to Lena. She decided not to
bother to explain what that meant to a city shrink. It seemed ludicrous in
that office where if you spoke too softly you couldn't be heard above the
traffic noise outside.

When she was twelve Ginger's family had moved to Florida, built a house, moved in, and guess who was there, across the street. Elly, the writer, who Ginger's Dad said collected rejection slips and Harriet, the nurse, who didn't work except in emergencies. That is, if there was a hurricane in Louisiana or a flood in Mississippi, she went on special duty for the Red Cross. Elly was an insult to the concept of neighboring; she rarely came out of the house. Ginger's Dad attributed her failure as a writer to this. Ginger's Mom was hurt by the fact that she could never get her to come in for coffee so she could get a better look at her. Harriet did come in for coffee and talked about where she had been in the Army or sometimes a recent disaster. Ginger's Dad had once said to her, "Harriet, why don't you get yourself a man?" Of course, he thought he was complimenting her. He thought he was telling her she could be likable to a man.

"Dan," she had said, "there's not a thing in this world that I want or need from a man." Harriet with the steady eyes, unequivocal. Years later he was still impressed. "She looked me straight in the eye ... " he would say.

This was probably the only instance Ginger knew of when her Dad's big mouth had been left hanging flaccid with no words, no grunts, no hisses, nothing coming out of it. "Harriet was fantastic," Ginger told Lena.

"I can understand why you'd feel that way," Lena said.

It was one thing to be a dyke-watcher child when the watched ones were old enough to know what they were doing. It was another thing to be in college with the two Lindas' three rooms down the hall of the dorm, Joey and Daniella up at the other end, Sparks upstairs and a friend sitting on your bed asking you to scratch her back. Ginger traveled with her best friend and in the motel room just before they went to sleep their feet touched. She read in her psychology book, ten to fifteen percent. That meant one in every corner. Scary. She often listened to the bedsprings squeaking in the Lindas' room. She had to pass it to get to the bathroom.

Ginger could see from her historical research that it was at this point in time that she had commanded her feet to leap into the trench of heterosexuality, though she had remained a virgin for several years to come. She hooked herself up to a gay man and dragged the relationship out for as long as possible. He, having just barely escaped a Trappist monastery via a blessed nervous breakdown, was still wandering around in a fog of purity. She, relieved to find orgasm possible fully clothed, the main stimulus being his leg, dreamed of living happily ever after though they both flinched in biology class at such words as *homo sapiens*. Eventually they got around to taking off their clothes and then of course the penis became more conspicuously an extra member that got in the way and they knew what they were supposed to do with it (and his shrink said it would mean progress) so finally they did, quietly and without much hoopla and for short periods of time, keeping in mind pregnancy and the possibility of defective rubbers. Neither of them ever managed to tell the other that even though that was the part that had to be done in the most private, that was the part they were doing for the public. In the end he was the one who had recognized the contours of a closet while she had denied it and thrown herself into the ring with the bulls and collected a series of miserable experiences.

Her "Lesbians I Have Known" list showed the gap which extended until consciousness-raising and the word spoken, purred, sometimes shouted—lesbian, lover... especially lover made her dizzy. It was a word from books, not from her experience. She lived with a man she could hardly stand. Her defenses were flabby from disuse and she fell in love with every other woman in the group. She condoned bisexuality, the bridge, but no one tried to seduce her. Lena, the shrink, would have loved her at this time. She would've said, "Why is it necessary to choose a camp? Why does it have to be such an issue?"

Lena would have said, "It doesn't. Don't make it be. Just do what you want and keep yourself open."

The reason Ginger knew that's what Lena would've said was because she was saying it now, four years after Ginger's consciousness-raising group had disbanded, mission supposedly accomplished. But let's not get down on Lena because she was really okay for Ginger. She was just dealing from an abstract seat. Her words were less important than her eyes which had held fearlessly to Ginger's that first day when Ginger had announced just after her name and occupation, her sexual identity crisis.

Ginger told Lena about the softball game. She'd found it advertised in *Majority Report*. After she'd finally dragged herself out of bed that Sunday morning and stared at herself in the mirror for a while, the question punctuating her expression, she'd trudged to the local newspaper store and tried quietly to sneak a *Majority Report* out of the big clip they were hanging in but the whole batch had slipped out and there they were swimming all over the fucking floor. Ginger, red-faced, had felt the store lady's eyes on her back while she stopped, gathering them up, the word *lesbian* glaring from the front page headline.

Such incidents must either build courage or contribute to the demise of the external world view (if you're out to your newspaper lady, that's one less to worry about) because Ginger went to the softball game and she never would have done that the Sunday before.

"They were all a bunch of dykes," she told Lena.

"How could you tell?"

"Most of them were real tough and when they were waiting to bat they sat around on each other's laps kissing and hugging."

"I see," Lena said, convinced.

"And I was freaked out and trying to fake having a good time the whole afternoon," Ginger said. "I thought I was going to have a cardiac arrest every time I had to run the bases. I was so hyped up with adrenalin I hit a home run."

Lena looked impressed and Ginger couldn't tell whether it was her proximity to so many dykes or the home run that was turning her on.

"So what freaked you out the most?" Lena asked.

"They were so tough."

"Playing tough," Lena contended. It was an idea that had not occurred to Ginger.

Between the fifth and sixth innings a woman from the other team had stopped Ginger as she was going out to the field and asked her what she was doing after the game. Ginger had felt about ten years old and she said she wasn't doing anything because that was the truth and at ten she'd been an honest Catholic who thought that telling a lie would bring on some dread disease like homosexuality. So the woman had asked her to come to Chinatown for dinner with her and it wasn't until she was out in right field that she realized fully she'd just made a date with a dyke. "The rest of the game was agony," she told Lena. She'd kept her eye on the woman and after each inning thought she'd sneak away but the woman was keeping an eye on her too. Definitely, she'd decided, the woman wasn't her type.

"So what happened?" Lena said.

"Oh, nothing much. As soon as we got to the restaurant I told her about my confusion. She turned out to be pretty fuzzy about herself."

"Altogether a courageous adventure," Lena said as Ginger got up to leave at the end of her time. Walking home Ginger wondered about the possibility that she was leading some part of Lena's life for her.

Her tightrope grew more and more taut. She found some Lesbians to hang out with but she told them she thought she was straight. She told some of her straight friends from the past that she thought she was a Lesbian. Then she hated everyone for being in a club—she hated labels, she commiserated with Lena and her clubless ideals. She stayed in bed even later on weekends mulling over her "Lesbians I Have Known" list, adding the new ones. The list was becoming staggering. It produced butterflies in her stomach and a tingling sensation in her thighs. In between lying down with each woman on the list, she sat with someone she cared for in the past and said, "I'm a lesbian. What do you think of that?" Then she imagined answers for every possible question. Finally, her own answers woven round and round her, she felt snugly wrapped, an embryonic creature.

The next day, if you leave off measuring days by dawn and dusk, she was camping with three dykes. She was in love with her tent-mate.

She'd slept three nights beside this small, soft breathing woman who whispered sweet good-nights. Her body floated light on the leaf bed beneath the sleeping bag. She touched her own cheek. She touched the cheek of the woman lying next to her. No questions came. She was a lesbian.

Excerpt from "Coming Out Regular"

20

Frieda Werden

At first I was not gay. That is to say, some might say I was at first gay, but others might say one does not begin gay, but only later has to become gay to be gay in the usual way. At first I was not gay, but they did say I walked funny, that it was not right. I also did think about women all the time when I masturbated at night (yes and in the day), but to think about a woman when you are a woman is not gay unless you say it is you and another woman and that all women are not you and whoever that is out of the picture behind your eyes is somebody, probably a man. You see you can think about women if you are a woman, in fact they say that is how they do it, the woman thinks about herself, the beautiful woman, and the man is in there, he thinks about the woman, too. But if nobody is thinking about the man, they might as well not have him. If somebody is not thinking about the man, she might be beginning to be gay.

E-DU-CA-TE they always tell you is to draw out. I have been educated, that is if that is to be drawn out. I have come out, I have been drawn out. My drawing out, too, has been drawn out. The first time I saw Joyce was at the women's center, then a neglected suburban house a few decades old on Baylor street. They came to the center in a white van, and they were out of another everything. I say a white van, this a piece of the fiction, they came to the center in a *red* van. White van or red van? You help me decide. Here is a dream:

> I am in a large hotel, and there is a middle-aged woman there whom I admire and am courting. I get her to agree she will go for a drink with me, but when I come to get her she says no, she won't go after all because she

has to pack her husband's suitcase. Dejected, I go down to the street and get into my car—the car I have in real life: a red-and-white '56 Chevy. As I get in, a red car drives up and it is in such a hurry to get into my place it doesn't even wait for me to pull out but just smashes into my car. Now my car turns into a white VW van, but all crumpled up. I try to signal through the murky windshield to a white station wagon that is pulling away, to get help—but it leaves me. Despair, rejection.

Here is another dream:

> Ben Barnes—former lieutenant gov. of Texas, and a notorious womanizer—is in my apartment and I have agreed with other plotters to kill him. I look down and see my red-and-white car in the street. I feel a little sorry for Ben, because he is only human, but I kill him with an icepick in the back of his neck like they did Trotsky in Mexico. Then I have to get away—I go down to the street and I can't find my car, all I can find is a big white van. There are cowboys and frat rats milling around the van—I push through them and get in. How can I get away? This van will only go 20 miles an hour. I discover that someone has taken the gas pedal and replaced it with the footpedal of an electric sewing machine—a machine with no subtleties of control for acceleration: it is either on or off. Extreme frustration and fear.

From those and others, I drive the conclusion that red cars are masculine egos and white cars are feminine egos, my red-and-white Chevy my androgynous ego. Doubt not.

Dream of baby in the car says it's Otto-auto-self. So, by god real life is just as symbol-laden as dreams, we can analyze waking symbols just as we analyze the sleeping ones. By god, you see those words there not in vain. Whatever god there is is a pattern of cymbals, a god of words.

Joyce played in the corner, with her harmonica, perhaps, or other toys. Robin came to the other end of the long room to discuss with the women, sometimes checking on Joyce. I think maybe Joyce whined. I thought she was very strange to be so shy to have to be put over in a corner, but later realized somehow she retained the integrity of purpose of the kid that made her not ashamed to do something else in the same room and not constrained to attend whatever did not interest her. This quality seems to have been at once the source of the relation to Robin as it was structured and its collapse to Joyce's disaster. Joyce was interested in me. I was little and black-headed and very curious with big brown eyes and not a little afraid of Joyce who was so strange. Fear of another is such an endearing trait. Indeed, all of love is composed of balanced or unbalanced components of fear and pity. My fear drew Joyce. When she stood near me in the doorframe, she could see me draw back half a pace in fear of accidentally touching her. I had never seen anything like her and I didn't know if fear or pity was in order.

Joyce is little. She is four-foot-ten, perhaps, a good two inches shorter than I even though I am sure I looked little to her, judging by the norm as we do all persons five-three or -four look short to me, too, though I cannot look at the tops of their heads. Joyce is little, but strong, her wide sagittarian shoulders holding up her muscular arms. She had her shirt cleft low and I could see her chest, the breasts small so that I looked and looked at first to see if I could see them, wondering at first as she and R. came in what category of people they were by sex, age, relation.

Once some years later I saw Joyce dance naked with her head shaved, and it reminded me to see it of a lizard, delicate and swift and bald. But very feminine with no hair, just the same, the wide shoulders, the muscular arms, the tiny breasts she had had "removed," above the rib cage, the suddenly-narrowing waist, the woman-wide hips, the short legs, with the short powerful thigh and calf muscles bulging, the profuse golden brown hair on her legs, and at crotch and armpits. As I write this I am thinking many shoulds I should check, like to use the feminine pronoun, to not write male-oriented-porno-interpretable things, these more robiny as well as others. "What is feminine?" asks this critic, "look out how you are using it, where did you learn those words, from a man?" Robin the separatist, even then she was a separatist, working at the women and withholding any energies from the man, except rarely when something overrode the no, like art or sometimes other work or political things. She came to the women's center, their first day in town or at least before they had made a home of their own outside their truck, they were really just passing through and living in the van. Robin had one or two teeth missing on the upper side.

K./D. was there with one or two teeth missing from the jaw, too. To have teeth missing and still smile, talk, go about in public if you are a woman, make new contacts in the world. That is a revolutionary act. That was the first time I had known it to happen, and I felt fear and pity.

Since that time they have both gotten their teeth put in. Going about without your teeth is revolutionary, but not pleasant or fun. K. and Robin have the same birthday, this I discovered much later. Truth is stranger than fiction, I swear it.

K. I met when I was 19 or 20. I don't remember who introduced us, how we met, what was said, all I remember is walking down the sidewalk with her swept along by her energy, her fast walk, her forceful way of talking. She was trying to organize waitresses then, one of those sweeping-the-sands jobs since the profession has so many transient members, so many working for a short time while aspiring to upgrade themselves through escape into marriage, college, etc. So many women who are used to being discriminated against and know there is no way out but to suffer. And the history of the trade, the myth of tipping—as I later discovered, rarely honored—that allows the employer to pass the buck of pay to the patron. A minimum-wage law had recently been enacted by the federal government, but restaurant and laundry workers—those worked-to-death bodies mostly women—were exempted.

On 19th Street was the laundry I had lived beside, walking by it every day and seeing the women working there in the sweaty shop, feeding the sheets into the mangles, standing on their feet and feeding the sheets all day, carrying and loading and catching and fetching and sweating and all for 75¢ an hour in 1966. In 1967, K. swept me down 22nd Street talking about unions and communism, about how it was necessary to sweep the sands, her long full brown hair trailing behind the thin, muscular live-wire form of her. I knew she was going to seduce me. I felt sex from my loins to my fingertips. I would have followed her for twenty blocks just to give her a chance. I don't remember how she disappeared.

This, then was that K. My confusion was just beginning to resolve. In 1971, I had left my husband in the country house with his dog and taken a room in town, for the greater convenience of having an affair with Leo. Leo was not really it, but he made a good excuse, being a type I was comfortable with, a hanger-about in coffee and beer joints spinning tales, and giving off that warmth of goodfellowship which is the hallmark of good Leos everywhere. To run into Leo, and to run into anyone who would stroke me with talk, without complications, I began hanging about in the Chuck Wagon both noon and night, and almost all times when I was not actually working. It became, as it had before I married, only more so, an addiction to the cafe society, a chance to talk without threat, a chance to be recognized, a chance to see the pleased expressions of greeting and be invited to sit or ask to sit. There was a woman who came there named D. A lean woman with very very short hair and dangerous-looking eyes. She hypnotized me. She had hair on her legs. She walked like a commando suppressing the urge to kill. It began to be that I came to the Chuck Wagon hoping to see D., watching D. from other tables, nerving myself to ask to sit with D., etc.

There are things you can know and not know. There are things you can want to know and never ask. You can sit staring at a door, day after day, night after night, if you are a woman, waiting for it to open, but never actually testing it yourself. Certain women are like doors. Walking around among the ordinary people, one can see them and sense that they could swing out into knowledge, into rooms, into worlds inhabited by other people who live the way you dreamed it for yourself. D. I watched and sat beside as if she were a door. D. was married and had a child. D. was a German translator who came into town to sit only for brief periods, to discuss academic matters with a few friends, to rave briefly about theoretical socialism and smoke many many cigarettes in a short span of time, then, true to her discipline disappear to home. I listened to everything, but D. was a door that never opened in the Chuck Wagon.

Once Jody was a door that never opened in the Chuck Wagon. When I worked in the book store for $1 an hour in 1966, Jody and Cristie came into the store in baseball caps, holding each other's hands. They skulked around the aisles, defiant. I had to watch them. I had to watch everyone strange in the store, to prevent shoplifting. They never seemed to look at me, they were sullen and they never met anyone's eyes. I was afraid of Jody and Cristie, but they were a door.

Jody came to the Chuck Wagon. She had black eyes. She was adopted. She had an aunt who was a famous librarian. We talked, but I never said, "I know you are gay." I didn't want to be rude. I didn't want her to say "go away" or something defensive. I wanted to be her friend, to say I feel so isolated on my side of this door that you go through. Jody was a Scorpio. No one can find out secrets from a Scorpio; she was a door that never opened.

The door of the women's center opened again, and in walked A. Now, Ray used to say back in Berkeley, "If you need something, make a place for it and it will come to you." This is one of the earliest forms of everyday or real-life magic I learned the use of. Ray says he needed a chest of drawers so he cleared a space for it in his house and a visitor said, "I have a chest of drawers that would fit nicely in that space." In the same way, to make a women's center was for me a magical act to attract women to come together, it was a place to hold a women's world. I wanted an opening of a door, and here in this house there was a door that could be opened. Robin opened the door, D. opened the door and Donna said, "O yes, I remember you, you're K. aren't you? How have you been all these years? etc." and merged my magical D. with the remembered magic of K. And A. opened the door.

A. was a professional photographer. She wore loud shirts, and men's glasses. She had a friendly but brusque manner, like other women who are Leos. She had been operated on for cancer and lost her lover of many years, and was coming out into the community to talk with women, to be stroked, to pull her ego together. She was in therapy, and she believed in the uses of psychology to cope with change. She was older, in her early forties, than most of the women who came to the center, but not older than some.

One cold night in the very early spring it happened that there was a meeting after the meeting. The women who were at the meeting left early, except for Robin and Joyce (who was playing in the other corner), A., K., Karen, and me. It was the night Robin and Joyce first came in, and they began the talk that opened the door I had been sitting by. They began to talk about coming out. Karen said nothing, except perhaps to ask one question. I was all ears, for once said nothing at all but sat slouched upon the daybed at the north wall, amazed that my prayers were getting an answer. Emboldened by their majority in the room, the three talked among themselves. They talked, for the first time in my hearing, about the life of Lesbians.

Those Lesbians were all smart Lesbians. They figured out how, with nobody to tell them or support them, to become what they knew they were. Their stories were long and wide-ranging, some beginning in childhood practice; they were stories of mischief and defiance, and knowing where happiness lies and going after it (A. especially) and also of pain and rejection of self and by self, and trying and doing and seeking and finding despite tremendous odds and general expressions of nonsupport and disbelief (Robin especially). None of them, however, had ever simply sat by the doors, year after year sometimes more and sometimes less doggedly, hoping for someone to open it up and shove them inside.

The stories inspired me. Yes, I wanted to be a Lesbian and now I had a better idea of how. I could hardly imagine that any woman would not be wanting the same. I looked at Karen, sitting there beside me about to fall asleep while she waited for me to give her a ride home, and could hardly credit that she or any liberation-minded woman was not actually aspiring to the same goal that I was: to be a Lesbian and make love with women and never have any more to deal intimately with the penis-carrying sex. Many Lesbians believe this; many Lesbians say that all women are Lesbians and if they are not yet they will be, they are just preLesbian women. Some Lesbians who are feminists say that feminism is the theory and Lesbianism the practice and that Lesbianism is the ultimate in Liberation. But recently Jody came back from San Francisco saying she finally believed that there was such a thing as a straight woman, that all women are not Lesbians and that heterosexuality is perhaps more difficult but ultimately just as difficult and in its own way a valid way of existence. Not for her, but still for someone and after all these years, after all the changes in proportions of political pressure, it is possible to be a normal Lesbian and still believe that there are valid straight people in the world. At this time it is daring to me to say that. But at that time, perhaps four years ago, it was impossible to say that because it was impossible to say Lesbian, it was impossible to think Lesbian in the same hour as to think straight. I had spent a lifetime keeping the two ideas completely apart from one another, and now that I let Lesbian into my mind, Straight flew out just straight away as the former had formerly.

I became convinced that my doctor and her assistant lived together as Lesbians. This seemed to me to be a positive good. I thought to myself and wrote down in my journal, that a man will never encourage a woman to achieve. A woman who wishes to be encouraged, to be grounded to be fed in order to achieve in the world must be encouraged by another woman. The men just don't know how to feed, and won't. They are all trained into being one-up on women, and on each other. To get support from a man, a woman would have to act like a man, and then she would only get the support like men give to men. The support to get down and get up again, that is the support one wants. Men's culture supports one to get up, to mount and ride. Women's supports one to get down and rest. The extremes of each are unseemly.

All the women talked about being Lesbians except Joyce. Joyce was the only one who knew I wanted to be a Lesbian. How did she know it? She just knew it. Perhaps she would have known it whether I wanted to be a Lesbian or not.

I did want to be a Lesbian, because I was a Lesbian, as I said before. My husband had stopped making love with me, I think because among other things he could not please me, that is, he could not make me come, neither could he please me very much, though neither was I pleased by not being touched at all, because one needs to touch and be touched, even if the bodies do not fit right, do not feel right, it is better than not to touch and be touched at all. In fact, I believe a great variety of mental illnesses have their source and their potential remedy in touching. Not touching for sex, perhaps, just holding and being held. He used to do that with me, and then he stopped. But it was all not too much use, because I wanted to touch and be touched with/by a woman. This is pure prejudice, you might say. This is neurosis. People are people—a man can be your mother, everybody knows that. Yes, but. Yes, but a woman can be your everything. Why not, if you want it? A man could be your mother, but would he? Would you? Meanwhile, some neuroses are worth changing but some are not. A neurosis that says you have a sexual preference is okay. If you have one lover, it will be one or the other. A neurosis that says not a man is no worse than a neurosis that says not a woman, etc.

Joyce backed me into a corner at the women's center and let me sense that she looked at me as one sexual person to one sexual person. She knew and I knew. I was scared, but it was plain. I knew. I could smell her sweat and her clothes, although she did not touch me.

I could smell her sweat. Believe me, we deny ourselves more pleasures in this life than just Lesbian sex. We deny ourselves the smells of women's bodies, our own included. Women don't smell like roses. I like the smell of roses, but why should it replace the smell of hot armpits, the green smell of the vagina, the familiar smells of scalp oils, of urine drops, the bite of ammonia or the metal smell of iron-rich menstrual blood? The toasty smell of sleepy skin that lives on in the pillow case. The dusty smell of sun-dried flesh in the afternoon. Now, at this climax of my love odyssey, I bury my nose in my lover, all her various parts and creases, as often as I can every day, inhaling her essences and reveling in the arts more subtle than perfumers' craft that speak to me out of her body.

But that is now. Then I was afraid to smell. The odor of Joyce's sweat reached me strange as a wild bird's odor to the senses of a handfed fowl.

They gave me books. I was not afraid to read books, at least not very afraid. They took me into their truck. The red truck (truth is more stranger than fiction) which was fixed, carpentered inside to house tools, bunks, their clothes, a self-sufficient truck not only for traveling, but for living, giving, fixing, a most self-sufficient truck. They had books under the seats, and they gave me two books as little alike as night and day. One was Charlotte Wolff's *Love Between Women*, a dry tome that was written like any clinical psychiatrist is likely to do, and reassured me that one could be a Lesbian whether or not one had or did sex at all. But the one I read first was a little paperback that got me very excited, little short clinical-pretending but really porno stories about different kinds of Lesbian couples and how they made love together, the suburban couple with the children, the butch and femme, the s-m, etc. I don't remember the name of it, but it was the most valuable primer anyone ever put in my hand, that is, primer, in the sense of becoming primed.

There are so many things, and the time sequence is confused in my mind. There was B. who with Nianne and me went to Mexico before I divorced, saying "Haven't you ever thought of just switching preferences?" Saying, another time, "You don't get enough support at home." So when I knew she was right about all of it, I went to where she lived with her friends female, where they lived in tandem with their various wasted friends male, putting up with the general laziness and abuse of the friends male, and I wanted her. I had told Stella that I wanted her, that I was in love with her (B.) and she just said oh, and was sympathetic, and said B. was going to go to New Mexico with the particular lizard male who lived on her. B. was slender, short, brown of hair, a great doper and a great one for cussing, and also accident-prone.

When I got there, I didn't know what to say and I didn't know what to do. I wanted to touch her, but I was afraid to touch her and I didn't know how. I wanted to say what I planned to say, that is Don't go to New Mexico with that lizard, he's not good enough for you, why don't you come away with me and we'll figure out what to do, etc. But I had no authority. I said Don't go away to New Mex with that lizard, he's not good enough for you, and she said "Yes, I know, but it's only for a little while and just to have fun" and I was sitting across the table from her, with a tray of marijuana between us and my feet up on a chair because I always put my feet up when I can, and she reached under the table and stroked my legs. Since I didn't know anything else to do, I went home.

It was later that I wrote to her. She stayed in Colorado after all, and as soon as I was sure what it was to do, I had tried it, I wrote to her and said I love you madly, please come back I know how to do it and let's live together, etc. She wrote back very noncommittal about how it was a good job market there and how the lizard was doing. I wrote back very agitated, no, don't you understand my letter, that's not what I meant, I meant I'm in love with you and we could live happily ever after, it is so much better with women than with those yickky old men, etc. And she never wrote back, but when Nianne went to visit her she came back and told me B. says you are insane. I had written to her that I believed women could achieve greater understanding between themselves than with men. I guess she showed me.

She looked like Jane Fonda.

All this time, I was knowing and not knowing. When I left Noble, I knew it was for sex and for women, but it was being for sex and men, for sex and freedom and for freedom. It was because I had my first orgasm in 7 years while imagining making love with a woman. It was because the thought of having babies and living in the country was like a nightmare of walking in a dark tunnel. It was because of B. saying You don't get enough support at home. It was because everything creative in me had fallen asleep. It was because I finally had learned how to drive and got my own car, and suddenly I had an ego again. I took a room in town that had separate entrance/separate bath. I promised myself that I would never get off my own path for any man again, and wrote some songs and poems about it. It took a while to recover the ability to write songs and poems. I bought Stella's banjo and began trying to learn to play it. I talked to strangers. I wanted women, but I was agressive to men.

There was one, for instance, who was an only child; he lived alone, he built domes and made soup. I never was nice to him if he came to my house, but if I wanted to be with someone I would go to his house and sleep with him. He had soft, curly hair all over his body, softer because he bathed in Dr. Bronner's Peppermint Castille Soap. I was aggressive to him and unkind in the same ways that men are aggressive and unkind to women. I hurt him in just that way, of not caring what he was like as a person and not taking an interest in his needs for intimacy. Finally he got another woman and I left him alone. There were other men like this. The world is full of men that can be used like this, men who would be the mistress of an aggressive woman and suffer the masochistic daydreams of that role. I had several over the years, imposing my revenge on the sex through my rapes of their bodies and their time. I felt not guilty but a little ashamed. In bits and pieces I learned how the roles lurk around us for anyone to use. There is nothing that is a necessary integrity in either sex.

Wendell, the gay communist, says that relations between the sexes never get out of roleplaying. If the roles are not the same roles, then they are the reverse roles. Reversal shifts are the easiest changes for rats to learn in maze-running. Left for right, and vice-versa.

Then I got a divorce and changed my name. Then I moved to another house, with a former roommate and also a man named Sweeney. Sherry said "You seem like you're trying to turn into someone else. Well, I liked you better the way you were." She worked in a child nursery. She fell in love again, the night of the worst lightning storm and flood in years. She painted and decorated her room, and set up her plants. The house was an old house that could absorb years of work and not show a difference. I didn't give a damn for it, except I did like to have a room on the 2nd floor and look down in the yard. Sweeney or somebody had left the upstairs bathroom full of men's photo-sex mags, which I read incessantly. He said one of his friends was a Lesbian, but Sweeney was such an apeneck I had no interest in meeting any of his friends. I worked on my car in the yard a little; overcoming my fear of car-dirt was something, some progress. Also, with a different name, nobody could intimidate me by saying my name at me any more. The landlady said "Frieda, clean up the yard," and I backed her right out the front door.

I was trying to turn into somebody else; Sherry was right. Some time later, Letitia said "you used to act like Uriah Heep." There is something, that false humility, that makes the heterosexual woman role no good for me. I think maybe that is also what makes it not good for the heterosexual woman.

I was trying to turn into somebody else, but still there was a lot of the old self about me. Once a woman poet from Virginia was introduced to me as Frieda Werden, but after about half an hour she called out "Linda" and I didn't respond but then realized what she had said and said "What did you say?" She said, "Linda. That's your name, isn't it?" So the old names hang around in the air around your head just the same. Margaret says she sees it there herself, sometimes.

21

Letter
Merril

March 28, 1977

Dear Julia:

Deadline approaches, and I want very much to be able to write a brilliant statement of my coming out. I have lots of paper filled with notes, almost illegible, jotted in careful answer to the questions in your form letters or during moments out of the reverie which usually followed, but I am having a difficult time getting it all together. Probably one reason is that I feel very inadequate, because I am not well able to make a strong and articulate political statement and raise pertinent, well-defined questions that will be a source of inspiration to other wimmin who are in the process of coming out (by whatever definition they choose), and I feel awkward in my manner of communication with sisters who speak in a different vocabulary and are brilliantly feminist in their expression. All I can really do is describe my own memories the way I remember now them being then. Then I was unaware of oppression affecting me as womin and Lesbian, unaware of my own entrapment by stereotypic roles and games. I enjoyed these, practiced them, and became expert at some. All roles that have since been exposed to me by myself and others as being artificial, superficial, gamey, and suffocating were very real to me then.

Probably another reason is that coming out is getting old for me by now, since I have been doing it for eighteen years. *Then* extends back through time in countless strands of remembrances so strong that I can close my eyes and *be* there. Remembering, sinking into pasts, I find the flow organic, orgasmic. I feel like a womb during birth, dilating and contracting, squeezing out little different aspects of me:

Miami Beach was a gay paradise in the late '50's when I came out (made my debut, so to speak—entered gay society). Gay was romantic. Gay people were brilliant, sensitive, aware. The veneer was superb. We were strong in our numbers, our togetherness, and our superiority. If we noticed the staring, heterosexual public, we didn't discuss it. Bravely we endured the raids at the public gay beach where we drank beer and danced on the long pavillion under the sun and the raids on the gay bars where we, underage, clutched our phony i.d. and paired off to appear heterosexual (Oh, heh, heh, no, officer, I just came in here with my husband to have a drink, I mean, I had *no* idea ...). We were secure in our togetherness and our sharing of traditional patterns which brought a feeling of power or, at least, somewhat lessened our sense of helplessness. Pride grew in me as a defense with each police raid, each scandalous newspaper headline, each flung insult from a passerby. All my paranoias were dissipated by the intellectual superiority and artistic sensitivity of the main of my companions. I was seventeen years old. Although in our ignorance we might feed into one another's sicknesses, our togetherness in force of numbers and our caring for one another was a source of strength that those who come out alone at first must, I feel, suffer for the lack of.

There were many different gay "sets." Countless gay bars entertained suntanned, white-ducked Lesbians and homosexuals day and night, night and day, and the gay beach offered excellent cruising all year round. Always there were parties, cliquey, of course, but there were so many Lesbians that it didn't matter. Parties at Penny's were notorious, famous, beyond gossip.

Penny was my first love, and she brought me out well, carefully teaching me the rules, roles, and lingo of the gay subculture. I learned how to "read" another gay person and also reveal myself through an intricate language of signals and subtleties and how to camp and carry on. I learned to use conversational gay slang terms and to sprinkle my conversation liberally with gay innuendo. We must have been quite a sight in large groups, camping and carrying on, wimmin mimicking men who mimicked wimmin, all presenting the same parody.

My Lesbian friends and I practiced developing masculine move-ments, aping and emulating the men we professed to despise. To be a man meant to be strong and to have power. The best we could do as wimmin was to be like men, since we had not yet learned of wominstrength and wominpower. Butch/femme role definition in the Lesbian culture around me was very important. In general, butches looked and acted more-or-less like men, wore ducktail haircuts and men's clothing, were aggressive, drank, swore, led when a couple danced (always a very sensitive point), held doors open for the femme, lit the femme's cigarette, etc. There was a great deal of public embarrassment and ridicule of a butch who "went femme," and often the derision was enough to prevent many butches from allowing their lovers to touch their bodies in lovemaking.

Then Mother Found Out, and there were weeks of trauma and a long, slow healing.

Mother Found Out. I was 18 and away at college most of the time, home on holidays, and had been coming out for two years.

Mother Found Out, and this, to me, was what finally made everything real. This was the commitment, the marriage vow, the final plunge.

Among some of us young dykes, this was a very important and often-discussed subject:

"Does your mother know?"

"Oh, God, No! Does yours?"

"I think she might suspect."

We could talk about it for hours, speculating ways to do it, to Tell, fantasizing situations involving Finding Out and What Would Happen Thereafter.

"I could never tell mine. She'd die. It'd kill her."

"Mine'd crack up for sure."

"I don't know about mine. Maybe she would Understand."

"Do you think she already knows?"

"Wouldn't surprise me if she did. I mean, she's *seen* Lillian and me ..."

"Yeah, mine told me she knew even before I did."

"Well, I haven't seen mine in seven years. She called me a freak and a pervert, and I walked out and never came back."

"Yeah, I hear Janet's folks pay her to stay out of the state."

"Mine just cried. She wanted to know what she'd done wrong."

Mine and I had it out one night away from home. She asked me. I was not surprised. For over a year mannish wimmin and effeminate men had paraded through her house, and she had made comments. Of course I had in secret from myself wanted her to find out, and I was indiscreet enough to hasten the time of confrontation by arousing her suspicions. I told her. She had wanted me to deny it, of course; to set her mind at rest. I didn't. We both wept bitterly, for reasons that were the same and not the same—she because I was me, and I because I was me.

I felt—I feel—her revulsion, her repulsion. My Mother! Her rejection! Then what could be worth all my seeking of and for wimmin, what mattered all my devotion and pursuit, when my closest, strongest, and most complete love of my existence grew to despise me? Mother,

we are we, in part of us each the other, sharing memories through
genetic archetypes, sharing growth and knowledge of each other
through our experiences of our years together, sharing so much more
than the reality of our differences! My greatest love then grew to despise
me, I that was she, I that was me, and all that was I. And besides all this, I
knew that I had caused her great pain. By only being me, I have hurt her.

She says, "I thought I would die," her voice a shamed whisper.
"Didn't you hear them when you passed?" I didn't. "They said, 'Look at
the Lesbian'," she hissed. "I was so embarrassed ... " We sat together at a
table in a small luncheonette. I could only eat my meal.

Sue got married. It was a marriage of convenience, since Sue was a
dyke and her husband a fag. Days later, Mother spoke to me on our front
lawn as I passed her on my way out. The green grass smell filled air warm
from Florida sea breezes in spring. "So now everyone is saying how
surprised they are that Sue is married—they thought she was a Lesbian."
Her voice was not quite a whisper this time. She looked at me, her head
tilted sideways. "I wonder what they are saying," her voice choked off
for a moment and tears spilled over, " ... about you," she finished
abruptly.

But time did heal, and I feel fortunate in my wealth of pleasant
memories, thoughts warm with sunshine and the feeling of wimmin's
bodies on beaches, beds, and dance floors, slick with suntan oil, naked,
or lightly clad in Florida hot nights. Aromas of liquor and sweat, cigarette
smoke, tanning cream, and Canoe perfume recall the feel of bodies
grinding close dancing slow fish to sounds from the juke box. I smell hair
fresh from sun and salt air and press breasts and bellies and thighs close
together as we sway in slow celebration to the rhythm of the music.

Merril

I Have Four Coming Out Stories to Tell

22

Susan Madden

I have four coming out stories to tell about myself, not one. I understand my coming out as a process which has been unfolding my entire life. I can tell you about four important parts of this story, three in my past, one in my present. I trust there are more to come.

I am 37 years old and celebrated my 36th birthday last year with special significance because I had then been a Lesbian half my life. My four coming out stories span the 19-year history of my Lesbianism, from my first physical involvement with a woman at 18 to my current involvement at 37.

I know the coming out process begins long before one's first genital contact with another woman: with feelings of being different, which can occur at very young ages (These feelings didn't consciously come to me until my teens); with wanting to be a boy (My parents allowed me to live this dream, complete with boy's clothes and a boy's haircut, for several elementary school years); with crushes on older women (I felt an enormous, life-enveloping and supporting crush on all active, attractive women rather than focusing exclusively on a series of single crushes); with very close friendships with other girls (I have several continuing intimate freindships which were formed in my early teens). The story I would like to tell begins with some of these pre-coming out feelings, but it is more a series of stories of the emerging consciousness and integration of one Lesbian life, most of which evolved after that initial coming out experience.

I interpret my successive comings out as four interrelated but different integrating experiences: I have come out through experiences which brought together my emotionality, my identity, my need for security, and my sexuality.

Emotionality: Ellen

I begin the story of my Lesbianism with Ellen, not because she was the first woman I touched with passion—she was—but because it was through my feelings for her that I learned I could feel love for another person that would take me beyond myself. Ellen's and my relationship was all quivering emotion. I have never, since that love, doubted my capacity to love and to express love.

It was a terrifying thing to be told one's whole young life that one's destiny is to be attached to a man and yet to feel nothing for men. Well, not quite nothing, but nothing compelling, nothing that I could build my life around, nothing that could attach me intimately to another person. I felt warmth toward the boys I dated, I enjoyed their holding me and touching me, but there was no real desire within me to be close to them, to know them, to love them. I felt flat, pleasant but flat.

I remember vividly one afternoon in my early teens looking up from the book I was reading, overwhelmed with some auguring of the future. It began as an assessment of my pleasant (but flat) life and my pleasant (but flat) prospects. I remember thinking that I was intelligent, good-looking, rich, well-liked and athletic (I might have added, vain). Everything boded well for me. I would obviously live a successful, pleasant life, successful and pleasant by all the standards I'd been taught.

And then came the thought that made the experience memorable: I wonder what is coming to me that will ruin it all. I remember I had no doubt at the time that something would, and I anticipated discovering what it would be with dread but also with some desire to get on with my destiny.

When I found myself in love with Ellen a few years later, I immediately recalled this experience and knew I had found that destiny. Of course. What was going to ruin my well-laid-out life was that I was a woman who loved other women. As I look back on it I believe the auguring and the discovery of my destiny were the experiences which first gave me a sense of *me*, the sense that I existed as a person distinct from the conventional life models I had been shown and the conventional achievements I had performed. Discovering my Lesbianism did not ruin my life: it gave me a life uniquely mine. But the sense of me was not uppermost at the time. What compelled me was a complex of love and guilt.

This was 1958 and, as we all know, there wasn't a dyke in the land. Well, I wasn't one either. Ellen's and my love developed from friendship to inseparable friendship to touching to making love to an absorbing love according to its own dynamic. Our increasing intimacy was not directed by external definitions of what we should or should not be doing with each other. It felt very natural, but, deep down, I knew it was also very unnatural. I knew because I continually denied it, both to myself and to Ellen. I recall writing her a long letter once on a train after we'd spent a college weekend together, justifying—and apologizing—for my touching her. I was explicitly assuring her that I touched her only because I loved her so much. I was explicitly assuring her—and, more importantly, myself—that we weren't both perverts. I steadfastly avoided reading psychological studies of "inversion" or any other reference to homosexuality. I wanted to do what my love told me to do; I didn't want to face what others called it or thought about it.

I believe there are some advantages to this highly private mode of coming out. One has the time and the emotional space to allow love to grow in its own way. It can be its own justification. I learned, through Ellen, that my capacity to love was an enormous and vital personal resource, and that this energy existed to be given to women, and through other women, to myself.

My emotional coming out was thus a private experience I shared with only one other person, Ellen. My relationship with her lasted about three years, the graduating from high school and early to mid-college years. She somehow—we didn't talk enough then and don't now for me to tell you how—became more interested in men and finally married. I became involved with a college friend who was interested in me as one female relationship among many male relationships. I went crazy. My going crazy was due to a combination of too much college performance and too unsatisfactory a love, but when my family's psychiatrist said I should quit all the intellectual effort, come home, and see him, I made the grave error of telling him I wanted to be cured of being a Lesbian.

Identity: Dorothea

I've said there are advantages to the privatized mode of coming out. There are also serious disadvantages, and I fell victim to them at this point in my life. When there isn't a dyke in the land, and you're not one either, except secretly you're the only dyke in the land, troubles with love and women are easily misinterpretable as messages that your choice of love object is at fault. If I would only change to be like everyone else (I told myself), I would be happy.

I stayed home for a year, worked, dated men, and saw the psychiatrist weekly. I can scarcely remember a thing from that year, except for a few pleasant moments and an overall sense of emotional dullness. I was trying desperately to achieve conformity, and my life reflected it: it was again pleasant and flat, as it had been before my first coming out. I had exchanged pain for depression.

My introduction to Dorothea was symbolic of what my second coming out—my identity coming out—would be about. Dorothea had told some of her friends she was a Lesbian (By this time it was 1963, and there were a few dykes in the land), and I was introduced to her by a mutual woman friend because, "Dorothea's homosexual, and you might be interested." My attraction to Dorothea was immediate, but the implications of that attraction terrified me. The rising excitement in me told me that I was about to lose my battle to be straight. It had been an honest battle, and I dreaded the knowledge that I was again going to have to experience, and this time recognize, my own Lesbianism.

I occasionally have an experience I call my "death vision." It's that moment when you know in your gut you're going to be obliterated someday, and your whole self recoils in horror and disbelief. It's momentary, and it passes, but it's a shock that leaves me breathless. For at least the first half of my life as a Lesbian I would have experiences equal in intensity and shock which were my "abnormal visions." Suddenly my attention and my sense of self would be assaulted with the conscious realization that what I was was to others disgusting, unnatural, perverted, an abomination. If they knew about it, they would kill me. The realization stunned me for, of course, I accepted some of the judgments of others as my own judgment of myself.

My attraction to Dorothea meant I would have to face those judgments, both of others and of myself, and this time I would have to face them openly. The time when I could hide my love in a private world peopled by only Ellen and me was gone. I was older, I had accepted the painful parts of my Lesbianism by explicitly asking to be cured of them, I had told my parents, I had told myself. And now I was going to choose being a Lesbian all over again, this time knowingly. I made the choice a long confusing process, but within a few months I had begun to reclaim my destiny, this time not only emotionally but consciously.

Throughout the previous six years of being a Lesbian I had—while simultaneously loving women—dated men, touched men, considered marrying men, and occasionally fucked men. At the very beginning of my love for Dorothea I brought up some date I was about to have with some man. Dorothea looked at me as though unable to comprehend such an anomaly and said something like, "What makes you think you're going to both love me and date men?" I don't believe I have, ever since that question, been on a conventional date with a man. The question, the claim on my love it implied, and the challenge to my identity it posed freed me from a vain attempt to live my life both ways, split between what was true for me but threatening and what was false but acceptable. I was being asked to be faithful, a demand no other woman had made of me. And, although Dorothea was asking me to be faithful to her, the consequence was that I learned to be faithful to myself. I learned to know my identity as a Lesbian, and I began the process of identifying with and developing solidarity with other Lesbians.

My relationship with Dorothea lasted about three years, during which time I was in love, afraid of intimacy, troubled by the wide emotional swings of our relationship, anxious, and eventually exhausted.

Security: Carrie

I believed that Lesbian relationships were, by their nature, relatively short-lived affairs (three years was my norm). They began with promise and with promises, and then ran their course until the painful breakup a few years later. I believed that, because I was a Lesbian, this pattern was natural to me. I fell in love with Carrie in part because she didn't believe any of this. She was a widow, had liked married life, and any relationship she chose would have that quality of marriage about it. I found the prospect attractive, frightening, and calming. Carrie was offering me the chance to make a life-long commitment, and I took it.

Carrie also argued that there was no essential difference between her love for and permanent relationship with me, a woman, and the love she'd felt for and relationship she'd had with her husband. (She would not now make that argument.) If people were happy to accept her relationship with a man, they would have to be happy to accept her relationship with a woman. I established a home with Carrie, I bought things with her, and she and I began a process of telling our friends and families about our relationship. The reactions varied from a hesitant and wondering acceptance to an outrage bordering on disinheritance. But we steadfastly persevered in our campaign to be just as normal and acceptable as any heterosexual couple.

Such an objective would now be regarded with suspicion, but in the mid-sixties, prior to the women's and gay movements, it was for us a radical and courageous effort. Over the years, and we were together ten years, our patience triumphed over the disapproval of those significant to us. This acceptance by straight people around us, especially our families, was an important source of support for our relationship. I learned to expect from others respect and approval of my choice of partner and life style. I enjoyed a love that was dependable, rational, and normal. And somewhere in the course of my ten years with Carrie my "abnormal visions" simply evaporated.

Through my first coming out experience with Ellen I learned to feel and to trust my own emotions—the loving ones, that is. And I developed the courage to express my love for women with one other woman. Through my second coming out with Dorothea I learned to define and to face my own identity as a woman who loved women. And I shared that identity with other Lesbians and with close straight friends, women and men. Through my third coming out with Carrie I learned to believe in my ability to commit myself to another person, to develop an intimate relationship, and to sustain it over a long period. I came out as one partner of a couple and was able to accept and contribute to the security this produced for both of us. And I built outward from this couple-security to demand and eventually assume acceptance from significant other persons. In the course of fighting for acceptance for Carrie and me as a couple, I came to accept myself as a Lesbian.

A few years ago I realized something about myself which fills me with an inner security and strength that is a constant joy to me. If you had asked me fifteen years ago what was most special to me about myself, I would have said "I'm intelligent." Had you asked me the same question five years ago, I would have answered, "I'm a woman." Ask me now, and I'll tell you, "I'm a Lesbian." Through the security of a long love that I see as my third coming out, I learned Lesbian pride.

Sexuality: Pierre

Coming out stories usually have something to do with sex. It's true that Ellen and I touched each other wherever we wished, but ours was essentially an emotional, not a sexual love. I had been a Lesbian for five years before I experienced the glimmerings of my first orgasm, with Dorothea. With Carrie sex was competent and satisfying but, after the first while, infrequent and fairly routine. Our important physical relationship was one of warmth, of hugging and support, not passion.

I am now in the midst of my fourth coming out experience, and it is my sexual coming out. Last fall I was explaining to someone that I'm not really a sexual person, if what one means by sexual is a genitally-sensitive, orgasm-oriented woman. Two months later I was free to explore all my feelings for Pierre, and these feelings were then and are now energized by a constant passion. I am learning something of the power that is in my body.

For me, being a Lesbian means that I, as a woman, find commitment, love, and excitement in relating intellectually, emotionally, and physically to another woman. Feeling sexual about another woman is, perhaps most clearly, what Lesbianism is about. It is the sexual attraction that is so compelling, but it is this sexuality that is also so terrifying.

I believe that a full exploration of my sexuality is just beginning. I am beginning to feel my body as me too: I am not just my mind or my feelings. I am making what had been life-long sexual fantasies into real behaviors that can be shared and are thus more accessible to me. I am following what my body tells me, not about sexual desire alone, but about food and sleep and anxiety and anger and intimacy. I feel vital, and friends around me sense and enjoy and want to share in the energy

Pierre and I radiate.

I do not believe I could have embarked on my sexual coming out before now because I had not yet achieved a secure and prideful sense of my own identity as a Lesbian. I had to struggle for many years before I could feel good enough about my choice of sexual preference to allow sex itself to assume any role of major importance. Until I could be joyful as a Lesbian I could not give full rein to the sexual energy which was one powerful source, after all, of my love for women. Until I knew the implications and consequences (or enough of them to feel secure, anyway) of this drive for my identity and my survival, I could not let it flourish.

But then, I am a fairly cautious person. At least cautious given that I am a Lesbian, a life choice that demands a degree of courage that I marvel any person can call up. And so many of us women do, not once, but throughout our whole lives.

23 Coming Home
Sarah Lucia Hoagland

I ran smack into my first Lesbian encounter eyes wide open and totally blind. I was expounding my then current theory that sex is a natural extension of friendship, and she agreed. My oblivion to the fact that recent friends had not been women caught us both off guard, and the subsequent Lesbian/hetero two-step must have been tragically amusing to the Goddess.

The will to have female friends had long since been exorcised as I watched best friends dissolve into nearby males, a process which included a two-year recurring nightmare of my own dissolution in marriage. Of late the existence of females in my life had been a function of the tolerance of their boyfriends and I knew better than to reach out. Jealousy, I was told. But that was inaccurate. When I gave my trust, I expected the bond to be safeguarded. Woman with man, it seemed, is proscribed/absolved from obligation. The only bond that remained strong over the years did so in spite of me. But then one's mother never is a measure.

Thus at 27 I was quite unprepared for England, Lesbianism, and Dianna, and I blush now as much for my sin as I did then from embarrassment, and I wonder how many others...

But in spite of my embarrassment and rejection, I was tantalized. "What's this?" I whispered from the bottom left drawer of my soul. Like a child I wanted to crouch unobserved in a dark corner and absorb— unobserved because I did not want to be confronted, I did not want to hurt again, and because I did not want a witness to my metamorphosis.

This I arranged by having myself appointed for a year as an instructor at Vassar College and placing myself in the care of Lesbian students, where I was not hassled. How was I to know that, having been labeled PDOF (Potential Dyke On Faculty), I was being carefully nurtured, complete with student assigned to bring me out? (While she did not actually bring me out, still her mission was accomplished a year and a half later.) And these were strong women. Oh they had their problems, but one had a sense that they would not dissolve. Here I went through growing pains while the mystery was dispelled. ("But Maria ... Debby, Lesbian couples have the same problems heterosexual couples do. So why should I risk my profession for the same old problems?" Silence.)

Forgotten dreams became possibilities as my first feminist perceptions, having snatched my attention two years earlier, now settled solidly in my gut. I had never quite buried my childhood rage at grown women acting like two-year-olds around men. Nor had I soothed frustration arising from the fact that married women perceived me as a threat; and now I began to understand. That summer I returned to Boulder, intent upon discovering a woman I had known as a graduate student. Gwen's became my first friendship since childhood which no man has touched.

Yet coming out for me had to center around the sexual experience, not because that was to be the essence of my Lesbianism, but because it was an obstacle in my path. I was not then physically attracted to women.

Having hastily constructed a closet, that fall I moved to Nebraska and prepared in good faith for my right of passage. I went to lots of dances, and this time I recognized the nurturing. I began to intellectually overcome what I irrationally resisted, arguing vociferously in my feminism classes that political Lesbianism was a legitimate alternative. I constructed a very good argument.

Her lips were softer than anything I had ever imagined. I was held suspended while butterflies danced madly about. I blushed full for two weeks, and as I recall, ate during only one of them. The magnetism was so strong that it (miraculously) overcame my inhibitions from being watched by my nurturers as well as a certain inane insecurity (I remained fully clothed most of the first night, complete with hiking boots, being uncertain I was expected to stay).

It was the most natural thing in the world. I wondered where I had been all my life, yet I did not regret one moment spent in arriving. To this day I wonder why it is not called, "coming home." For the first time I was at ease with being a woman, body and soul were united—healed ... or was it, completed?

There are on this earth sisters of mercy who, happening upon gnarled souls, stop to tend. If they act with no concern for the future, they also act with no concern for the present. They stop time, for there is work to be done. Theirs is not the gift of permanency, healing is not made of such stuff. They nourish one's soul until it is reflected back that one may marvel at it. But, task completed, they move on, as Judy did. I cried.

Realizing this would never do, I found another and settled in to continue my explorations. The next day her lover materialized and on the third day she dissolved. No one had warned me how exhausting it all could be. But I had not been labeled PDOF in vain. As I wrote my former students, my honorary status in the Lavender Menace had changed to regular.

I was just shy of 30. And as I write this, exactly two years later, I slip easily, if slowly, into the last lap of my journey. I was never good about shutting doors.

24

I Am Born: Excerpts from a Journal

Minnie Bruce Pratt

3/2/75

Sitting down at the Employment Securities Commission, I'm getting ready to draw my pennies, having quit my job of ten years, my marriage, by sleeping with a woman last night. Crowds around me, retired vets, snuff-toothed old men, kids in Halloween masks, factory women in polyester slacks, all seem to be chatting like comrades about the problems of living in immobile homes. And the women are saying "When the children are gone... I'll be alive... a medical degree... handing the instruments to the surgeon... assistant to anesthesiologists... try to run a computer register at the Winn Dixie... always stole when I was little," while I feel like a Hardy character who took the wrong footpath into a Dickens subplot. The retired Lt. Col. who interviewed me noted my Alabama hometown and chortled that he had spent many a summer there playing baseball with cousin John Percy Kennedy: had I known him before he died of cancer at Walter Reed? No, but, of course, "My mother did." What would she say if she could see me now? or last night with S?

I'm a waking nightmare and thriving like a mushroom on detritus, decay, rotten emotions and fertilizer of tears. I'm what? not an Amanita, nor a Russula, something more inconspicuous. Am I poisoning myself with this soma? I slept with S last night: madness, bliss, treachery, honey, delirium. I plotted how to get to her apartment, or her to me without other people, without M, without the children.

For two weeks I've been bewildered about my feelings toward her; I tried to think they were just sexual fantasies because she was mysterious, because I couldn't get at her, because I was married so she was 'safe' and I could indulge in day dreams. But I haven't felt this before with any other female friend, not even E when so close at work, we talked about Firestone and feminism and she tactfully told me she was having a 'relationship' with another woman. Leaning over the green wall of oak under our office window and listening to her stories of love and politics, I learned the idea of being a lesbian. I even went to her parties, danced with other women, and felt that first intense attraction-repulsion at watching a brunette in a mechanic's cap kiss another woman on the floor behind the endtable. But I never felt like this: all I have done for the past two weeks is drive the children to school and lie on my bed, stare at these oaks' green unleafing, and think about touching S. I want to hold her. I have had dreams: a blonde woman and I sit together looking at a book, we kiss and I am permeated by that sweet moment in dreams when there is no sorrow; and I orgasm. But I couldn't imagine this happening to me awake; what would I tell M? We have been working for four of our last ten years on non-sexist marriage, but I still have dreams of him murdering me, drowning, blowing me up. Still I lie on my bed, masturbating in the damp spring air, all my energy flowing toward S. I divert just enough to get into the VW and pick the kids up when school is out each day, only to walk staring around the house, thinking that the last ten years have been a dream and these two boys are phantasms.

So I plotted to see her ("Come over Friday night for a beer after work, S") and sat on the front steps in the March chill to catch her before M did. We leaned back against the porch pillars, watched the oak branches twist together against the purple light, and exchanged tentative touches, oh so ambiguous, friendly, and seductive—her hand pausing on my foot, mine on her hand—a few words, about dreams. We made plans to go to the karate tournament and I felt like, ridiculously, 16 or 20, wavering through the stylized bow and retreat of courtship, trembling with lust like a mockingbird. When she left, I leaned to hug her, hand and arm merging into her side; that was making love with her the first time.

When have I ever touched a woman? My mother and my aunts, the kiss on the cheek at coming and going. Sally when she broke down over the cat's death and I held her tightly while she cried and then never touched her again. My cousin Anne, tender interludes with her blinds drawn, our heads and consciences conveniently detached from our mouths and hands by the fiction of pretending to be various heroes and heroines, until her mother burst into the darkness, "What are you doing in here?" Men touch me all the time: M for sex only, my advisor grabbing my shoulder, another teacher patting my head on his way to coffee, scaly feet on the back of my neck.

But no one has touched me like S did yesterday. We came back from the Salvation Army gym, opened the windows to the narcissus, drank pink chablis and beer on the couch, and I went under. She stroked my arm through my denim jacket, and we talked about Russian and Brodsky and the party when she had left the white camellia on my car window. I had gone with M to an art-and-newspaper party where friendly journalists tried to talk to me about George Wallace and all I could concentrate on was S flirting with Bonnie or Kate. After I got quite drunk, M took his embarrassing wife home, white camellia clutched in hand, where I made up the guest bed drunkenly for the friendly journalist and raged, wept, shrieked for S, for the chance lost, for being walled in by my family, for being alone without S to touch my hair. As we sat on the couch, I bent over and talked into S's palm, talked about the shrieking, and kissed the palm of her hand, while she kissed my hair. Then we went up the stairs to my room and my bed, and I saw as I lay next to her that her arms were fleshy and white, just like mine; they are a woman's arms.

And, of course, lunatic with love and the waning of the pattern of being a married mother since 19, I told M, who walked in from Greensboro just as I was saying good-night to S. I really didn't think that he would care; there seemed so little connection between me as the cog in the family wheel and me flowering from my fingertips. The first is his idea of me, and why shouldn't that continue? But despite our former, admittedly skimpy, conversation about affairs, he collapsed; he said, "I have no identity; you have taken it away. I am nothing without you; I don't exist."

We lay side by side in our bed, talking into the night until the morning greyed, his fears of madness, weakness, dependency leaking from his mouth. I was killing him; he is dying in my arms. I cannot speak, for to comfort him is to reject myself. I love him, but I want to sleep with S, not live with her; and I think I can still desire him. But, "You have made me impotent," he says. "I am second choice sexually."

I called E last night, in Atlanta, who rose from her lover's bed and long black hair to say, "This is the last thing in the world I expected to hear from you." We talked for a while about the break from a monogamous relationship, with E hinting delicately that I face a different problem because M is male; the breaking bowls and plates certainly must make it louder. I know now why we say, "My heart is breaking." I'm cracking right through the breastbone and turning inside out, leaving the shell of the skin of ten years of marriage and habit behind. I would change back if I could but I've metamorphosed into this stage and can't crawl back into the chrysalis. I desire S, and can't say I love her, but maybe I do. She says she loves me and maybe she does. Desire and friendship seem enough now.

3/6/75

I'm more collected now after turmoil this weekend. After my wanderings through the labyrinth of ESC, M drove off to see a psychologist and returned talking of "feeling enslaved, vampirized." I, in turn, felt like a cannibal, so I agreed to see ditto psychologist, female, and thought hard on the drive up of my motivation. The therapist's questions clinched my resistance: "Have you thought of the results of your action? How can you sleep with them both? What about your mother and your alcoholic father? Was she quilty about doing something to your father and thus felt she caused him to drink? Do you think M might become an alcoholic? You could arrange it." I hoarded my anger and summoned up Lessing, gathering energy, resisting the inertia of the individual 'sickness.' I chanted Horney, Weisstein, Chesler, went home and read Abbott and Love on Lesbianism and Women's Liberation, and concluded: I don't need therapy; put society, put M in analysis. I do need more feminist support. I feel I have to try to be fair to M; because of his good faith in attempting a non-sexist marriage which most men sneer at. But he has to choose to change his masculine conditioning, to struggle with his acquired male expectations. And I have to choose also; S is the result of my independence. But now how can I choose to live with him, on him financially? M will have to recognize and suffer that I will see S, perhaps not to go to bed, but to see her. Sex now is a political act, and my allegiance is divided between the woman and the man. I've thought of remaining celibate for a while. Sex with M will mean that he is trying to re-possess me, a couch, a car, a used TV. It is hard for me to love M now because we are the microcosm in conflict, man against woman, where there is no solace, and no hegemony. I'm tired of expending my energy in justifying myself to men, to M, the anger spilled wastefully, when it could ignite and burn away in the torches of women. I am afraid to love S. If I let go and love her, I'm afraid I won't want to sleep with M, I will only want to be with her. Then I will have to decide about the last ten years of my life and the children.

4/10/75

Right now, all I feel is insensibility, numbness. I'm writing to come out of that death, in the middle of Cross Creek Mall, deafened by the fountains. Last night M staggered in after drinks with G and gummed, "Do you care for me? I hate myself. Why do you keep me around? To help with the kids? Can I not excite you as S does? Isn't this more than a casual affair? Aren't she and I mutually exclusive? You have to choose," and fell up the stairs.

I sat down on the bottom step and chose. He wants more, always more; he feels weak with me because I'm strong, independent? Because

I'm no longer all his. It seems that one of us has to be in control of the other, that we can't be together without a power struggle. He can't accept me as the person I am now, in my idependence, and this wouldn't change if I never saw S again. But, mostly, giving up S would mean giving up thinking, feeling, choosing for myself. To be with M would be to cringe, to hate, to feel defeat, to respond when response would come only from his threats. I would be choosing a life of daily suicides.

I see S as completely removed from my decision; I must decide for myself, so I don't want to know how deeply S cares or how little. If I leave, I'll have to be alone. I have considered myself a feminist for a long time; perhaps this is what I have been growing up towards, perhaps this is what it is to be a Lesbian, though that name seems awkward to me. I easily consider myself a feminist, but to call myself a Lesibian makes me another person; this is, perhaps, what I want.

The kids, the children—but my heart won't break. I just don't want the confusion for them; to be without one of us, and to need that one. Where shall I live? What about a phone, electricity, heat, room for two boys, work, money? But I can manage, perhaps without them for a while, until I get a regular job, or perhaps live on my $64/week unemployment in a room in Haymont, until I can afford daycare. Maybe I really want them to be with M to have solitude for me.

I have chosen, and now I feel the back of my head gone, sheared off, cut away. I might fall face forward, Chaplinesque into the fountain or onto the orderly, well-swept tiles of the Mall. I feel better for this outline, but I can't know if my observations are true, or if I am underestimating the expense of this choice to me, the loss of the children, the stability, the ten years with one person. I'll give myself until Sunday; I see S in half an hour and M tonight. I will look for work this afternoon.

At least I'll never have to use birth control pills again.

25 Debbie
Full Moon

Deb was my next door neighbor. I was eight months pregnant when I met her. My husband was working extra shifts, away a lot. We became very close, closer after the baby came. Seems she was always there when I needed someone.

I was 24, she was 20.

I really don't think, looking back on it, we knew how important this relationship would become. After my son came, we needed more room. My husband, two male friends, Deb and I rented a big old house. The friendship became stronger. We did everything together. Usually, it was her and I, sometimes Garry (my husband) was included. Now, this sounds crude, but it wasn't then. We wound up one night with the three of us sharing a bed. This happened very "innocently." We had been to see *The Exorcist. She* didn't want to sleep alone—and I didn't want her to.

So there we were. One of those "want to touch—not wanting to" things. Garry went to sleep. We couldn't. We lay there all night just holding hands.

This scared me. The feelings were too new. I wasn't ready for it. So I reacted strongly and also the wrong way. I wouldn't be alone with her. I was fighting my own head and my own feelings but at the time I didn't know that.

Deb became very hurt, understandably so. My willpower did not hold up. I had to be with her. There was a magnet drawing us together.

Deb was a Cancer in the fullest sense. Very gentle, very strong, and very loving. Jake, my son, adored her.

The relationship slowly evolved into a threesome—physically and mentally. We were all very happy. We learned from Garry and he from us.

But then something went wrong. Garry grew insecure. Deb began to make him feel threatened. Garry was brought up very macho—sex-role type thing. Here was a woman that could do anything he could do (he was a mechanic) and some of it better. Plus his wife was in love with her. He couldn't handle it—began working longer hours. Stayed away from us. Started sleeping in the den. All this drew Deb and I closer together.

When Jake was 2½ I left my husband, moved to Florida. Deb did the ride down with me. She stayed two weeks, left with a promise to come back. She went back to North Carolina, and joined the Army. The guilt she felt for my marriage falling apart—she couldn't handle. It's been over a year since I heard from her.

I've had several relationships with men before Deb. (This was my second marriage.) But nothing comes close in the intensity of the emotions we experienced. I miss it very much. She taught me a lot. There's a million things I wish I would have handled differently, but alas that's that.

Women are very much my life. I couldn't and wouldn't change that.

26 Confessions of a Country Dyke

Elana

I flash back to the loneliness of my young adult years as I watch Amy, who has just turned 18, walking down the windy path arm in arm with her lover. I envy her at her age living with other Lesbians in this feminist community, feeling proud that she is a woman and feeling comfortable loving other women. How long it's taken me to feel this way! The many guilt-laden years when I felt I was a misfit, a queer or a pervert. And now at 55 years I live with my lover, a woman my age who like Amy, "came out" in this Lesbian community. She suffered guilt too, but in another way. She chose to deprive herself of intimate relationships, had repressed her feelings and lived alone. Her decision to love a woman in the context of this rural women's setting was for her a natural and joyous one.

It is difficult to say when I decided I was a Lesbian. I spent many years trying to go "straight" while I was still having Lesbian relationships. Throughout my childhood and adolescence I had my share of crushes (all unrequited) on girls older than I or on my teachers. At the same time I suffered the boredom of trying to feel romantic toward boys. The only knowledge I had about Lesbians came from Radclyffe Hall's *The Well of Loneliness*, which my mother gave me when I was 14 and in the throes of a serious crush on a girl in high school. Later on as a college student I thumbed through the smudged and worn-out cards in the UCLA library catalogue, tracking down psychiatric books which described in gruesome detail the case histories of "female homosexuals" and left nothing to the imagination.

I was 21 the first time I felt physically attracted to someone of my own sex. I had met Judith in the summer of '41 at a Quaker workcamp for migrant families in California. I quickly responded to her warm and friendly manner. She was both gentle and strong—a nice combination of feminine and masculine qualities. Her hair was plain, cut off at ear's length, which in those days was considered short. She expressed a deep concern for the people we were helping and showed a sensitivity that went beyond her years. We shared sleeping quarters in an old converted chicken house and sometimes we talked for hours after the lights were out about our past. She had grown up in India with missionary parents in contrast to my Jewish Beverly Hills background. But one night after sharing confidences I found I couldn't sleep. Finally I got up and sat by the window and began to sob.

"What's wrong?" she asked in a soft voice.

"I can't sleep," I answered and then added hesitantly, "I want to be near you."

She slid down from the top bunk and came over to me and laid her hand on my shoulder.

"I don't know what to say," she replied.

I could barely look at her; I felt so ashamed.

"I've never felt this way before toward anyone," I said and waited for some gesture from her to reassure me that it was all right to have these feelings. But she just stood and stared at me. She dropped her hand from my shoulder which I took for rejection. I quickly moved away to the other side of the room. "I'll leave tomorrow," I said defensively. She didn't answer for several minutes. "If you think that's best," she finally replied.

I was hoping she'd disagree with me but she hadn't. I could feel my tears coming and I rushed to my bunk and tried to smother my cries in my pillow. She stood there silently and then returned to her bunk. I felt that my whole world had suddenly caved in. I dreaded the thought that I would have to face Judith the next day. But my world did not collapse with my first Lesbian confession as circumstances arose that allowed me a reprieve. Our group had planned to go to a spiritual retreat that weekend and Judith felt it was important that I attend.

Sunday was a day of silence at the retreat. In the late afternoon I walked up a hill and sat beneath a tree. I felt the need to be alone. I was finding it hard to live with these feelings I had for Judith. I knew then that if it wasn't her it could easily be someone else in time. What made it hard was that there was no one I could talk to. I can see now that all my years of feeling alienated had its roots in my Lesbian loneliness of that first awakening. As I meditated, Judith approached and asked if I was all right. Hesitantly I replied, "Yes, I think so." I took a deep breath and added, "I feel I have the strength now to control the feelings I have for you."

"I'm glad," she said and took my hand.

Our friendship grew and as our love intensified we became affectionately and sexually close. We joined a pacifist living cooperative in the black ghetto of San Francisco, which was formerly the Japanese neighborhood until the residents were forced to leave to be imprisoned in concentration camps. Judith and I organized a recreational program in our basement and backyard for the children of these displaced southern sharecroppers who had come to work in the shipyards during World War II. She and I had our own room, slept together, shared our incomes, while we spent our waking hours in a completely heterosexual social community. We never saw ourselves as Lesbians, nor thought about other women who might be in the same kind of relationship. Although our relationship felt natural to me, it did not feel that way to Judith. After two years she became emotionally involved with one of the men in our house and later on married him. I was devastated.

"I thought you loved me," I cried over and over again.

"I did. But I am really not that way," she said emphatically, "I never was, not really."

I couldn't pull out of the deep sense of rejection I felt with the loss of Judith's love. She moved out and I broke down. I committed myself to a local psychiatric hospital. It was the only place where I could get support. I stayed there two weeks and the following poem I wrote while there expresses the state I was in.

On the brink I stand.
Between normality and abnormality,
Between life and death.
In a state of nothingness.
Where there is no past, nor future.
Where life is in a vacuum state.
I go when the wind blows,
I cease when it stops.
Nothing to lose, nothing to gain.
Helpless, hopeless and lifeless.
Waiting, waiting, waiting.
Waiting for those forces
Which shall act upon my life
And determine my destiny.

A sense of powerlessness sums it up. All I wanted now was to be cured of this affliction that had caused me so much pain. No one told me I had a choice in terms of my sexuality. The only respectable and acceptable thing to be was a heterosexual.

I tried therapy for over a year. It didn't seem to help for I became attracted to my roommate in a campus cooperative in Berkeley where I had resumed my studies. The development of our Lesbian relationship followed a similar pattern to the one I had with Judith. It was Ruth's "first," and her initial response to my affectionate gestures was one of resistance. But our friendship overcame society's taboo.

I remember the day she moved into my room. We were both excited about the prospect of being roommates. As I watched Ruth put away her things in the closet, she turned to me and said, "I have a strange feeling about you."

I looked at her for a moment stunned.

"What do you mean?" I asked.

She paused a moment and answered, "I don't know," and continued hanging up her clothes. Her remark took me completely off guard. I felt myself trembling inside. I knew damn well what she meant. Her "strange feelings" about me were very well grounded as we both discovered a few weeks later. Our picnics on Sunday in the Berkeley Hills, when it was still a wilderness, were just the beginning of the many things we did together. Holding hands while hiking, lying side by side in the tall grass, were the first steps toward a more intimate physical relationship. As with Judith, I still had no identity as a Lesbian or an awareness that other women on and off campus might be in a similar situation. We had to hide our feelings in public to ensure that our sense of closeness was not interpreted as "strange." Feelings of guilt were always there but unspoken. In time Ruth, like Judith, could not take the pressure and restrictions that society placed upon her. I constantly felt threatened by the men she knew, even when they became my friends too. Everything in heterosexist society jeopardized and invalidated my feelings of love for another woman. I had even been brainwashed to believe Freud's theory that homosexuality was narcissistic and an immature stage of development.

When Ruth fell in love with a pre-med male student friend of mine, I again felt total rejection, and could not deal with it. This time I took an overdose of sleeping pills which I had stolen from a drugstore where I worked part-time. It was after midnight when a friend found me, face down on the floor in my locked room. She had noticed my light on and after I didn't answer her knock, she climbed through my window from the fire escape. In the hospital, they pumped my stomach and I lay in an oxygen tent unconscious for 20 hours. I really didn't want to die—I wanted to escape from my pain. The university social worker and psychiatrist still believed they could cure me. The need to find an "all-loving mother" was their reason for my homosexuality and of course I agreed—they were the experts.

My mother too saw *it* as purely a psychological problem that would eventually go away. Since I had had boy friends, she never believed that I was a true Lesbian in spite of all my women lovers whom she knew and was very fond of.

I was well aware of the "goodies" I could have as a heterosexual. With a man I had acceptance and respectability in the various social and recreational functions I attended. If I was alone or with a woman it felt different. Each time I "failed" in a relationship with a woman, I found a man and vice-versa. The concept of bisexuality had not been fully developed in our culture. It was either-or. I had no choice of an "alternate life style." My choice was social isolation or social acceptance.

I had seen women whom I suspected of being Lesbians (those who fit the stereotyped "butch" image) particularly my gym instructors at UCLA. I remember the times I had watched them, fascinated by their air of self-confidence. But I always felt uneasy in their presence. They represented the kind of sexuality I could not accept in myself. I once went to Mona's in San Francisco, a Lesbian night club. I sat in the corner clutching a glass of coca cola, staring at the women dressed in men's suits and with men's haircuts. Was I like them? It was the same question I asked when I read those case histories in psychiatric texts. It was hard for me to feel I was one of them and belonged in their world. Yet I didn't feel at home in the world of the heterosexual woman either. What kept me going with all this self-doubt and confusion was the goal of a college degree and the desire to be a social worker. I identified with those who had emotional problems and were economically deprived. By helping them it helped me to feel better about myself.

When I was around 26, I made a conscious effort to be heterosexual. This happened after my third Lesbian relationship. I had worked for a year in the Public Welfare Department. It was there I had met Sarah and moved in with her and her father. She was six years older than I, but had never had a close relationship with a man or a woman. We got along well but for some reason I was not so dependent on her as I had been on Judith and Ruth. Through her encouragement, I applied for and received a county stipend for graduate training at USC and moved there to live on campus.

Had I now found this "all-loving mother" the psychiatrist said I was looking for and could I now go on to the more mature relationships—meaning with men? I thought for two years that I could, but my feelings for men were never so intense or spontaneous as for women. I was always conscious of what I should be feeling or doing as a female—playing a role. Sexually, I was not attracted to them although I continued to believe that I would change or that Mr. Right would some day appear.

Just when I became convinced of this fact an unexpected incident occurred which ironically jerked me out of my invisible closet and into gay life. The episode happened in 1949, when I was in Germany with the American Friends Service Committee. I was doing recreational work with refugee children in a TB Sanatorium and later in Children's Village. It was heart-breaking but gratifying work. It is amazing that the scars of war and the concentration camps had not destroyed the spirit and trust of these children. I worked a 14-hour day for room and board and $25 per month and felt, at times, I should have done more. This was a rare period in my life. I gained a great deal of confidence in myself due to the success of my work and also the fact that I could work and live with women without getting emotionally involved with them.

I'll never forget how proud I felt the day I was chosen to go with our team leader to a conference at our AFSC headquarters in Frankfurt, 500 miles away. We spent the night on the train, and the next morning met with our two supervisors. As we sat down together in the conference room I suddenly became aware of a certain tension in the air and that their attention was focused on me. My first thought was that someone in my family had died and they had called me to headquarters to break the news personally. But that wasn't the case at all. The State Department had discovered my psychiatric record of homosexuality and demanded my expulsion. AFSC officials in Philadelphia at first refused to act on hearsay. They had used an inside connection at the hospital in San Francisco where I had been a patient 7 years previously to verify the information.

The State Department threatened to inform the military authorities in Germany if my organization refused to recall me. AFSC had no choice. A plane ticket for my departure had been bought. I was to leave that afternoon. I was stunned—unable to believe their words. I denied to them I was homosexual but they said their hands were tied. "But that was years ago, " I pleaded. But it was useless. I looked into the faces of these three women and saw only pity and embarrassment.

I wept bitterly as I sat in the plane with its roaring motors while it taxied around the field for what seemed to be an incredibly long time. "Why doesn't it take off so I can get away from here, " I thought to myself. But it kept taxiing around and around. (For years the noise of a plane would send me back to this moment and to this day I have a fear of flying.) I cried the entire journey. I felt ashamed. I felt I had failed again. I was met by an AFSC staff member and driven to our headquarters in Philadelphia. I told them that I was no longer a homosexual and submitted to an interview with their psychiatrist. Although they appeared convinced, they would not send me back to Germany. I not only wanted to be in good standing and finish my 18 months' service with AFSC but I had planned to hitch-hike around the world. I turned down the offer of a clerical job in their office and with my small rucksack (my belongings were still in Germany), I left for New York City. If I was to be persecuted for being a homosexual, I was going to be one! I headed for the Village and stumbled upon Mona's, which I figured might be a Lesbian bar since the one in San Francisco had the same name. I was right. Again, I sat in a corner, gripped a glass of coca cola and tried to feel a connection with the women around me. One of them asked if I was "gay" or "straight" and another asked if I was "butch" or "femme." I didn't know what they were talking about. I had to learn a whole new language. I had to learn to be a Lesbian. I had to learn the art of living in the sub-culture of the "gay world." I went to the bars every night and fortified myself with "boilermakers." I was confused by the butch/femme roles and the way Lesbians related to each other. I had one-night stands for the first time in my life. Bar closing time was 4 a.m. in New York. I'd make it home in time to get a few hours of sleep before I dragged myself to an eastside Settlement House where I was a counselor in a summer daycamp.

If going to gay bars and having Lesbian relationships is "coming out," then my story should end here. But I feel with my new consciousness that "coming out" is only a small step toward a much greater one, that of being "up front" about one's Lesbianism; to have a sense of pride in being one. It was 25 years later after my summer escapade in Greenwich Village that I accomplished this. In a very condensed version I shall describe the many changes I've gone through to make this possible.

By September, when my job was over, I bought a one-way ticket on the *Mauratania* and with $209 began to fulfill my dream of hitchhiking around the world. During my six months in Paris I fell in love with a very gentle Frenchman at the same time seeking out gay bars on the Left Bank. But I was still too shy to make real contacts with other Lesbians and in my travels, which got me as far as Israel, I never came to know any of them. Two years had gone by and I returned to the U.S.A. and settled in San Francisco where I entered gay life with a flourish. My successful shoe-string adventures in Europe and the Middle East had sufficiently washed away the ugly memories I had connected to my expulsion from Germany.

My gay relationships patterned themselves closely after the heterosexual model. My various lovers and I spent beautiful times together at dinner parties, restaurants and bars, at the latest art films, stage plays and Sunday brunch in Sausalito. I "passed" as a "straight" at work, on committees of mental health organizations, in folk dancing classes, on Sierra Club hikes and in the coffeehouses of North Beach. I led a double life. I didn't particularly like it, but at that time it was my only choice. It was the upheavals of the '60's that freed me as well as thousands of others to break away from the status quo and to search for new answers.

I first questioned my professional role as a social worker and joined the War on Poverty at the grass roots level. The Blacks, the Chicanas and the Indians convinced me that the old ways of social change didn't work. The youth of the Haight-Ashbury said something more. "Just open yourself up and listen," my hippie niece demanded of me one day and I did. This new awareness became a backdrop for an unexpected incident in my life. One day I came home from work and discovered my lover of 4 years had suddenly moved out. The wall of barren bookshelves reflected an emptiness I felt in myself. It was time for another change.

I "dropped out," left my job, home and friends and walked across the country with the Peace Torch Marathon to the Pentagon, to protest the war in Vietnam. Two years of demonstration in the streets, the bloodshed I witnessed at the Chicago Convention and a trip to Cuba, radicalized my politics. I experienced gay pride when I donned a purple ribbon on my arm and joined the first Gay Liberation demonstration in Washington Square, NYC. I turned from the city and farmed for five years in New Mexico, consciously looking for new values.

I loved my farm but the feminist revolution began to draw me in another direction and I returned to the Bay Area to put my energy into the women's movement. I found I could not adapt to city life and met country Lesbians when I attended a country women's festival in Mendocino. Six months later I decided to visit the women's community in Southern Oregon where I have lived ever since. Here I found I could garden, folkdance, and be involved in political and social issues with feminist Lesbians. The different parts of my world have come together and I now feel my strength and see my beauty as a Lesbian/woman and feel my confidence growing as a writer.

27 Dear Mother

Jane Sipe

Coming out as a Lesbian is a process that began when I was a child and was mostly unaware of what homosexuality meant. Looking back it is easier to see the patterns, which were very fuzzy, even unidentifiable at the time, as more in focus now. "Queer" was a name my sister got spanked for calling me. I knew why, but didn't know that such people really existed; sexuality in any form was practically unthinkable then. In spite of that, when I was ten and my sister was seven, we managed to get into some sex experimentation together. The interest was mostly mutual, but when she said she didn't like it anymore, we stopped. I *did* like it and was disappointed.

My mother taught me, primarily by example, that women could and should be strong. She was and is an aggressive woman and worked during most of my childhood, usually earning more than my father did. She told me that men's bodies were not beautiful, that men were dirty in their personal hygiene, and that women could get infections from men. And, after all that, *I* had to learn how to wrap my used kotex properly because if they were visible to a man, it would just confirm *his* ideas of the uncleanness of women! Mother had a close friend whom I always admired. I envied their relationship, which seemed to mean more to them than did their marriages. It taught me that women were worthy of each other's friendship, trust, and energies beyond what any man was.

As a pre-adolescent, I did not like boys; in fact I felt superior to them and to the girls in my class who were starting to like boys. In spite of all that should have discouraged interest in boys, I began dating at sixteen and was married at nineteen, much to Mother's dismay. She predicted that I would get pregnant right away and therefore never finish college. She stated her strong opposition and would not attend nor allow my two sisters to attend the wedding. She did not want to look at the pictures afterwards because she said it would be like seeing me in my coffin. Mother often said how much she resented her own marriage and children for preventing her from fulfilling her needs and doing all that she would have wanted to do.

I completed a degree in psychology, perhaps limited to that because that was all that was expected. To do that much would prove Mother wrong and satisfy her all at once. The degree led to a career counseling teenage delinquent girls. Early on, Diane was assigned to my caseload; she was fifteen, I was twenty-two. Rapport was almost immediate, and we found mutual enjoyment in our sessions. She was then in the process of coming out, and her experiences gave me a first glimpse of Lesbianism. Our relationship grew beyond the official one as we came to be quite intimate with each other. Sometimes our visits were as therapeutic for me as they were for her. I read what I could find on the subject of homosexuality to try to understand where it came from, what it meant, and how I could "help" Diane. My husband observed my books, and could see that Diane was very important to me. He pushed—no, pounded—on that emotional button: "Just what does this girl *mean* to you, Jane?" Repeatedly I tried to explain that she was like a sister (my own were 2000 miles away with a still angry mother in between), but he would push harder until I'd cry and confess I didn't know. Diane's coming out evoked many unexplainable responses in me: puzzlement, curiosity, worry, excitement, envy, a desire to experience what it was that affected her so deeply, fear of acting on that desire, and therefore repression of it. I loved her. I respected her judgement finally, and felt that she knew what she was doing in making this choice. I wanted to follow her, but felt that I could not because of my job, our ages, my marriage, the fear that it would mean that I was abnormal.

We continued to be friends over the next few years. I felt self-conscious when, after her mother began living with a woman, Diane said that I was the only straight woman left in her life. Within one year, the husband and I were divorced, I was remarried, and Diane had gone into the service. The second husband and I discussed my feelings for Diane. It was due to his encouragement that, upon her return, she and I talked more openly than before about Lesbianism. We went to see *Emmanuelle* together and it aroused a great desire in me to love her. My fears of what would happen to me gave way to wanting to touch her and her life, hopefully in a way she'd never been touched before. Later she presented me with this poem that she had written that evening, and it was amazing to see how our feelings and perceptions of the incident matched:

Emmanuelle

I need only stay between the lines
This road will lead me home
Am given room to think/feel
Don't know what you're about now—exactly
Reading your eyes has never been too
        difficult
my friend
You're not hiding the feeling
But we look at one another little
        since the coming of this small confrontation.
We get closer at every meeting
        and parting

To what
        I'm not sure.
I'm supposing you don't know either
If becoming closer than we are and have been
finds us on another plane
I won't object
And it's not for me to worry
        about ? after that
Tho at times I do
Gambling never was one of my favorite pastimes.
Step light
        my friend
Beautiful woman-child
Willing to learn
        and eager

I'm here
I won't move first
But I'm here

                                    Diane Francis
                                    1975

Shortly after *Emmanuelle*, we took a weekend trip together, and
finally allowed ourselves to express, verbally and physically, what we
had been feeling. It was wonderful. There was none of the guilt or fear
that I had once thought to protect her from. The only complication, it
seemed, was that we couldn't ride off into the sunset together to live
happily ever after because I still had a husband, and a house in the
suburbs, and a job. That was distressful, but the one real obstacle was
easily cleared; the husband moved out so Diane could move in. It was a
fairytale summer: living together, doing yoga, learning self-hypnosis,
cooking healthy foods for each other, and making love. Later she went
off to see the world and seek her fortune and the physical intimacy
terminated. With little more than a noticeable stumble, our friendship
recovered, and it has endured and grown.

Since then I have generalized that first love of a woman to loving women and what we have to offer each other. There was one aspect of coming out which I had not faced and I wasn't sure if I could face it until I had written this story: being open with my mother. I had discussed my Lesbianism with both my sisters, but Mother's rejection was, until very recently, an experience I did not want to risk.

Dear Mother:

My, my, my. I've been wanting to write you a letter or somehow communicate where I think I'm going and my feelings about that. Unless I do, I fear that you'll have an incomplete and inaccurate frame of reference for looking at what's happening in my life. And that doesn't feel good to me. Also, I don't want there to be large gaping holes in your understanding of me and what makes my life meaningful anymore. It just now occurs to me that my not sharing all of myself with you has probably been responsible for much of the distance over the last few years.

I consider myself to be what is called a woman-identified woman. That means that I recognize and value the strength, power, sensitivity and all that I am as a self-actualizing woman. And I reject male values, do not wish to associate myself with anything having to do with the patriarchy any more than I absolutely have to to survive. My friends and I don't need men, to define how we live, to define how we should look or be, to take care of us, to provide us with a purpose in life. We define ourselves, we recognize our own beauty which comes from a source much deeper, much more permanent than what the boys would define as "beauty." We heal each other, care for each other and ourselves, and we determine our own purposes.

I cannot support any institution that contributes or is entirely directed at keeping women in an inferior position. That's pretty far-reaching. Includes: marriage, heterosexuality, religion which worships male god figures, government (of the boys, by the boys, for the boys), conspicuous consumerism. What I need or want I will buy from the boys, but no more lovely homes in the suburbs, no more playing that competitive game.

What will take the place of all that is a very affirming community of strong, beautiful wimmin (who reject the word wo-man) who love themselves, and each other. Finally free from all the male-imposed ideas that we used to be expected to live up to. I am proud to be part of such a community; I am proud of loving wimmin; of supporting my sisters and finding loving support in them; I am proud to be a Lesbian.

I realize that this will be a difficult thing for you to accept, but I feel that you have given me much of what I needed to be this strong, fine womon that I am. I think you can also recognize that you are a strong womon and your mother is a strong womon, and I certainly come from a fine tradition.

I hope you will have read this far with an open mind and an open heart. I want you to know me, I want you to know that I am not alone, not a loner. That love and community and relationships are very important to me. And that my needs are being filled. This lifestyle feels right to me on all levels and I feel very confident. If I didn't, I don't think I'd yet be ready to risk so much in telling it to you.

Love,
Jane

This is About How Lesbians Capture Straight Women and Have Their Way with Them

28

Judith Katz

I.

1. The first thing that dykes do is they hang out in places where there are a lot of women of either sexuality. If it's in a place where there are women's centers and women's bars, then they hang out there. You can generally tell the dykes in these places because they run around like they feel real comfortable and own the place. A lot of times they have real short hair and they wear leather jackets and a lot of times they do not. You can usually be sure that a woman is an actual dyke if she is hugging one or more other women and liking it. Some times, especially in bars, the dykes hang out around the pool table and sometimes they can really shoot pool and sometimes they cannot, but if they aren't shooting pool they are playing pinball, and if they aren't doing that they are dancing, and then, if they aren't doing any of those things, they are sitting and drinking either beer, tequila, wine, coca-cola, ginger ale, gin, or something else, depending on whether they are a working class dyke or a jet-setty dyke. Most dykes do not drink pink ladies, pink squirrels, but I know one who drinks something with a silly name like that. If they are in a women's center and not doing anything I mentioned above, they are having a meeting. Okay. If dykes live in places where there are no women's centers or women's bars, they probably hang out behind parking meters or in shopping centers, or else at the library.

2. After a dyke is hanging out in a bar or a center or at the library, the next thing she does is set a trap with her friends. She does this by getting a butterfly net and some very subtle, sexy perfume (Charlie, Aramis, Chanel, Patchouli). Then, she and her friends hang out, just

before closing, in the parking lot. They pick a late model Volkswagen, and splash a little perfume on it. Then they hide behind the Volkswagen. When the straight woman comes out of the building and walks into the parking lot to find her car, she is suddenly struck by this subtle sexy smell in the midst of all the pollution (in the case of Omaha, the oatmeal cookies) and she drifts immediately toward the Volkswagen. The dykes begin to giggle a little bit in gleeful anticipation, but then they shush each other and become quite somber. When the straight woman approaches the Volkswagen, one of the dykes jumps out behind her with the large butterfly net. Ever so gently, she drops the net over the straight woman. The others emerge from behind the Volkswagen and cheer and clap with enthusiasm, but softly. They bring the straight woman to the biggest car, ask her if she needs to sit near a window when she is riding in a car. If she says no, then they place her in the middle of the back seat. One dyke holds her hand to reassure her, one puts her arm around her, one drives the car, and the other one starts asking her what her sign is. She explains that she herself is an Aquarian and that she trusts the straight woman is going to have a great time.

II.

Rose arrived stoned, carrying two Rachel Faro albums under her arm. She forgets what jacket she was wearing, she knows that she was not wearing her brown leather jacket with the fur collar because Barb did not give her that until the next morning, but she was wearing some jacket because she pulled it around herself for reassurance. She looked for a doorbell and there was none, so she knocked on the door. She was sure no one had heard her because she could hear the stereo playing inside and she knew her knock was a weak one. She rapped on the window and waited. Just when she had gathered up all the courage it takes her to walk into anyone's house before they answer the door, just as she was putting her fingers on the door knob, Barb came to the door. Rose tripped over the door jamb and walked in.

"Here are those records."

"Good. Come in."

They sat down, Barb in an arm chair, Rose on the floor. Rose took off her jacket and Barb began to talk easily and then Rose began to talk easily. They smoked a joint and played the Rachel Faro albums. Barb wanted to know where Rose wanted to go to eat and both of them decided on Chinese food. They smoked another joint and Barb made tea and they drank tea and smoked the third joint and then they decided that it was too far to drive to Council Bluffs, so they went to Chu's in Omaha and Rose drove, apologizing profusely for the pitty condition of her car. Barb told her that it was okay because her car was a pit too (although Rose says she can hardly call a newspaper lying on the backseat of a Volkswagen grounds for calling anything a pit), but anyway, they made it to Chu's and they talked all the way there. Then they found a parking space and Rose apologized profusely for the nature of her parking job, but then she realized that she had done a pretty good parking job for having been stoned, so she took the apology back. While they were walking up to the door, they saw a yellow Mercedes (still warm), and Barb remarked about how she wouldn't mind having enough money to have a Mercedes and Rose agreed. Then Barb said, as they were walking up the sidewalk, "Have you ever tried to walk on this ramp when it's icy? I can't do it. I got these shoes so I can walk on the ice, but the soles are ridiculous. I can't do it." They walked into Chu's and were seated immediately in the very back of the dining room. They began to order dinner, and then Rose realized that she was too stoned to know at all what she wanted. They both finally decided on something...three things, and then they continued to talk. Rose remembers that she was afraid to look at Barb too carefully for fear she would make herself and Barb uncomfortable. She focused her visual attention on her cigarette, and when the food came, she focused on it. But all the time she was listening to Barb and taking long monologues herself. It was somewhere in the middle of dinner, after Rose had gotten over her anxiety about using her chopsticks poorly that the conversation began to get serious. Rose noticed that she was beginning to talk about being a dyke.

III.

3. Then the dykes go to the cleanest apartment of the group, or if all the dykes live together, then they go to their house. They are real gentle about bringing the straight woman into the house, but they are also firm. They ask her where she wants to sit, and they try to clear the most comfortable space for her. They sit her down and do not ask, but rather bring right away a cup of herb tea, some marijuana cigarettes, and, if weather and laws are permitting, a spoonful of cocaine. They smoke the marijuana cigarettes and drink the tea, they cavort and carry on and have a good time. By this point, the straight woman is usually laughing right along with them, and maybe she is even telling jokes about what a lunkhead her boy friend is. The dykes pick up the cue from there, and begin to talk about what lunkheads their old boy friends were. This usually dazzles the straight woman for a minute. 'You mean you've had...er...

"I used ta fuck a lot. I used to love to fuck."

"Sure, me too."

"Na, not me...I used ta hate ta fuck...men don't know how to kiss." The straight woman agrees on this point, as do the other dykes. "Nope, men sure don't know how to kiss."

By now, the straight woman is really loosening up. She is beginning to say things like, "I don't think you women are scary at all." This makes at least one dyke, probably the Aquarian, blush. The straight woman becomes real touched by this and starts to tell a few stories. She talks about how once when she was six, she and her best friend used to sit in the woods and hug and hug and hug. One of the dykes says, "Yeh, that happened to me, only I was about twelve, and it really freaked me out. I felt like there was electricity all over my back." Each dyke tells a similar story and then someone suggests that it's time to smoke another joint.

While one dyke gets the pot, another dyke puts some music on. They play the following albums in any order they please:

Lavender Jane Loves Women
Theresa Trull, *The Ways A Woman Can Be*
Cris Williamson, *The Changer and the Changed*
B-B K'Roche
Sweet Honey and the Rock (both albums)
Laura Nyro, *Gonna Take A Miracle*

It is perhaps wisest to put Laura on last, but any time the dykes put on any of these records is okay. After they have smoked the last joint and have been listening to the music for a while, one of the dykes asks another of the dykes if she can have a back rub. The second one says sure, and rubs the first one's back gently as the first lies stomach down on the floor. Pretty soon everyone is rubbing everyone else's back since it looked like so much fun the first time. Even the straight woman is having her back rubbed. Suddenly, one of the dykes (and there is no correct or incorrect timing here—it is never too soon) takes the shirt off of the woman whose back she is massaging. Depending on whether or not the straight woman is relaxing into the back rub,she will or will not become alarmed at this. Should the straight woman become alarmed, at least one of the dykes will give her another joint and rub the back of her neck gently.

Much laughter and giggling ensues as the back rubs turn into full body massages, and the dykes take turns getting up to change the records.

If the straight woman continues to be apprehensive, none of the dykes taunts or cajoles her. Instead, they stop massaging each other and come sit around the straight woman in a close, warm circle. They have their arms around each other. They hold each other. Then they take turns telling stories again.

IV.

Rose and Barb left Chu's and decided to go to Rose's house to get some more pot. When they got there, Rose told Barb that she could wait in the car or she could come in. Barb said she wanted to come in, so she did.

They went up to Rose's room, and Barb sat on the bed and Rose began to roll a joint, which she was apologizing for while she was rolling it. Barb said, "This room is nice, but you either have to get rid of these frilly white curtains or you have to get a canopy bed." Rose felt a little embarrassed, but had to agree. Barb had begun to look through the ten records that Rose had brought with her to Omaha from Massachusetts. She was holding *The Harder They* Come and looking at it intently. Rose looked up from her badly rolled joints and said, "Would you like to listen to that? I don't have a stereo, but there's one in MC and Gail's room we could use."

Barb said, "Let's go in MC and G.'s room," so they did.

Rose put the record on and lit a joint. Barb sat on MC and G.'s bed, and Rose, after thinking about it for a minute, sat on the floor. They smoked the joint and listened to the record, and after a little while, Barb said, "Why are you sitting on the floor?"

Rose giggled a bit and said she wasn't sure why.

Then Barb said, "Why don't you come up here on the bed?"

Rose did, and then for a while, just sat up very tall and hardly breathed. The record continued. No one was saying anything. Rose took Barb's hand and began to stroke it softly. Barb squeezed Rose's hand. Rose began to touch Barb's shoulder. Barb was lying on her stomach now, sort of, she had most of her face in a pillow. She looked at Rose out of the corner of her eye and said, "I don't know if you know this, but I guess since you know R.A. you must know this, but...I...Um...I've never had an experience with a woman before."

Rose said that she did know this. She touched Barb's hand again. "What do you want to do?"

"I don't know."

Rose looked out the window in G. and MC's room. "The moon looks pretty amazing. Let's go some place where we can really look at it."

They took another joint with them and got into Rose's car. Barb suggested that they drive through the park. Then she directed Rose onto a little road in that park that came to a tiny valley. They got out of the car, and ran down a hill. When they got to the bottom, they looked up, and there, smiling soft like a wonderful mama, was the moon, three rings around it, low, and in Aries.

V.

4. The next thing the dykes do is talk. Dykes are very good at talking and the thing they like to talk most about is being a dyke, unless they are into cars or cooking or music or Marxism, or Classism, or their job, in which case they will talk about that. But when dykes are together with the express purpose in mind of being dykes, that's what they talk about. So the dykes tell true tales of coming out and horrifying tales of true heterosexual occurrences, and pretty soon, even if the straight woman was apprehensive before, she has stopped being apprehensive. She likes it when one of the dykes begins to rub her neck and shoulders again. She likes it that someone else is being perfectly charming while talking about the first time she tried to use a Tampax. She likes it that the room smells like pot and peanut butter and musk. She likes it that everyone in the room is smiling and tickling her under the chin, and that no one has any knives or guns or fists for her. She lies back in one of the dyke's laps, and has a beautiful, beautiful dream.

VI.

Rose and Barb walked around the park and played on the swings and looked up at the stars and the moon. They talked and played and Barb was telling about how she really liked women better than men, but she didn't know…she was pretty sure, but she didn't know about sleeping with women.

Rose told about how she had slept with a lot of women, and she liked it a lot, it was a lot of fun, and about how she was afraid of men.

Barb nodded a lot, and occasionally made fun of the fact that Rose was so much shorter than she was. Rose thought this was pretty funny herself (the first three or four times), and kept looking at the moon and freaking out. She was afraid she was going to get sucked up into it and never come down. Her fear was alleviated as soon as she was near to her car. After one last look at the moon, through the branches of the trees and clear, they got into Rose's car and drove back to Barb's.

VII. The Straight Woman Tells Her Dream

Hah-hah, it was sooo wonderful, I dreamed I was riding to the ocean, faster and faster I was riding to the ocean and there were two of me, and the spray from the ocean was bubbling up and blowing through the air and I was riding riding riding to the ocean with my legs wrapped around my own thigh.

VIII.

There was a little hesitation when they arrived at Barb's house, but not too much. Rose decided to go in and they decided not to listen to any more records downstairs, but to go up to Barb's room and listen there. They had plenty of cigarettes and a lot, lot lot to talk about.

Rose told Barb that the first time she made love with a woman she felt like she had fallen into the warmest, softest river in the universe. Barb laughed and said that she bet Rose said that to every aspiring Lesbian. Rose giggled and said (she insists this is the truth) that she had never said that to anyone before, it just sort of popped out of her mouth. Barb said okay, and then she talked a lot about not wanting to have to be one thing or another thing, and Rose said that a decision to sleep with a woman didn't have to be a terminal decision. Barb said she guessed that was probably true.

Rose told some stories of lovers gone by, she told about how she suspected she wanted more from lovers than just hanging out and having orgasms, she told about all the times she was asked to leave and find someone else. Barb listened and agreed a lot and in between getting up to change the records and swearing at the stereo, she told some of her stories. She told about the women who she lived with now and before, she talked about feeling close to women, she told how she thought of Rose as a renegade rascal. Rose got silly about that, basically because she was very shy, and didn't see herself at all as a high school desperado, which was what Barb said her fantasy of Rose was.

Somehow, it got to be twelve o'clock in the morning and Barb said, "It must be getting really late."

Rose thought that that meant she should maybe leave, so she began to collect herself. She didn't really want to leave, she was really loving listening and talking and listening some more, she was thrilled that her time, this first time, with Barb had been so easy and comfortable.

IX.

5. The dykes all sigh and swoon and blush when they hear the straight woman's dream. Some of them have had similar dreams, some of them have had dreams, mostly about being arrested by men, and some of them have a hard time remembering their dreams, but after hearing this particular dream, they are anxious to know how to remember them. A long discussion on methods and theories for remembering dreams ensues.

X.

Rose said she was leaving, and Barb said, "I wish I could ask you to stay."

Then Rose said, "I'd love to stay." So, together, they went down to the end of the hall and picked out a suitable blanket. Barb showed Rose a beautiful quilt that she had bought for a very low price from an old woman down the street. Rose agreed that it was a wonderful quilt, then Barb said it would be too warm, so they picked out another one. Then they walked back to Barb's room.

Barb sat at the foot of her bed and began to undress. "Well," she said, "we could sit here and throw our clothes at each other." Rose giggled a little. When Barb got up, maybe to play with the stereo, maybe to do something else, Rose said, "Come here," so softly that Barb said, "What did you say?" She was very close to Rose now. Rose said one more time, still softly, "Come here." Barb leaned closer, and quite gently, a littly shyly, but basically easily, they kissed.

XI.

6. THE DYKE CHECK LIST

Do you like to be held?
Do you like to kiss?
When someone bites your finger, where do you feel it?
How do you like your breasts?
Your vagina?
Do you look at the face of the person you have just made love to, are making love to?
When you do, does it make you feel wonderful?
Do you like to make jokes in bed?
What does your mother think about all of this?

XII.

They spent much of that night holding and hugging and kissing and playing. They slept curled into each other. In the morning, they kissed and hugged and played some more. Barb gave Rose an incredible jacket. Rose gave Barb another kiss. They had of course given each other, in all of those hours, a great deal more, but some of those things are not easy to put down on a piece of white typing paper. There is more to this story, this is only the story of the first night. That the moon was in Aries and sun was in Libra is of course significant. But it should also be taken into account that there was a great tenderness stored up in both their hearts.

29 Come Again
Constance Faye

One

a coming out story would be
a chronicle of all the days of all my lives
it seems there is either nothing to tell, or far too much
how can i possibly capture any of it
stop the flow
march it out in lines for all to see and know
i am always coming out
endlessly unfolding on an infinite number of levels
i struggle and i persist

Two

coming out of the womb
i gave up warmth, security and insulation
for a new awareness
from between my mother's legs
i came out
to her embrace, her breasts, her loving
she nourished me, sustained me
and i grew

coming out of blissful innocence
to hide myself under sheets

wrap myself round and round with towels
lest i be caught
pants down
unprotected in my nakedness
coming out of innocence
into fear and shame of my own body
my own being

coming out at thirteen
into the young arms of another womon
kissing, caressing the fires in our breasts,
our bellies, between our legs our fingers
danced, never quite touching
the center, the love
was carefully compressed and hidden away
coming out into the delusions, illusions
the lies
we didn't mean anything
we were only practicing for the real thing

coming out of the nest
my spirit already broken
i fluttered through the man's world
buffetted by ill wills and unkind intentions
easily caught up in each passing storm
'til i crashed, raving delirium
so immersed in self-doubt, revulsion, fear and insecurity
i relinquished all claim to my future
rejecting any further responsibility
i came out in madness
to search for a new womb

coming out in love
with a woman touching
deeper than her male medicine taught
she nurtured, loved my spirit, my heart, my mind
but not my body
pushing and shoving me into my own
self-love, strength, beauty and honesty
and honestly i loved her, passionately i loved her
coming beyond those manmade boundaries
to which she clung
coming out with such unacceptable notions,
feelings, desires

into the threat of her fullblown rejection
i fled into denial

coming out from between a womon's legs
into a new awareness
loving the self loving the other
loving and beloved I am whole
a rediscovered self defined in terms of
acceptance and affirmation, struggle and sorrow
coming out of the silence to scream
to stand strong and proud
coming out of my gut
daring all
i will not be swept away
kept locked away in preconscious
i will come again

30 Untitled Story

Patricia E. Hand

Gay—Lesbian—Dyke. The terms represent the changing self-image I experienced in the process of coming out. I had entered therapy because of some personal and situational problems and eventually got around to dealing with the difficulty I had in relating to men on a social level. As my therapy progressed, I discovered that the idea of becoming involved with men was less and less attractive to me and, at age 24, I decided to explore the possibility of relating to women. This process took about a year; I talked about it frequently with my shrink, but the fear and anxiety I felt at the mere suggesiton of actively seeking out such relationships was enough to cause instant paralysis and retreat. I believed all of the myths and stereotypes about Lesbians that straight society perpetuates; when I finally gathered up enough courage to go to a gay women's discussion group, I was convinced that I would be walking into a room filled with "crazy women." Instead, I found a group of warm, supportive and accepting women who looked just like my straight women friends. At first I thought that there must be something visible (clothes, jewelry, makeup?) that distinguished gay and straight women and I used to search for it at every opportunity. Unfortunately, no universal sign exists—it might make it easier for us to meet each other.

As I became more comfortable in this new identity, a feeling of euphoria set in—I knew who I was and it was great! I wanted to tell the world I was gay, but I was afraid of being rejected. I started coming out with a few friends and ran into a brick wall. My best friend (and whom I'd shared everything else and whom I'd supported during her heterosexual affairs) said that it was fine with her—and then stopped coming over for dinner. I was devastated and tried for months to work it out with her, but she was too afraid that I was sexually interested in her (I wasn't); eventually the friendship ended.

I gradually progressed from "gay woman" to "Lesbian" (the first time someone referred to me as a Lesbian it was a bit of a shock!) and with some anxiety about possible consequences (what if my students saw me?) I participated in the Gay Pride Parade in June, 1976. What a fantastic, up experience! I experienced a tremendous feeling of strength, solidarity and community with other Lesbians. My straight friends didn't quite understand. When I told one of my anxiety before the parade, she suggested I march wearing a pair of sunglasses!

I had told my sister about my Lesbianism because I felt it was a very positive thing that I wanted to share with her. We're very close and my sharing my feelings with her has brought us even closer together. My mother, however, was a different story. She never accepted my moving away from home and thinks that "my situation" (as she calls it), is due to my unfortunate association with and brainwashing by the women's liberation movement.

Working out my identity as a Lesbian has not been an easy process. At one point I remember experiencing an acute anxiety attack over the possibility that I might be a latent heterosexual. But, in general, I have been fortunate in coming out at a time when homosexuality is not automatically associated with mental illness by everyone, and for the most part it has been a very positive experience for me. I feel very good about my self and the friendships I have developed with other gay women. I am out with my friends, my family and my co-workers. The primary frustration that I feel is not related to my identity as a Lesbian but to the reactions I have encountered in straight society. Most of my friends and co-workers have "accepted" my gayness and say it is "OK." with them; but, with one or two exceptions, they do not see it in a very positive light, as a fantastic discovery, something to be proud of. Some friends have made it clear that my being a Lesbian is fine with them as long as I don't bring it up in conversation. Another friend, of eight years standing, was also accepting but requested that I not tell any of her other friends, because if her husband found out she would have to stop seeing me.

I used to be very tolerant of this type of reaction by straight women. I rationalized that it was new to them, that they needed time to accept it, etc.; but lately I've become very tired of all this nonsense. I don't understand what all the fuss is about; I'm tired of gently explaining my existence to insecure women. If I were black and people were uptight because of it, that would be their problem to deal with. As a Lesbian, however, I am expected to go out of my way not to "threaten" straight people and to understand that it takes them a while to "adjust" to my new status.

Friends have suggested that I would avoid some of the pain and frustration by not "mentioning" my Lesbianism. As one put it, "I don't tell everyone what kind of sex I like or who I'm sleeping with." Well, neither do I; I talk to people about my identity because I don't like it when I am relegated to the category of unmarried (translation unwanted) straight woman. I also feel a very strong political commitment to being open about my Lesbiansim. I believe that it is very important for dykes to be out because this will eventually make it easier for all of us. In the first place it proves to the straight world that we do exist (gay men exist but most people don't believe in Lesbians). Secondly, it shows that we're regular people just like everybody else; and finally, that ignoring us won't make us go away.

31 Dragon Lady Speaks

Liza Cowan

When Peanut Butter and I first met we were so overcome that we could hardly speak. I was too shy, too passive to call her to meet again, but she called me. We became friends and I knew there was something special about her. I knew I wanted to sleep with her, but I had never slept with a woman before.

We talked a lot about Lesbianism. She had had affairs with women before. I knew she liked me and was attracted to me and I figured she'd know what to do. She did nothing except kiss me each time we met or parted. She always kissed me on the lips. My mind reeled in delight and shyness each time.

One night, after we'd been friends for two months, I told her I was attracted to her. She said she was attracted to me too. I went home and danced alone for hours, happy and secure. I knew everything would be wonderful.

Later that week she came to my house early in the morning (we'd been out all night talking on the radio about how the liberated woman seduces men. What a farce!). We sat on opposite ends of my big wooden bed. I wanted to kiss her, to hold her, anything, but we just sat and fidgeted, making small talk, forcing ourselves to smile at each other. Finally, I got up to leave the room. She held onto my shoulder, and I knew the time had come. We kissed.

As I said, I'd never kissed a woman before. I didn't know what to expect. Woman's Lips! Sweet mystery. But ... they felt like lips! I couldn't have been more surprised! I told her so. We lay down. I was terribly nervous. I felt wooden, awkward. I was too aware of how large i was against her. We didn't fit.

I said all the wrong things. I didn't mean them to be discouraging. I thought she knew how much I liked her. I wanted her to know how strange I was feeling. It never occurred to me that this older, experienced woman could be feeling more awkward than I.

When I came back from driving her home I felt wonderful. I was glad to be alone and thrilled at what had happened. She had told me before that she liked me and I believed it. I knew that eventually we'd be a great team.

The next week I went downtown to her house for dinner (we'd picked the day according to an astrologer's counsel of Venus in the something or other house). She greeted me at the door wearing a shirt that was more empty space than cloth. A net undershirt. Her breasts were clearly visible. This turned me on and amused me. What a rascal!

Several strange men and women arrived later and they all danced and carried on while I sat watching, embarrassed. I wanted to go home. Finally they left.

I had been so uptight with these strangers that I felt truly comfortable alone with Peanut Butter. We hugged and kissed, went to her bed. Everything was great. We were no longer awkward. I felt her breasts, her soft smooth skin. I loved her! I adored her! I still do.

Peanut Butter Meets the Dragon Lady

32

Alix Dobkin

She was getting off the bed. If I didn't move right away the seconds would pass along with the chance to find out exactly what was happening between us—and I hadn't had any idea of what that was since the moment I first laid eyes on her a couple of months before.

I moved. My hand went to rest on her shoulder. She responded immediately and easily. She was as curious and as cautious as I ... waiting for something to happen.

Kiss. And there it was; skin upon skin. Top lip to top lip. Bottom to bottom. Gentle, warm, but what was happening? Nothing except the bare presence of skin.

She said, "Your mouth is just like any other mouth."

I knew she was bold, outspoken, right-on, but I was not ready to hear those words out loud at that time. Undeniable as they were. My confusion, born of fatigue and bewilderment coupled itself with her phrase and all of my impulses went shooting to my head, blindly behind my eyes. I could feel them colliding with each other in their madness. I was feeling crazy: out of control. Oh shit ... oh shit ... oh what the *fuck* is going *on?* ... Oh *no!* ... what do I do now?

We lie down. Christ! Maybe that will help. We are going through the motions, but it is the same thing all over. Now it's whole bodies touching. Still. Deathlike.

But I am a stoic. I stick to something like peanut butter. I could barely appreciate the drama which seemed to be playing itself out for its own amusement, independently. Eyeball to eyeball with this devastating twist of events, I speak up. "I'd like to hold *you.*" Maybe this will make it better. After all, I have made love with women before. She has not. I'm supposed to know what to do and how to do it. We change positions.

"You're too little," she says.

I am feeling fragmented. My parts don't seem to relate to me or each other. My mind roars, "What can she *mean*?" and my body verifies her observation. It's a pity, but now that the words have been spoken, there seems truly to be no fitting together here. In a desperate attempt, my leg moves itself ... trying to get a better fit, and my mouth says, "What do you mean, 'too *little*'?"

"We don't fit!"

"Don't be silly!" says my confusion aloud.

"Are you comfortable?"

"Yes," she replies in a clear, unsentimental voice. Then, "Are you too exhausted to give me a back rub?"

It was then 6 a.m. We had been up all night doing a radio program while contending with the stress of our great unresolved attraction and the strain of our timidity.

"Yes," I say in truth. I really must go home. At least that is one reality I can deal with. I touch her cheek. She is so pretty. She says, "We'd better go."

Putting on my boots. Admitting in my weariness, my blues, I say to her, "I guess that was premature." I feel compelled to make some excuse.

The matter-of-fact voice comes bounding out of her room and says, "No it wasn't." The voice of clarity sails past me unfurling in its wake a legend which reads like a banner, "Premature lying in bed together."

I can see her words strung out in block letters dissolving before my eyes. The verdict in sky writing. "Guilty of premature lying in bed together." It makes me smile in the face of my misery.

I tell her that I was confused by the whole thing. "No floods of recognition," I explain. Our bodies and our mouths had revealed only that which we already knew about each other.

"What did you expect, divine inspiration?" she says at the elevator. (I had.)

She drove me home. I talked all the way. She hardly said anything. When we parted she said, "Don't worry about my not talking."

I said, "Don't worry about my talking." I felt like a fool in a comedy of errors.

Epilogue

The following week was a marked improvement. We gave ourselves enough time and space. There were other people to be with at first.

There was dancing and I was relaxed. What else did I have to lose? More important, there was the knowledge that we were together and turned on and that the disaster of the previous week had not driven us apart.

When the party broke up she stayed. We lay down on the bed and embraced. This time everything was right. I had come home to the warmest, most comfortable, most secure, most exciting place in my life. All the juices flowed. I was alive in every molecule.

Although my insides were celebrating riotously, on the outside nothing much seemed to be happening. Hugging, whispering, giggling, and then—kissing.

To me there is nothing approaching the wonder of a woman's kiss. The kisses we had that night were beautiful. They were soft, slow and delicious. They tasted of an ancient forgotten sweetness.

I had held and cuddled several women in my past and had experienced a wide range of feelings from very turned on to very turned off and a couple which fell in between. Never before, though, was I more open and innocent than I was on that memorable night.

In college, when I first embraced a woman in bed, we were both so thrilled that we dared not move all night, but lay in each other's arms as stiff as boards, our hearts pounding furiously. This time I could move, but I didn't want to. The force of our energies so charged us that to move seemed almost like resistance, and I wanted all of my being to fully experience this dream come true. I had emerged from the shadowy closet into the light of my own joyous existence as a Lesbian woman!

33 La Güera

Cherríe Moraga Lawrence

> It requires something more than personal experience to gain a philosophy or point of view from any specific event. It is the quality of our response to the event and our capacity to enter into the lives of others that help us to make their lives and experiences our own.
>
> *Emma Goldman*[1]

I am the very well-educated daughter of a woman who, by the standards in this country, would be considered largely illiterate. My mother was born in Santa Paula, Southern California, at a time when much of the central valley there was still farm land. Nearly thirty-five years later, in 1948, she was the only daughter of six to marry an Anglo, my father.

I remember all of my mother's stories, probably much better than she realizes. She is a fine story-teller, recalling every event of her life with the vividness of the present, noting each detail right down to the cut and color of her dress. I remember stories of her being pulled out of school at the ages of five, seven, nine, and eleven to work in the fields, along with her brothers and sisters; stories of her father drinking away whatever small profit she was able to make for the family; of her going the long way home to avoid meeting him on the street, staggering toward the same destination. I remember stories of my mother lying about her age in order to get a job as a hat-check girl at Agua Caliente Racetrack in Tijuana. At fourteen, she was the main support of the

---

[1]Alix Kates Shulman, ed., "Was My Life Worth Living?" *Red Emma Speaks* (New York: Random House, 1972), p. 388.

family. I can still see her walking home alone at 3 a.m., only to turn all of her salary and tips over to her mother, who was pregnant again.

The stories continue through the war years and on: walnut-cracking factories, the Voit Rubber factory, and then the computer boom. I remember my mother doing piecework for the electronics plant in our neighborhood. In the late evening, she would sit in front of the TV set, wrapping copper wires into the backs of circuit boards, talking about "keeping up with the younger girls." By that time, she was already in her mid-fifties.

Meanwhile, I was college-prep in school. After classes, I would go with my mother to fill out job applications for her, or write checks for her at the supermarket. We would have the scenario all worked out ahead of time. My mother would sign the check before we'd get to the store. Then, as we'd approach the checkstand, she would say—within earshot of the cashier—"Oh honey, you go 'head and make out the check," as if she couldn't be bothered with such an insignificant detail. No one asked any questions.

I was educated, and wore it with a keen sense of pride and satisfaction, my head propped up with the knowledge, from my mother, that my life would be easier than hers. I was educated; but more than this, I was *la güera*: 'fair-skinned'. Born with the features of my Chicana mother, but the skin of my Anglo father, I had it made.

No one ever quite told me this (that light was right), but I knew that being light was something valued in my family (who were all Chicano, with the exception of my father). In fact, everything about my upbringing (at least what occurred on a conscious level) attempted to bleach me of what color I did have. Although my mother was fluent in it, I was never taught much Spanish at home. I picked up what I did learn from school and from overheard snatches of conversation among my relatives and mother. She often called other lower-income Mexicans *braceros*, or 'wet-backs', referring to herself and her family as "a different class of people." And yet, the real story was that my family, too, had been poor (some still are) and farmworkers. My mother can remember this in her blood as if it were yesterday. But this is something she would like to forget (and rightfully), for to her, on a basic economic level, being Chicana meant being "less". It was through my mother's desire to protect her children from poverty and illiteracy that we became "Anglo-ized"; the more effectively we could pass in the white world, the better guaranteed our future.

From all of this, I experience daily a huge disparity between what I was born into and what I was to grow up to become. Because, as Goldman suggests, these stories my mother told me crept under my *güera* skin. I had no choice but to enter into the life of my mother. *I had no choice.* I took her life into my heart, but managed to keep a lid on it as long as I feigned being the happy, upwardly mobile heterosexual.

When I finally lifted the lid to my lesbianism, a profound connection with my mother was reawakened in me. It wasn't until I acknowledged and confronted my own lesbianism in the flesh, that my heartfelt identification with and empathy for my mother's oppression— due to being poor, uneducated, and Chicana—was realized. My lesbianism is the avenue through which I have learned the most about silence and oppression, and it continues to be the most tactile reminder to me that we are not free human beings.

You see, one follows the other. I had known for years that I was a lesbian, had felt it in my bones, had ached with the knowledge, gone crazed with the knowledge, wallowed in the silence of it. Silence *is* like starvation. Don't be fooled. It's nothing short of that, and felt most sharply when one has had a full belly most of her life. When we are not physically starving, we have the luxury to realize psychic and emotional starvation. It is from this starvation that other starvations can be recognized—if one is willing to take the risk of making the connection— if one is willing to be responsible to the result of the connection. For me, the connection is an inevitable one.

What I am saying is that the joys of looking like a white girl haven't been so great since I realized I could be beaten on the street for being a dyke. If my sister's being beaten because she's black, it's pretty much the same principle. We're both getting beaten any way you look at it. The connection is blatant; and in the case of my own family, the difference in the privileges attached to looking white instead of brown, are merely a generation apart.

In this country, lesbianism is a poverty—as is being brown, as is being a woman, as is being just plain poor. The danger lies in ranking the oppressions. *The danger lies in failing to acknowledge the specificity of the oppression.* The danger lies in attempting to deal with oppression purely from a theoretical base. Without an emotional, heartfelt grappling with the source of our own oppression, without naming the enemy within ourselves and outside of us, no authentic, non-hierarchical connection among oppressed groups can take place.

When the going gets rough, will we abandon our so-called comrades in a flurry of racist/heterosexist/what-have-you panic? To whose camp, then, should the lesbian of color retreat? Her very presence violates the ranking and abstraction of oppression. Do we merely live hand to mouth? Do we merely struggle with the "ism" that's sitting on top of our own heads?

The answer is: yes, I think first we do; and we must do so thoroughly and deeply. But to fail to move out from there will only isolate us in our own oppression—will only insulate, rather than radicalize us.

To illustrate: a gay male friend of mine once confided to me that he continued to feel that, on some level, I didn't trust him because he was male; that he felt, really, if it ever came down to a "battle of the sexes," I might kill him. I admitted that I might very well. He wanted to understand the source of my distrust. I responded, "You're not a woman. Be a woman for a day. Imagine being a woman." He confessed that the thought terrified him because, to him, being a woman meant being raped by men. He *had* felt raped by men; he wanted to forget what that meant. What grew from that discussion was the realization that in order for him to create an authentic alliance with me, he must deal with the primary source of his own sense of oppression. He must, first, emotionally come to terms with what it feels like to be a victim. If he—or anyone—were to truly do this, it would be impossible to discount the oppression of others, except by again forgetting how we have been hurt.

And yet, oppressed groups are forgetting all the time. There are instances of this in the rising black middle class, and certainly an obvious trend of such "unconsciousness" among gay men. Because to remember may mean giving up whatever privileges we have managed to squeeze out of this society by virtue of our gender, race, class, or sexuality.

Within the women's movement, the connections among women of different backgrounds and sexual orientations have been fragile, at best. I think this phenomenon is indicative of our failure to seriously address ourselves to some very frightening questions: How have I internalized my own oppression? How have I oppressed? Instead, we have let rhetoric do the job of poetry. Even the word *oppression* has lost its power. We need new language, better words that can more closely describe women's fear of and resistance to one another; words that will not always come out sounding like dogma.

I don't really understand first-hand what it feels like being shit on for being brown. I understand much more about the joys of it—being Chicana and having family are synonymous for me. What I know about loving, singing, crying, telling stories, speaking with my heart and hands, even having a sense of my own soul comes from the love of my mother, aunts, cousins....

But at the age of twenty-seven, it is frightening to acknowledge that I have internalized a racism and classism, where the object of oppression is not only someone outside of my skin, but the someone inside my skin. In fact, to a large degree, the real battle with such oppression, for all of us, begins under the skin. I have had to confront the fact that much of what I value about being Chicana, about my family, has been subverted by Anglo culture and my own cooperation with it. This realization did not occur to me overnight. For example, it wasn't until long after my graduation from the private college I'd attended in Los Angeles, that I realized the major reason for my total alienation from and fear of my classmates was rooted in class and culture. *Click.*

Three years after graduation, in an apple-orchard in Sonoma, a friend of mine (who comes from an Italian working-class family) says to me, "Cherríe, no wonder you felt like such a nut in school. Most of the people there were white and rich." It was true. All along I had felt the difference, but not until I had put the words *class* and *culture* to the experience, did my feelings make any sense. For years, I had berated myself for not being as "free" as my classmates. I completely bought that they simply had more guts than I did—to rebel against their parents and run around the country hitchhiking, reading books and studying "art". They had enough privilege to be atheists, for chrissake. There was no one around filling in the disparity for me between their parents, who were Hollywood filmmakers, and my parents, who wouldn't know the name of a filmmaker if their lives depended on it (and precisely because their lives didn't depend on it, they couldn't be bothered). But I knew nothing about "privilege" then. White was right. Period. I could pass. If I got educated enough, there would never be any telling.

Three years after that, another *click.* In a letter to a friend, I wrote:

> I went to a concert where Ntozake Shange was reading. There, everything exploded for me. She was speaking a language that I knew—in the deepest parts of me—existed, and that I had ignored in my own feminist studies and even in my own writing. What Ntozake caught in me is the realization that in my development as a poet, I have, in many ways, denied the voices of my brown mother—the brown in me. I have acclimated to the sound of a white language which, as my father represents it, does not speak to the emotions in my poems—emotions which stem from the love of my mother.
>
> The reading was agitating. Made me feel uncomfortable. Threw me into a week-long terror of how deeply I was affected. I felt that I had to start all over again. That I had turned only to the perceptions of white middle-class women to speak for me and all women. I am shocked by my own ignorance.

Sitting in that auditorium chair was the first time I had realized to the core of me that for years I had disowned the language I knew best—ignored the words and rhythms that were the closest to me. The sounds of my mother and aunts gossiping—half in English, half in Spanish—while drinking *cerveza* in the kitchen. And the hands—I had cut off the hands in my poems. But not in conversation; still the hands could not be kept down. Still they insisted on moving.

The reading had forced me to remember that I knew things from my roots. But to remember puts me up against what I don't know.

Shange's reading agitated me because she spoke with power about a world that is both alien and common to me: "the capacity to enter into the lives of others." But you can't just take the goods and run. I knew that then, sitting in the Oakland auditorium (as I know in my poetry), that the only thing worth writing about is what seems to be unknown and therefore fearful.

The "unknown" is often depicted in racist literature as the "darkness" within a person. Similarly, sexist writers will refer to fear in the form of the vagina, calling it "the orifice of death." In contrast, it is a pleasure to read works such as Maxine Hong Kingston's *Woman Warrior*, where fear and alienation are described as "the white ghosts." And yet, the bulk of literature in this country reinforces the myth that what is dark and female is evil. Consequently, each of us—whether dark, female, or both—has in some way *internalized* this oppressive imagery. What the oppressor often succeeds in doing is simply *externalizing* his fears, projecting them into the bodies of women, Asians, gays, disabled folks, whoever seems most "other".

> call me
> roach and presumptuous
> nightmare on your white pillow
> your itch to destroy
> the indestructible
> part of yourself
> *Audre Lorde*[2]

But it is not really difference the oppressor fears so much as similarity. He fears he will discover in himself the same aches, the same longings as those of the people he has shit on. He fears the immobilization threatened by his own incipient guilt. He fears he will have to change his life once he has seen himself in the bodies of the people he has called different. He fears the hatred, anger, and vengeance of those he has hurt.

This is the oppressor's nightmare, but it is not exclusive to him. We women have a similar nightmare, for each of us in some way has been both the oppressed and the oppressor. We are afraid to look at how we have failed each other. We are afraid to see how we have taken the values of our oppressor into our hearts and turned them against ourselves and one another. We are afraid to admit how deeply "the man's" words have been ingrained in us.

To assess the damage is a dangerous act. I think of how, even as a feminist lesbian, I have so wanted to ignore my own homophobia, my

[2]From "The Brown Menace or Poem to the Survival of Roaches," *The New York Head Shop and Museum* (Detroit: Broadside, 1974), p. 48.

own hatred of myself for being queer. I have not wanted to admit that my deepest personal sense of myself has not quite "caught up" with my "woman-identified" politics. I have been afraid to criticize lesbian writers who choose to "skip over" these issues in the name of feminism. In 1979, we talk of "old gay" and "butch and femme" roles as if they were ancient history. We toss them aside as merely patriarchal notions. And yet, the truth of the matter is that I have sometimes taken society's fear and hatred of lesbians to bed with me. I have sometimes hated my lover for loving me. I have sometimes felt "not woman enough" for her. I have sometimes felt "not man enough." For a lesbian trying to survive in a heterosexist society, there is no easy way around these emotions. Similarly, in a white-dominated world, there is little getting around racism and our own internalization of it. It's always there, embodied in some one we least expect to rub up against.

When we do rub up against this person, *there* then is the challenge. *There* then is the opportunity to look at the nightmare within us. But we usually shrink from such a challenge.

Time and time again, I have observed that the usual response among white women's groups when the "racist issue" comes up is to deny the difference. I have heard comments like, "Well, we're open to *all* women; why don't they [women of color] come? You can only do so much...." But there is seldom any analysis of how the very nature and structure of the group itself may be founded on racist or classist assumptions. More importantly, so often the women seem to feel no loss, no lack, no absence when women of color are not involved; therefore, there is little desire to change the situation. This has hurt me deeply. I have come to believe that the only reason women of a privileged class will dare to look at *how* it is that *they* oppress, is when they've come to know the meaning of their own oppression. And understand that the oppression of others hurts them personally.

The other side of the story is that women of color and working class women often shrink from challenging white middle-class women. It is much easier to rank oppressions and set up a hierarchy, rather than take responsibility for changing our own lives. We have failed to demand that white women, particularly those who claim to be speaking for all women, be accountable about their racism.

The dialogue has simply not gone deep enough.

I have had to look critically at my claim to color, at a time when, among white feminist ranks, it is a "politically correct" (and sometimes peripherally advantageous) assertion to make. I must acknowledge the fact that, physically, I have had a *choice* about making that claim, in contrast to women who have not had such a choice, and have been abused for their color. I must reckon with the fact that for most of my life, by virtue of the very fact that I am white-looking, I identified with and aspired toward white values, and that I rode the wave of that southern Californian privilege as far as conscience would let me.

Well, now I feel both bleached and beached. I feel angry about this—the years when I refused to recognize privilege, both when it worked against me, and when I worked it, ignorantly, at the expense of others. These are not settled issues. That is why this work feels so risky to me. It is a discovery. It will bring me into contact with women who will invariably know a hell of a lot more than I do about racism, as experienced in the flesh, as revealed in the flesh of their writing. This process has already begun.

I think: what is my responsibility to my roots—both white and brown, Spanish-speaking and English? I am a woman with a foot in both worlds; and I refuse the split. I feel the necessity for dialogue. Sometimes I feel it urgently.

But one voice is not enough, nor two, although this is where dialogue begins. It is essential that radical feminists confront their fear of and resistance to each other, because without this, there *will* be no bread on the table. Simply, we will not survive. If we could make this connection in our heart of hearts, that if we are serious about a revolution—better—if we seriously believe there should be joy in our lives (real joy, not just "good times"), then we need one another. We women need each other. Because my/your solitary, self-asserting "go-for-the-throat-of-fear" power is not enough. The real power, as you and I well know, is collective. I can't afford to be afraid of you, nor you of me. If it takes head-on collisions, let's do it: this polite timidity is killing us.

As Lorde suggests in the passage I cited earlier, it is in looking to the nightmare that the dream is found. There, the survivor emerges to insist on a future, a vision, yes, born out of what is dark and female. The feminist movement must be a movement of such survivors, a movement with a future.

34 My Life as a Lesbian

Julia Penelope Stanley

I am one of those wimmin for whom there was never any doubt about my sexuality: I've always loved wimmin, and my mother was my first womonlove. My first conscious expression of my Lesbianism occurred when I was four or five. It was during World War II, and there was a song about "the girl that I marry." I was standing on our front porch, singing the song to myself, when I turned to my mother and said: "I want to marry a girl just like you." She said, "You can't marry a girl. Girls can't marry girls. Only boys can marry girls. You'll have to marry a boy." I decided then never to marry, because I had no intention of marrying a "boy." If I couldn't have what I wanted, I would have nothing.

My mother took me to our family doctor to make sure that there was nothing physically "wrong" with me. I had convinced her that there had been a "mistake" somewhere along the way. I remember the doctor examining me, tapping my knee with his rubber hammer; he assured my mother that I was physically a female, that everything was "in my head." So it was, and still is.

All of this had to take place before my father disappeared in the Bermuda Triangle in 1947, days before my sixth birthday. I remember him as a kind, gentle man who taught me to swim at three by throwing me into the water at Silver Springs, Florida; who had taught me to read by the time I was four; who had promised to teach me to play golf on my sixth birthday.

By the time I was nine, my mother and I were back in Miami, back in the house in which I spent most of my childhood. On Saturdays, I would go down to the Miami Public Library in Biscayne Park; I was reading my way through the stacks, starting with the A's. I got as far as the H's, when I discovered the books on "homosexuality." Few of them mentioned Lesbians, but I read and re-read the passages that described "mannish" wimmin with short, cropped hair; who wore men's clothes; wimmin who were "tough" and "swaggered." Wimmin defined by their love for other wimmin. And I thought to myself, "That's me!" I was excited. I knew what I was! I loved other wimmin! Now I had a "name" for it! I was a "homosexual." The knowledge was priceless to me, and I carried it secretly and proudly inside me.

Other things happened when I was nine. Till then, I had been weak and thin, sickly; most of my first- and second-grade years had been spent at home in bed. That summer, my mother sent me to Ohio to spend the summer on my godparents' farm. There, I "filled out." I learned to swing a scythe, to load hay, to carry five-gallon cans of water from the spring down the hill. The food I ate was fresh from the garden outside the cabin, strawberries heavy with cream from the two wimmin across the road who raised turkeys together. And I spent that summer fascinated with the large, pendulous breasts of my godmother. We played a game called "sneak-a-feel"; I loved it, delighted in the soft sensuality of her breasts.

When I returned home to Miami, R., a womon, had moved in with us; she had taken my room so my mother and I slept in the same bedroom. On Sundays, we got up and went down to Crandon Park to watch the sun rise over the ocean. We would leave before the crowds got there and filled the beach. Every Sunday morning the three of us had the beach, the water, and the sun to ourselves.

And during this time I had a best friend, M. I remember nothing about any sexual feelings I might have had for her, and doubt that I did. But we did everything together: hunted and collected butterflies and moths; collected rocks, seashells, spiders; played basketball, at which we both excelled; played in the swamp near my house (which was "forbidden" to us); raced prams up and down a small canal off the Miami River; snuck into the Indian villages that lined the river, finding there treasures of peacock feathers, porcupine quills, alligator teeth; and fantasized about what we would be when we grew up. I would be an oceanologist, an entomologist, a geologist, an astronomer, an archaeologist, a baseball player with the Brooklyn Dodgers. It *was* all in my head.

My mother bought me a microscope kit, had bookshelves built into my room so that I could display my many collections, bought me books on natural history, paid for my annual subscription to the *Junior Natural History* magazine. She, too, chased butterflies with me; saved "tomato" worms for me, learning from me how to feed them until they went into their chrysalis stage. My mother nurtured all of my fantasies but one. She carefully explained that my feelings of being a "homosexual" were "just a phase."

In the fifth grade, I became the "protector" of all the girls in my elementary school. I was big, I was strong, and I gloried in my ability to "beat up" the boys, and, yes, the other girls who bullied those smaller than themselves. I sent at least two boys to the hospital for "picking on" girls, one with a broken collarbone, the other with a cracked skull. Never did I start a fight without provocation; I defended those who could not, or would not, defend themselves. As a consequence, I was often suspended from school, and spent many days in the principal's office, where the teachers taught me to run the ditto machine for them, or let me take their classes for them while they went to the teachers' lounge.

In the sixth grade, the "crushes" began. I mooned, courted, wrote poems, and followed numerous girls around. Some of them would let me walk them home, but eventually their mothers would forbid them to speak to me. The mothers knew what was happening. I had entered what was to be a painful, confusing adolescence. When I was eleven, I had my first "experience" with another woman, my babysitter. We had grown up together. She was about three years older than I, and my mother would ask her to stay with me when she went out on dates. One night, M. J. began to act very strangely. She put on what she called "sexy" music, and started to do a striptease show for me. I was her rapt, if astonished, audience of one. She stripped down to her underpants and draped the rest of her body using a crocheted tablecloth as a "veil." I don't remember how long this went on. I do remember that she finally suggested we go to bed. Once there, she began to squeeze and stroke my yet unformed breasts, and urged me to do the same to her. I complied. Then I suggested that I lie on top of her, and I did. But suddenly she pushed me off, saying, "Only men can do that to women!" I shrank from her, confused, ashamed, bewildered. I didn't understand what I had done "wrong." We never spoke again.

While I was still in the sixth grade, my mother remarried. He was a bitter, violent, nasty man. Two months after the marriage, she had to have a hysterectomy. One night E. came to my room, drunk, and started asking me if I "liked" him. I lied. I said "yes." I hated him, but I understood perfectly well that expressing my hatred would only make *my* life miserable. He asked me if I would "be nice" to him. I understood this to refer to our new life together as a "family." I answered that I would "try." He kept urging me to "be nice" to him, and promised me a much longed-for first-baseman's mitt if I would. I said "yes," I would be "nice" to him. The next thing I knew, he had pushed me down on the bed and was thrusting away at my body. I was repulsed, and *angry*. I began to kick and flail under him, and must have gotten one good kick in where it hurt the most. He screamed, and I pushed him off of me onto the floor. He got up, cursing and yelling, and left. I locked my bedroom door, and slept with my bedroom door locked as long as I lived with him and my mother. I stopped going to the hospital with him to see my mother, because I didn't want to be in the car with him alone. I don't think my mother has ever forgiven me for not coming to see her in the hospital during this time.

When my mother had been home for a couple of weeks, I told her what had happened while she was gone. She was sitting in the living room. My stepfather went into the kitchen to make drinks. She tried to convince me that I had "imagined" everything; I refused to withdraw my account of the events. Finally, E. called me into the kitchen, urging me to "forget it"; "Let's be friends," he said. Later, I learned that his version of "being friends" would be to try to turn me against my mother. For a while, in fact, he succeeded.

After that, I spent as little time at home with "them" as possible. I became an avid church-goer and sang in the choir. I was also taking voice lessons, and had become a soloist with the First Methodist Church of Miami. There was a red-haired girl who was also in the choir; her name was N., and she was my first "serious crush." I followed her everywhere I could, found out where she lived, and lurked on the street waiting for a glimpse of her. Not much happened, though, beyond surreptitious hand-holding in the back of cars, until Christmas. I had two solos on consecutive Sundays, and I got through the first without error. The next Sunday, I was to sing "O Holy Night." N. and I were sitting on the front row, so that I could leave quietly to don my robes. We were holding hands, touching; I was alive with feelings. But when I sang that night, I cracked on the high note. Somehow, I got through the rest of the song, and made it back to the warmth of N. There, on the first pew of the church, we kissed and cuddled. She gave me the consolation I needed for my pain and humiliation.

After that, she stopped speaking to me, and I didn't understand until one Sunday I read either Ann Landers or "Dear Abby" in the *Miami Herald*. There, for everyone to read, was my humiliation. A "concerned mother" had written a letter about this "queer girl" in the church that no one knew how to deal with. My body went clammy, my hands sweated, my heart stopped. She was describing that night at Christmas as "shameful." I was "pitiful" and "queer." The columnist told the "concerned mother" to call my mother and have me taken to a psychiatrist for "help." I was "obviously in need of professional help." I closed the newspaper and decided to ignore it. But I never went back to the church.

Later that week, my mother asked me if I was the girl described in the newspaper the previous Sunday. By now, I had learned. I lied. I said no. She asked me if I was *sure* that it wasn't me. Again I lied and said no. And that was the only time my mother ever questioned me about the incident. But I carried it inside me, a hard, sharp pain that wouldn't leave me. It was the first "betrayal," and the hard place that remains still makes it difficult for me to completely give of myself. I probably never have. And the one thing I cannot psychologically tolerate is "betrayal."

From that time on, I constructed various theories that would explain me to myself, seizing anything that would make my love for wimmin "all right." When I was thirteen (or thereabouts) Christine Jorgenson became "hope" for me. I reasoned that I was "really" a man, the soul of a man trapped in a womon's body. An operation in Denmark would ease my pain. I asked my stepfather to pay for the operation. The response, of course, was horror and denial of my request. He and my mother assured me that I was "just going through a phase."

We had moved by then, and I began my ninth grade in a new school, Hialeah High School. In that year, I fell in love with S. Again, I courted and pursued, and was denied by her, at first. She had a crush on our chorus teacher who, it later turned out, was gay. In order to divert her, he pushed her in my direction. By the time she became interested, I had developed other interests of my own, but nothing that kept me from responding. Thus began a torrid affair that scandalized the entire school. I was oblivious. She loved me!

We exchanged poems with each other, read Edna St. Vincent-Millay to each other for hours over the phone, *This is My Beloved* by Walter Benton, and listened to classical music together. By now, we were in the tenth grade. S.'s best friend, L.A., hated me, and constantly threatened me if I didn't "leave S. alone." I was interested in several other girls, but S. was "it." I had no intention of backing off. Nothing physical happened, though, until Christmas, when S. came over to give me her present. We spent the day together, talking, reading, and listening to music. We were on the couch in the living room. I was sitting up and she was stretched out with her feet in my lap. I was innocently and absentmindedly stroking her legs. Suddenly, she jerked herself upright, grabbed me around the shoulders, and kissed me on the mouth. It was my first kiss and my body burned from the contact. My feelings that had been so vague and undefined crystallized when she kissed me.

I wanted more and more of the same. Everything in me surged upward to continue that kiss. But she abruptly drew back from me. "That can't happen ever again." "Why?" I wanted to know. "It just can't," she repeated. "I love you, S." "Yes, I love you, too. But it can't happen." In spite of her denials, I did kiss her once more before her mother came and picked her up. After that, I remember nothing except the lostness, the daze, the dreaming of kissing her.

Months passed. Spring came, and with spring came the annual state chorus contest in Tampa. We were both going. But S. was rooming with L.A., and I was to room with J., who belonged to the Church of Christ and worshipped Pat Boone. (I, too, joined the Church of Christ, because wimmin couldn't dance or wear lipstick. It was a "perfect cover.") On the bus, S. and I sat together, across the aisle from the chaperones. We *had* to touch each other. S. had the cunning to spread her coat out across our laps, and underneath her coat we held hands and touched constantly on that long, eight-hour bus-ride. Beyond thinking to cover our hands with her coat, neither of us thought of anything else but the strong, physical burning in which we were engulfed. (Later, the chorus teacher recounted to me the anxiety of the chaperones who knew perfectly well what was going on.) I could think of nothing but the touching of our hands under that coat.

When we finally got to Tampa, neither of us could really walk when we got off the bus. Somehow we got into the Hillsboro Hotel and went to our separate rooms. I was putting my clothes in a drawer when L.A. came into the room that J. and I were sharing. "Do you want to room with S?" she asked, her voice full of hatred and venom. I mumbled something like "Yes. But you're her roommate." She said, "I can room with J." And so, we switched rooms. I was alive with anticipation, but frightened and confused, too. I had no idea what would happen. I didn't know what to do. All that I did know was that S. wanted me.

I don't remember that we even left the room that night. I wish that I could truthfully say that "love found its own way." Perhaps, in a way, we did manage to "find ways," but I was less sure than she, clumsy, and embarrassed by my body. In spite of the exhilaration of at last being free to hold and touch her, I was afraid to undress except in the dark. Afraid that the sight of my body would so repulse her that she would reject me. I was overwhelmed by feelings of inadequacy and ignorance. I was not a man; I couldn't make love to her as a man would. And, looking back, I had no knowledge of my own body. I hadn't yet discovered masturbation, and I'd never heard of a female orgasm. Yet, all that I did know was that I wanted to touch her, to love her, and I discovered that night, amidst my own fears and insecurities, the joy of being inside a womon. I learned that night the intense and intimate presence of a womon's sexuality. Later that night, we stood together naked in front of the hotel window and danced in the moonlight, swaying and touching. We were together!

S. and I remained lovers until the end of our senior year in high school. Yet, in all that time, I never made love to her with my mouth, nor did I ever allow her to make love to me. I was ashamed because I wasn't a man; I don't know what she thought. By then, I had read *The Well of*

Loneliness for the first time, and every other paperback novel on "twilight love" that the male media published during the fifties. I fantasized that I would have "the operation," I would become a man and marry S.; or, alternatively, I would "pass" as a man, I would support her, and we would, either way, "live happily ever after."

We touched each other whenever and wherever we could. Her parents had, by now, forbidden her to see me, but we made love in houses under construction when I walked her home from school, in the bathroom of the Dade County Auditorium when we served there as ushers for ballets and concerts, the chiffon and taffeta of our formals rustling and whispering on the tiles. We made love in my bedroom to *Swan Lake*, Grieg's *Concerto in A minor*, the *Moonlight Sonata*, *Romeo and Juliet*. I wrote my first book of poetry, now destroyed. During our junior year, I heard of a bar for "queers" called Googie's, and I determined to seek out others "like me." S. swore that if I went there she'd never speak to me again, and so I lied, even to her.

My mother and stepfather went fishing in the Keys almost every weekend, and I had stopped accompanying them on their trips. On one of those weekends, I slicked my hair back, borrowed one of my stepfather's shirts, put on my jeans, and found my way to Googie's, on 17th Avenue. I paced with fear on the sidewalk in front of the bar, occasionally trying to see inside through the clouded windows. I couldn't see much. Finally, my fear won out and I went home without having set foot inside the place. Two weeks later, I was more successful. At fifteen, I walked into my first "gay" bar. I was petrified. And repulsed by what I saw. I stood by the door, trying to look "casual." Finally, a marred woman approached me and asked me to dance. She had few teeth, and the ones she had were rotten. Her eyes were bloodshot and hard, and she staggered as she walked. I had no way of knowing then that she was one of the "crippled." I reflexively recoiled from her and turned and fled. I vowed never to become "like her," hard, maimed, and grotesque.

After that, I restricted my attempts to meeting other "homosexuals" to waiting outside my house for the lunch wagon that went by every afternoon: The driver was a very "masculine" woman! As time passed, she came to recognize me and would wave to me as she went past. Beyond that, we did nothing, but the recognition was there, the recognition of sameness that I craved.

During this time, S. and I were still lovers, our passion continued unabated, and I had sworn to her that I'd never go to another "gay" bar. But, one night when I was ushering at the auditorium, a night that S. hadn't come, I was approached by W., a friend from school. He had intimated earlier that he had "a question" to ask me, something "personal." We sat in the lobby, I in a chair, my formal rustling around me, he in his "tux," kneeling by the chair. We tried "small talk," but tension surrounded us. Finally (this must have taken tremendous courage on his part), he said, "Are you and S. lovers? Are you gay?" I'd never heard the word "gay" in this context, yet I knew instinctively what he was asking. And I sat there. And sat there, and sat there. In silence. W. shifted uncomfortably on the floor. I thought; I thought long and hard, and finally lied to him. "No," I said. "No, I'm not gay." All he could say was "Oh. I'm sorry I asked you that."

But the matter didn't end for me there. I continued to think about his questions, and finally realized that he was asking because *he* was "gay." Two weeks later, in the lunch line, I said, casually: "W., remember that question you asked me a couple of weeks ago? The answer is yes." And his eyes lit up, his face beamed with recognition, he whooped, threw his tray in the air, and hugged me! And I had my first "gay friend." Through W., I met the other faggots in the school, discovered that they went "cruising" together downtown, and soon joined them in their nightly excursions to the center of Miami. There I met the other "gays" from Miami's high schools, and we formed what I can only call a "gang." We went and did everything together. (Well, almost everything.) There was an apartment building close to the downtown area called "Sex Manor," where gay people lived, and we "hung out" there all of our free time. On Sundays, we went to the gay beach on 21st Street, and there I began to meet other wimmin. I managed to get false I. D. by registering to vote (and lying about my age) and getting a driver's license (again with a false birthdate on it). In this way, all of us gained access to the many gay bars that flourished in Miami during the fifties. And so, I was introduced to "gay life."

I had a new word for myself, gay. I wasn't "homosexual," or "queer," I was "gay." It's hard to explain now the tremendous freedom that word bestowed in those years. More than anything, I now knew for sure that I was *not* alone, that I wasn't the only "one" in the world. The year was 1957. Armed with my new identity, my new belonging, I sat my mother down one night and said, "There's something you should know, because I can't lie to you, Mother. I'm gay." I guess then she knew that I had discovered "others." But her response swept the rug out from under me. Very confidentially, she said, "Well, I've known that for some time now, and I was gay, too. Remember R., the woman who came to live with us for a while when you were young? She and I were lovers." I guess if a mother had told her daughter that at any other time, it would have been cause for rejoicing. But what she said next chilled me thoroughly. She asked me if I'd ever done "that" to another womon. I didn't understand what she meant. She said, "you know, kissing her 'down there' with your mouth." I said, honestly, "no," that I hadn't. Then she told me, "Don't ever do that, or I'll never let you kiss me again." And it was several years before I did.

In other ways, however, my life improved. I now had friends, a lot of friends, and I'd never had many friends at any other time in my life. On the weekends when my parents went fishing, W. and all of us would troop downtown and announce that I was having a party. And everyone would come! And every time the cops would bust up the party. Once they caught two of the men out in the backyard on a blanket. Soon, I had a "record" down at the police station. But my mother took care of that. *She* started staying home from the fishing trips, too, and acting as "chaperone," which meant that when the cops turned up, as they always did, she could turn them away. Thus she protected me, and all my friends, during my senior year in high school.

Virtually the only time I saw my mother that year was on those weekends. The rest of the time I was either at school, having chorus practice, or at volleyball, basketball, or softball practice, or busy with one of my "honorary" societies. I had learned by then what was to become my major weapon that would protect me from the society that would try, more than once, to destroy me. I had a brain, and I knew that I could do almost anything as long as my brain performed well. I honed it, sharpened it, strengthened it, and learned to use it. (And I still carry it before me like a brandished sword.) For that reason, I spent my days, from dawn to dusk, at school. I went home to eat and left again, to roam the streets and bars of Miami, often returning just in time to catch the school bus, and so hung over that my French teacher, who was also gay, would have to give me aspirins before I could manage to sit upright through class. (Let me say here that I owe much to my high school teachers who were gay men. They knew what was happening, and they nurtured me through those difficult years. My P.E. teachers, on the other hand, ultimately saw to it that I was ostracized and discouraged from further participation in athletics. I was "too obvious.") So it was the gay men who took me in, befriended me, and introduced me to other wimmin. Without them, I would have still been "alone."

Except for S., and she backed off during the spring of our senior year. I still loved her. I couldn't imagine loving anyone else. But one day, after a rehearsal of the senior show I had written and was directing, she called me backstage in the auditorium before we went to class, saying there was something she had to tell me. I no longer remember her exact words, but the gist of it was that she couldn't stand to be ostracized and live outside society. Furthermore, she revealed to me that she was doing this because E.M., a boy she'd been dating to allay her parents' suspicions, had threatened to go and tell the dean of women that we were Lesbians and have us kicked out of school. She was afraid that he'd really do it, and he probably would have. And she tried to make me swear that I wouldn't "do anything." I left her standing there in the wings of the stage, and I ran to our next class, which the three of us shared, College Prep English. I ran into the room, stopped in front of E.'s desk, and started yelling. I no longer clearly remember what I screamed at him, except that I taunted him, asking him exactly *what* he thought he was going to tell the dean of women. And I dared him to do it. He turned purple, and tried to get up out of his desk to get at me, but he got caught in it, and wound up falling on the floor, desk and all wrapped around him. I went and sat down. S. walked in seconds later, took one look at him on the floor, still writhing with anger and humiliation, and strode to her seat, giving me only one hostile glance. Thus ended my three-year relationship with her. I heard several years later that she and E. had finally married, after they graduated from a music college in Louisiana, and that's all I ever heard of her. Often, though, I think of her, and wonder if she remembers as I do, or whether she's one of those who has tried to forget that she loved another woman in high school. I often wonder what she's doing now.

My life, then and since, has been a continual process of "coming out." When I was sixteen, my mother asked me if I planned to "spend the rest of my life butting my head against a stone wall," and I said, truthfully, "yes." She told me then that I would lose, but I've never believed her, and I never will.

But there's more to the story, in spite of all that I've left out, like the summer that my mother sent me back to my godparents' farm in Ohio to get me away from S., or the other wimmin I loved during high school. There's always more to the story. I met Merril during Christmas vacation my first year in college; it was her first year, too. She said she was "straight," I determined to "bring her out." I fell deeply in love with her. She accepted me unquestioningly as I was; with her I could be all of my selves, and she never harshly criticized me or ridiculed me. (By then, I was a "butch," as a result of letting another womon touch me. The next day I had arrived at the beach to learn that she was telling everyone that I'd "gone femme" for her. Except for sporadic attempts by various lovers to change me, I was a "stone butch" until 1972.) Merril threatened all of my carefully constructed defenses, and, in panic, I ran from her, stopped corresponding (we were at different schools) without explanation or good-bye. I've never forgiven myself for my cowardice and fear, nor have I ever told her this.

Shortly after I broke off communication with Merril, Florida State University (in Tallahassee) was "visited" by the Charlie Johns Investigating Committee on Communism and Homosexuality. Only the "homosexuals," however, were purged from FSU, and every other educational institution in the state. I was among them, although my fate was easier than that of most. The wimmin in my dorm circulated a petition, asserting that I'd never bothered any of them, and that they didn't think that my "personal problem" was just cause for expulsion from the university. It was 1959. By then I was notorious across the state for my wild parties and "indiscretion." But the dean of women promised me a "clean" transcript if I'd transfer to the University of Miami, where she knew the dean of women and could get me admitted (with a psychiatrist's approval).

Only eight weeks into the fall semester, however, the university found out that I had my own apartment off-campus. The old woman across the hall had turned me in to the dean because I had "men sleeping in my apartment."(!!) I was kicked out of the University of Miami, but not before the dean urged me to "seek help," because, as she put it, "society needed my mind." My rejoinder was: "How can you ask me to change, to not be myself, so that the very society that wants me to change can then have the use of my brain?" She didn't have an answer for that; no one ever will. I decided then that society might have the "use" of my brain, but it would be on my terms, not theirs.

I did, finally, get through college, and graduate school, and I even got a job, in 1968, at the University of Georgia. In the meantime, I had a lot of help from a lot of people. One of them, the dean of night students at City College, helped get me admitted to day school. I had also joined the New York Chapter of the Daughters of Bilitis, and it was DOB that provided funds to pay for my textbooks from the Blanche M. Baker Scholarship Fund. (I hope they believe, as I do, that their money was well-invested.) I subscribed to *One* and to *The Ladder*, and had articles published in both in the early sixties.

But in 1968, I was "in the closet." At least, that's the way *I* thought of it. Then the Women's Movement began, and in 1969, Stonewall happened. And my students happened to me. In 1972, I came "out front" as a Lesbian on campus, an Assistant Professor, untenured, but defiant. Again, I brandished my intelligence, this time in the form of publications. The rest is now herstory, our story. I have written and spoken of those events elsewhere and at other times.

I have written much more here than I planned to, but I wanted to include what I consider the "important" points in my coming out process. I must still "come out" every day at work, in my classes, at professional meetings, in my writing. Too many people would still like to pretend that my Lesbianism is "irrelevant." But I know it isn't. It is too easy for many to dismiss words like *sexism* and *heterosexism* as "empty political rhetoric." But my life is contained in those words, and, while I have gained strength and support from the wimmin's movement, I am still aware that I am "crippled" by my early experiences. The healing process is long and slow, but with the help of other strong wimmin, I am healing. To all of the wimmin who have loved me, I dedicate my story. This is perhaps the third or fourth time that I've told it in anything approximating completeness. Too often I've trivialized it, or told it briefly; mostly, I've tried to make it funny. There is too much pain in it for much retelling, and so, for all the wimmin who will read it here, those who've heard only "pieces" of it, and now know that I failed to tell them "all," I ask forgiveness and understanding for my short-comings, for my silences, for my omissions, for my inability to give of myself. More than anything, I don't want another woman to have to seek her identity as I have, ever again.

Coming In or Will the Real Lesbian Please Stand Up?

35

Miriam G. Keiffer

I first realized I was a Lesbian in 1968 when I was 26 years old. I had always known that I loved, was attracted to, was comfortable with women, but before the Women's Movement I didn't have a word for someone who felt those feelings.

I had heard the word *Lesbian* before. My mother once told me that a very athletic high school friend of my sister's was a Lesbian and when I brought a very good college friend home with me, who I had spent long hours doing everything with (I mean we were inseparable), my mother asked, "Is she a Lesbian?" I didn't know. What was a Lesbian?

My high school Spanish teacher spent many afternoons teaching me and a small group of girls what she called *un poquito de culturita general* or 'a smattering of general culture'. We spent many hours learning the poetry of Sappho, a Lesbian, Garcia Lorca, a homosexual and Pita Amores, a Mexican writer/personality and also a Lesbian. So I thought that Lesbians had to be poets, jocks or large women, and since I was none of these things, I could not be a Lesbian.

Sexuality had nothing to do with being a Lesbian since only men were sexual, and in order for something sexual to happen, a male member had to be present. Males were the necessary ingredient. In any case, sex was dirty, demeaning and painful. It was also my duty to my husband if I ever got married. How did I know these things? My mother told me.

I first realized that there was great fear of Lesbians, when an acquaintance of mine who belonged to the same Princeton NOW chapter told me that she wouldn't go to the Congress to Unite Women because she had heard that there were going to be Lesbians there. I wanted to know why that would make a difference to her. She told me that they might proposition her. I told her that the chance of anyone propositioning her at a conference to unite women was highly unlikely, and besides if someone did, she could say "No" if she wasn't interested and "Yes" if she was interested. She never spoke to me again. (I think that some of the fear women have about Lesbians comes out of our own inability to say no to things, to be responsible for our decisions, to believe that what we want or don't want counts. I think we are taught we should not say no to a man who is aroused by us because it is somehow our fault that he is aroused and that if we don't take the responsibility and immediately help him to decrease his sexual tension, his balls will turn blue and his penis will fall off! Many women see Lesbians in this male, heterosexual light and think that it would be as hard to say no to a Lesbian. We must learn to take control of our bodies and take responsibility for our own sexual arousal.)

I went to the Conference with much curiosity. I had high hopes of seeing a Lesbian. And I did, I saw lots of Lesbians, and they didn't look very different from anyone else except that they seemed stronger, more articulate, more attractive, more powerful, and funnier than the other women. Rita Mae Brown was the first up-front Lesbian I ever saw. She was marvelous. Small, beautiful, strong, wearing a "Super-Dyke" T-shirt which she had dyed lavender, incredibly articulate and funny as hell. She was a Lesbian I could identify with. When she asked for women in the audience to join their Lesbian sisters at the front of the auditorium, I jumped up, eager to be counted as a sister traveler. A friend sitting with me, who I knew to be a Lesbian, would not join us. When I asked her why she said it was too dangerous. That made me want to be a Lesbian even more. After all if Kate Millett and Anselma Del'Olio were not afraid to be Lesbian-identified, why should I be? Besides I thought the Lavender Menace take-over of the conference was done delightfully and humorously. It was the best thing that happened. Far more exciting than the endless speeches and painful disputes about who and how many women would be allowed to speak. These women had seized the time and created a Lavender Happening. They were terrific! I am still in love with all of them, but I have never told them, of course. I am not that kind of Lesbian.

I first went to bed with a woman for the purpose of having a sexual experience when I was 27. I remember it well, because it happened around the same time that I learned to masturbate. I am dreadfully sorry that I didn't learn to masturbate until I was 27 because learning to masturbate helped me to like myself and helped me to feel powerful and independent and it would have been nice to have had those feelings and that *pleasure* at an earlier age, but I am glad that I learned when I did so that I didn't have to spend any more time feeling frigid and impotent. I had had a lot of what could be called sexual adventures with girls in my pre-pubescent days and in my early teens. I didn't think of these experiences as sexual, however, because they didn't involve men and they weren't genitally-oriented. I thought that men were the necessary and sufficient ingredient for sexual adventures and therefore I was ashamed, embarrassed, humiliated, inadequate, frigid and mystified, when I was involved in sexual adventures with men. I didn't feel anything except sometimes repulsion, sometimes fear, sometimes boredom, but mostly sweaty and frustrated, but pretending to have a great time. Which is not to say that I hadn't had some good times with men in bed, but these were all exceptional situations and the men were either very young, very old, too fat (by society's standards), too thin (by society's standards), too short (by society's standards), too tall (by society's standards), virginal, shy, Black or gay. The truth of the matter is that I have never had a good time in bed with a man who was a heterosexual mesomorphic macho male (society's ideal male sex-object) and until I thought of myself as a Lesbian, I thought it was *my* fault.

I had had a lot of loving feelings about women as a teenager too. I had crushes on girlfriends and older girl scouts and lots of infatuations with older women, some of whom were alcoholic. I loved my high school gym teacher, my Spanish teacher, my art teacher, my drama teacher, my algebra teacher, Maria Elena, Maria Elena's mother, the school nurse, and, of course, my mother. And all of the senior girls when I was a high school freshman. But I didn't think these feelings were sexual and I didn't think I was a Lesbian for having these feelings.

So when I was 27 and I thought I was a Lesbian, and I was learning how to masturbate, I was working on a project with a woman who thought she was a Lesbian and who was/is probably the world's most creative and committed masturbator. The project we were working on had to do with female sexuality and we kept having these discussions about how good it was for women to go to bed with women, how righteous, how beautiful, but neither one of us had ever gone to bed with a woman for explicitly sexual reasons and neither of us knew quite what to do. The situation became intolerable and we knew that we had to go to bed together, if only to be good researchers. So we made this rational decision to go to bed, and we did. I had a good time, and I thought she did too, only to find out five years later when we finally talked about it waiting for her train to come and take her away, that she thought I had had a lousy time because I didn't make a lot of noise and didn't say anything about the fact that I had enjoyed it. She had felt very disappointed, sad and impotent. We never went to bed together again and I thought, until I heard the truth in the train station, that it was because her interest in going to bed with me was purely clinical and once she satisfied her insatiable scientific curiosity, there was no reason left for her to go to bed with me. We were both very busy, anyhow, being buffeted by the politics of the times at our respective academic institutions—so I didn't even wonder about it too much.

After that when people asked me if I was attracted to women sexually, I said "Yes!" I gave a talk to a large group of clinicians on alternate life styles in which I discussed my own sexual orientation. People in the audience rushed at me saying "how brave" and "will you go to bed with me," others whispered, "how tacky" and "what a narcisssist." I got letters from small town fundamentalists on scented paper telling me that snakes like me should be beaten with large sticks back into the holes we came out of. Others told me they would pray for me, others wanted me to come to their town and talk to the Rotarians about my sexuality. A prisoner wanted me to be his way station in life. My mother saw the article about me in the newspaper and wrote me a note saying, "this is a life style?"

I joined the women's caucus of the Gay Academic Union and loved many of the women in the caucus, although I felt defensive about the fact that although I knew I was a *Lesbian*, some of the women thought I wasn't a Lesbian because I had a male lover at the time, and I also had been married and too many of my friends were gay males. However, I knew I was a *Lesbian* because of the way I felt about women and that the fact that I also had loved and was loved by some men didn't make me any less of a *Lesbian*.

One very conservative, uptight, male GAU member, angered by my feminism, my activism, and my power called a secret breakfast meeting to denounce me as a *false Lesbian*. The *Lesbians* at the breakfast meeting were incensed and gave testimonials about my Lesbianism. He screamed that sleeping with women doesn't make her a Lesbian. My answer to that is sleeping with men doesn't make me *not* a Lesbian, and men have a nerve determining who is a real Lesbian and who is not a real Lesbian, anyway!

I told my mother I was a Lesbian about a year ago. She asked me, "What do Lesbians do?" I told her, "they do everything!" "I mean in bed," she said. So I told her all that I knew a Lesbian might do in bed, and then because I am a sexologist and a compulsive educator, I told my mother everything that every combination of people and animals might do in bed, alone and in groups. "Oh!" she said, "I see!" And I knew that she did see. She admitted that genitals made her queasy, that orchids looked like female genitals and that was why she didn't like orchids. I forgave her for everything. And then she asked me whether some of her longterm friendships with women could be Lesbianic in nature. I said, "yes, they could." "Oh!" she said, "I see!" And I knew that she did.

36

Dear Mom and Dad

Wendy Judith Cutler

February 1976

Dear Mom and Dad:

You are asking me to explain to you why you don't understand me. Well, this is incredibly difficult, and probably impossible, because if I could express this to you, you wouldn't be so confused.

The basic misconception you have about me is that I am looking for a man to fulfill me, to make me complete, to fall in love with and to marry and make a family with.

This is not me. I am not in the market for a man. I don't think I ever was, but I didn't accept myself as much as I do now. Perhaps in a revolutionary or post-revolutionary society that has been struggling against sexism (*Sexism*—that word that I'm sure you've heard me say and write, but you probably don't understand its meaning or significance to me) and working towards the abolition of distinctions of male and female, I would be open to pursuing relationships with men.

The fact is that I do not feel that it is worthwhile to pursue relationships with men, not sexual or romantic ones, at least. I find that my friendships with men are most satisfying when we relate to each other as friends. Contrary to this, my relationships with women are most vital and of most importance to me. My closest relationships have always been with other women. And this is not merely because I have not yet found the "right man." As far as I'm concerned, he doesn't exist. I am not, at this time, open to marriage or to building a family with a man of my choice. And, I clearly realize that I *have* that choice.

In most ways, I choose to focus on my connections with women, and have found that my everyday life—at work, school, in political work, and my free time—includes mostly women. And this is mostly women who are women-identified, politically conscious and strong (or struggling to be strong and to overcome our weakness—*not* our individual weakness, but due to our reduced status as women in this society).

I realize that you take issue with most of the statements I make. And I am fully aware of our differences in outlook and perspective. I am not looking at these issues blindly and without looking at all viewpoints. You must remember that I am in an institution that explores, studies, examines and is challenging. This, at least, is my interest in being here, in doing what I am doing.

Everyone in this society (and in most, not all, cultures and societies—I have been researching this) is raised to be heterosexually-defined. To believe (however strongly and firmly) that if we are women we need to love, live with and marry men in order to become whole, complete, "real" women; for men, it is the converse. And those who don't conform to this culturally-defined (not biologically-dictated) category are considered "deviants," "abnormal," "queers," yes, homosexuals.

It has taken me a long time to get here. But, I reject the classification of heterosexual, and I mean a lot more than a sexual description. I am a woman and I am close and loving with other women. I identify with the term lesbian. (I expect you to cringe here and/or feel 1) disgusted; 2) guilt; 3) confusion; 4) anger; 5) scared *or* some or all of those.) Well, you must react however you react. I have no control over my decisions. I have decided—politically, emotionally, intellectually, physically—to relate to this word, *lesbian*. In a different sort of society (as I've tried to explain) there would be no need to use these labels. Because actually I find so-called sexual labels to be quite limiting. But in order to function in this society, I realize that I feel connected to certain kinds of people—who are working towards radical transformations in this society, *and* who are experiencing the limitations of living in a capitalist, sexist, racist, classist and heterosexist culture.

I am a lesbian socialist feminist revolutionary. And my life and lifestyle and political viewpoints are not "traditional" or regular. But I feel good about myself, my understanding of oppression in this society and my understanding of who I feel most connected with and who is working towards the same kind of changes I am. I feel *very* connected to other women who are challenging the basic assumptions that most of society conforms to.

I do not see myself as static, non-changing. This does not mean that you may not take me seriously as I am. If you are unable to do this, then I am afraid that we will not be able to get along. I do not want to feel defensive, because I am quite excited and feel good about myself and my friends. I am sensible, mature, sensitive and have good judgment. You may try to believe that I am uninformed, influenced, illogical, mentally unstable, physically unattractive and otherwise Sick and a Loser. Well, I do not fit any of those descriptions, and you will never (nor will anyone or anything else) convince me to believe those as accurate descriptions.

I do not see myself as part of a kooky, freaky, drug-crazed (and there *is* a distinction between "hard" drugs and marijuana) sleazy subculture. More and more women are affirming their connections with each other and are defining themselves as political lesbian feminists. The assumption I make about all women-identified-women is that we are confronting this system (the capitalist system) that robs us (robs everyone whether they know it or not—except Ruling Class White Males) of our freedom to live. To live a life that is grounded in our *real* needs, not imagined, designed, constructed, artificial, created needs. This necessitates changes in our consciousness and in the concrete economic-political system that is in charge. (It is the function of capitalism to *create* needs, and the supposed "way" to live to best satisfy our needs.)

Unfortunately, efforts to "liberate" women (I am assuming that you know the meaning of the term "liberation" as it is used in liberation movements) in countries that are experiencing revolutionary changes have not successfully destroyed male domination and forms of sexism that oppress all women (and, in fact, all men too, despite the fact that most men benefit from the oppression of women). So, I am speaking about the kind of revolution that has never occurred yet, and that is actually more revolutionary and potentially liberating than anything that you can imagine.

I don't look to the government, or even to the Revolutionary Radical Movement Groups to make these changes that I'm talking about. I look to myself and to my friends—a category that encompasses all of those who are close, caring, loving and supportive of me. You have probably heard me speak about them, but you never have listened to me very carefully because you have not valued my friends. To you, they are not important as long as none of them is a man—potential husband.

In closing, I refuse to be assaulted on the phone (that is how I find myself feeling) by questions about meeting men and how I haven't found the right one, yet. You see, nothing that I am involved in is anything that you can "relate" to. This is at once my feeling, and also my fear. For I don't want to accept that this is true, that I will become alien and removed from you. This is not my wish.

I hope this letter makes some things clearer than they were before. This is my hope.

In the spirit of keeping you informed,
Your daughter

Update

In response to the circulation and publication of the letter that I wrote to my mother and father coming out to them, I feel the need (and sense the responsibility) to provide an update. I will attempt to share both the reactions I've received from them and my responses and feelings about having written the letter, about my family, about my lesbianism. Naturally, I could not begin to thoroughly explore this rigorous goal, but will attempt to explore the highlights.

My mother's letter following the one that I sent began with the sentence: "The day we received your letter was the worst day of my life." I've memorized the words. The "story" (it almost seems like some fairytale/nightmare) goes on to explain that my father blacked out twice in the office that day (he's a dentist; she's his dental assistant), and the last time he fell and fractured some of his ribs. Then she continues with her reaction to what I've written: "You're not *like that*. Someone has brainwashed you into believing that you're *that way*." Towards the end, she says, "We love you very very much. Please don't hurt us." In the letters to come, "hurt" was to change to "disgrace" and I was starting to be taken seriously (though not really) enough so that my mother tried to convince me that "your [my] future is bleak."

Despite my protestations regarding the "bleakness" of my future and repeated assurances that my life "feels good to me. I really feel very good about myself and about what I'm doing. Really I am. I'm fine"—no sign of any particle of tolerance or acceptance was communicated. I admit that wanting acceptance is a little far-fetched. And when I think of it, I don't think that I really ever expected *acceptance*. I didn't know exactly *what* to expect. Except that I expected a lot of tears and disbelief (though knowledge of). But, if I had known that it would have been *this* bad—this strong of an indictment against my lesbianism, against me—I don't think that I would have written it.

It was painful (to say the least) to be forced, again and again, to lie in response (self-defense to the questions my mother would ask and the probing that she would put me through over the phone. "Met any boys?" she'd cautiously but blatantly press. When I told her that I had been accepted into the delegation that was chosen to visit the People's Republic of China next spring, she asked, "Are there any men going?" She was relieved to know that there were. Any glimmer of hope she can snatch that someday the "right" man will fall into my life (with my willful maneuvering, of course) she is determined to hold on to. I could have learned how to lie better, like some of my friends, whom I must say I admire a great deal sometimes, for being able to schmaltz it up on the phone or even in person. I've thought about the stories that I'd like to tell (like the one about having fallen in love with "the man" who is Jewish and just old enough and from a good family *and* is gay!).

So I'd run out of things to say on the phone practically just after we'd start talking. I have a herstory of being quite close to my mother. That heightened the distance and awkwardness I felt whenever we'd talk or be together. Shopping together—our great activity together— became anxiety- and nerve-ridden. I was sick of saying "no" to her "Anything new? ... anything else?" The "anything" meant a man, a potential boyfriend, husband, protector, *my* security. I have never indicated that I was preparing to be a wife and mother and was even quite blatant about my distaste and criticism of those roles as the *only* means of fulfillment and satisfaction for a woman. I always looked to my brother as a model—never her. Both of my parents were excellent providers and had little trouble (well, probably not really) filling their roles well and complementing each other as partners. But I never desired to recreate their relationship in a future marriage with a man. I don't know yet all of how I feel about the concept of marriage between women, but relationships between women are so complex and different (I believe strongly) that my parents can never serve as role models for my potential relationships.

Nevertheless, I am not validated so long as I do not procure a husband, a house, a baby. I am currently enrolled as a graduate student in a doctoral program called "History of Consciousness" at the University of California at Santa Cruz, and benefit by having work as a teaching assistant during some of the year, which has some very worthwhile aspects to it, and carries with it a reasonable amount of privilege—both economically and professionally. However, neither of them validates my work, but only see me as a single woman, alone in the world, outside and on the fringes of society, missing the love and security that a relationship with a man could provide for me. My rejection of that is unacceptable to them. They have a strong resistance and heterosexual training that prevents them from identifying in any way but tragically fearful to the term, *lesbian.* So, I am denied recognition as a lesbian by my parents; and at the same time, I am seen *only* as lesbian by most of heterosexual society. This is frustrating and makes any relationship with my parents nearly impossible for they will at once never accept *and* always only see my lesbianism from now on.

Much to my surprise, my mother's letters came to me with a weekly punctuality. This is unusual in that she nearly never writes me.

Contrary to my expectations, my father didn't write until over a month from when I had first written. His letter brought messages that struck me as being even more distasteful and dissatisfying than my mother's. He claimed to respect me and considered me intelligent and thoughtful. However, he stated (pleaded) that "*Our* only problem is mother." His request of me (he never asks me to do specific things) was to never again write and speak the words *gay* or *lesbian* to mother. "You must give her every chance to believe that you aren't that way. Your reaction will be most important to me. *Fuck*. He plays up to me by saying that he respects me, and then tells me never to be honest again, as his one demand. I felt more ripped off by him than by my mother. At least she's honest about her non-acceptance. He isn't. It struck me that he could be having the exact same feelings about me but never say that. In many ways my mother seems more honest and direct than him. At least I *know* what she's thinking, the horrid thoughts and fears that lurk within her mind. And, I can't blame her. Well, not totally. She has worked hard to acquire the good ol' American heterosexist racist classist sexist brainwashing. Her values and attitudes make sense to her. She can go anywhere and find validation for them. She does not know who's like me, other than depraved, immoral, sick stereotypes of queers.

What Did I Expect? I didn't expect what I've gotten—complete and total rejection. Well, almost. They say that they still love me, but "Please don't disgrace us" (Letter #2). Now *that's* getting down to it. They're not worried about *my* happiness and security. Well, to a certain extent they are. Predominantly they are concerned with *their* reputations, futures, the future that they want me to help complete for them. No gay daughter can provide them with the *nachas* they deserve. "You can't tell me that I raised a gay daughter." She doesn't know how I could ever turn out gay when I was brought up so heterosexually. She feels similarly about my politics. Where did she go wrong? she wonders. She feels as though she is to blame. How else can she make sense out of what has happened?

What Has Happened? I reject the classification of heterosexual. I identify with the term *lesbian* (my letter). I refuse to find my fulfillment in a relationship with a man. I refuse to focus my primary emotional, intellectual, physical, sexual energy on men. It isn't that I just "haven't found the right man, yet" (Letter #1). "He doesn't exist" (Letter #1).

I am a strange (hidden) breed in straight Amerikan culture. I acknowledge that. I can't go anywhere and see other lesbians. Not openly. Not yet. I do have a great deal of support from my friends and peers. I am no longer connected to the family in the way that I was. And yet, I am still in some strong and stubborn way connected, longing for a feeling of connection and identification that I once felt that I had, thought that I needed and wanted and treasured.

My decision to come out to my parents reflects my desire to be open, honest, direct about my lesbianism; reflects my need to express myself without the reservations, the repression that gay people are forced, coerced to succumb to. I am fighting that. And a lot more. *And*, I am not fighting alone. We are everywhere. We are coming out. More and more and always more after that. We have always existed just now starting to acknowledge each other, ourselves. And it is feeling wonderful and terrible and frightening and exhilarating and we are not alone and we are getting stronger and stronger, expressing, not repressing ourselves. Challenging, not accepting a system, rules that only bind and separate us.

These are but a few reasons I came out to my parents.

I don't want to be confused as being straight. I respect myself and my friends and the goals that we are struggling towards. An essential element of these goals is the right to be who we are, as we challenge this society that won't allow us our rights.

I have no illusions that by being open about my lesbianism and my rejection of straight society I am gallantly speeding up the revolution. I do not see lesbianism, in itself, as a political strategy for revolution. However, by being an open lesbian, who is also committed to making revolutionary changes in this society, I am helping to insure that the revolutionary changes we make will include the rights and legitimation of gay people, and especially, of lesbians. The destruction of capitalism and patriarchy hinges on the need for complete liberation of all peoples—all peoples including gay women and men. Up to this point in history, no revolution has guaranteed the rights and interests of gay people.

By being an open lesbian, I am doing what I can to lay my claim for the kind of revolutionary changes that *must* occur in order for gay people to be fighting in that struggle. Working towards a socialist revolution *is* my commitment, my struggle. No one is going to convince me that I should disguise my caring and love for women or my disgust at heterosexual repressive society. I do not expect my parents to relate to or understand this struggle. I do, however, expect all committed revolutionary people to be fighting against heterosexism, in all its subtle and blatant forms. *Because* it is all peoples' struggle, too.

37 Queer

Elizabeth W. Knowlton

Coming out—a process. *Coming out*—a happening. *Coming out*—a political step. Did I come out at 15 when my younger friend turned to me in the darkness of "sleeping over" and kissed me on the mouth? Or did I come out the summer I lived with my boyfriend in Seattle and tip-toed into the local Lesbian Resource Center to read *The Ladder*? Did I come out at 26 when I had a one-night stand with the visiting bi-sexual who spent most of our time together telling me of her good relationships with her ex-husband and her gay male friends? Or did I really come out when I began an extended relationship at 27 with my roommate of two years?

Am I "out" today when I tell some people I am gay (while they never have to tell me they're straight), and others (mainly men) whisper it anyway, and still others go on thinking I'm asexual? Why is it simpler to announce in print that I'm a Lesbian than to tell my neighbor?—to identify myself as a homosexual to public groups than to tell the woman at the next desk that I love women? It is almost easier to let people think that I only have violent sexual urges for women and feel no attraction for men than to try to communicate the experience of feminism to anyone who has not been affected by it over the past 10 years.

I do not happen to be 6 feet tall, do not have broad shoulders and narrow hips (à la *Well of Loneliness*), do not enjoy participating in sports. I wear my hair long, like dresses (although I no longer wear them in mixed company), and played with dolls until I was a teenager. I, like the average woman in this repressed society, have rarely had strong physically sexual passions—more in the head than in the body. I initiate new relationships. I welcome new friendships. I do not spend every evening in a bar. I go to work. I cook meals. I read, go to the laundromat, and watch softball games played by other Lesbians. Coming out to me is much more than expressing another sexual preference. It is finding and developing a whole self-identity and then becoming comfortable with it.

I have not been home in over four years. In a sense I cannot go home again. I don't mean that I cannot get off the NY bus on South Street by the three gas stations and the cleaners and walk the four blocks home along Leland Avenue. I don't mean that I can't go up the walk between the lilacs, dark and light in May, and the spruce trees planted twenty years ago. I tried that walk, every month out of NYC, then several times a year, then just at Christmas when I lived in North Carolina. And every visit followed the same pattern—boredom on my part with the surface interactions which my mother insisted upon, then irritation with my father's male self-confidence, the way he kept growing while my mother didn't, the way he would try to draw me into his omnipotent understanding of my mother's sad case—an arthritic cripple before she was 50, "and she just never will do anything to make herself better."

Soon I would be pushing my beliefs in their faces, unable to bear the bland self-satisfaction of their so ordinary lives. For they *were* ordinary despite my mother's continual class pretensions. She would refuse to deal with anything important to me—feminism mostly. Long before the word again became current, she and I were wrangling about sex, children, work, the neighbors, and my friends. Or I would wrangle, and she would freeze up, refusing to face anything outside the safe, known household, afternoon bridge parties, her silver service, situation comedies on television, fiction and upperclass biography from the local library, taxi rides to the doctor's. Sometimes sitting there in the living room, I would feel it all weighing down upon me, a pressing claustrophobic intensity. Upstairs alone was no better. There I heard the voices: "Now, Elizabeth—Can't you ever do anything but criticize?— Answer back, answer back, not another word—You know, Elizabeth, there's something a little *queer* about you." Tight-lipped. *Queer* in the old-fashioned sense she meant, of course. *Odd. Weird.* But unwittingly my mother had made what is to me an important connection.

The struggle with my mother involved my potential as seen in her. I begged for validation of what I could be without knowing why we fought. Over and over she would say that she cared about me, but at no time was she able to help me grow up. She was frozen in eternal souring girlhood herself, with no room to move, no happiness but in new babies who too soon fought her tiny nest.

The struggle with my father was more insidious. He was always so rational, so helpful, so right. He always won. Whether the argument terminated in a physical spanking when I was small or just with me in tears when I grew older, the message was always the same. There was no way I could win, certainly not without joining Daddy. To be like a man— to succeed in the "working" world and put down women like mother who did no "real work"—that was my only escape from being mother.

But I was not a man. No matter how well I competed on various levels with men—and I did not always compete well since I was an *average* woman, i.e. inferior to men—no matter how well I competed, I knew with my whole being from the time I was very small that men could always run faster, lift more, and, restrained by only the thinnest veneer of "civilization," hit harder.

It took me a long time to see that dedicating my life to overcoming these things could only end in frustration and bitterness. There is no way for average women to participate in a society where might is right and to feel good about themselves. Sleeping with a woman when I was 15 was easy. Realizing that almost any time spent on men was a dead-end took me until I was 27. Achieving a society of womenvalues will probably take centuries.

Even after that realization I went home a few more times. But I finally stopped going because I could see no way in that setting for me to relate proudly with my mother and to stop giving energy to my father and brother. I did not stop going home because I sleep with women. My family knows I am a Lesbian; accepting that seems to have been fairly easy for them. There would have had to have been a transition period while they adjusted to yet another of my supposed eccentricities (in actuality I was a boringly ordinary child who gave no trouble), and eventually as TV programs contained more and more gay jokes I would be only another minority served up hot by the media for interest in this more and more mass-produced world. As it was, they all sent letters and presents—"It's OK that you're that way. We love you *anyway*," meaning that it's OK that I'm queer.

But you know, I don't feel queer anymore. It's women who spend their *lives* on men who to me are queer. Human beings who spend their lives serving, listening to, cajoling, persuading, and mirroring back to another set of human beings. Human beings who in many cases plead with, beg for acceptance, and are beaten, raped, unwillingly impregnated, and deserted by that other group called men. Those women are queer, weird, odd, brain-washed. And I love *them* anyway. I know how difficult it is to leave all that horror on the intimate level, by becoming a Lesbian. I know how impossible it is to leave it on the societal level—I still deal with men every day. But as far as the strength of my sisters stretches, I have come out.

38

A Small
Detective Story

Judith Katz

I.

JUDITH: When did you come out?
BW: It's hard to know.

II. Interrogation

Q: Did you watch your mother putting on makeup, perfume, did you zip her up?

A: Oh yes.

Q: What else?

A: I used to put on my younger brother's sport coats and slick my hair back in the mirror.

Q: Did you masturbate?

A: Not till college.

Q: What else?

A: Jane K. in home room in the seventh grade—(Heavy breathing). Mrs. Y. in the eighth and ninth grades—French (Heavy breathing).

Miss C. in the eighth and ninth grades—Geography (Heavy breathing).
Holly J., Bayla W., Betsy L., Lynne F.,—Etc. Etc. Etc. Etc.

And then there was the summer the summer the summer I was going into the 10th grade and Jane K. and me and some other people went to camp for two weeks and I fell madly in love with N. E. and I knew exactly what it was and it wasn't fun because it was 1966 or something and a dyke was one of those *strange* women who hung out at the car wash with *vitalis* in their hair, with *cigarettes* rolled into their tee shirt sleeves who ate beercans with their teeth who wore wingtipped shoes and looked at you funny in the dark, and...

Q: Your parents sent you to a shrink.

A: Because I tried to slit my wrists, not because they thought I was queer.

Q: What did your shrink say?

A: I never told him I was afraid I was a lesbian so he never said anything. He sat in back of rows and rows and rows of pipe racks ... I don't think he smoked once the whole time I was seeing him ... he just nodded his head, and any time I cried he'd hand me a box of kleenex. He'd tell me I must have said the truth because it made me cry. One day I just decided to stop going. He asked me if I had any questions or answers and I said no and left ... I was a sophomore in high school or something.

Q: Then things were okay after that?

A: Not at all. Jane and I were locker to locker in high school, although she was in another home room. She started sneaking around with black young men who were members of student council and stuff, and basketball players and track stars. I didn't do anything but bum out. No one asked me out on dates or anything, and it was okay because I hated how everyone looked anyway ... except the girls ... I hung out mostly with Jewish kids and so there were lots of Sweet Sixteens ... which I hated because I had to get *clothes* for them, and a lot of times I had to try to find *dates* for them, and I wasn't easy about dates like everyone else seemed to be ... but I was losing my friendship with Jane and I never did *anything* on weekends because all of my friends were out on dates, and it was not fun. It got to be

more fun as I got a little older. By senior year I had found some
people I really liked who didn't scare the shit out of me. And
there were no more Sweet Sixteens.

Q: A Sweet Sixteen is what?

A: It's this party like where all these girls get to come out in the
       debutante sense, even if they're Jewish. Anyway, I stopped
       being hung up on Jane and on N. E. and I stopped thinking
       about sex as a weapon—

Q: Sex as a weapon?

A: Sex as the only sure-fire way to intimacy—

Q: Why did you think that?

A: I don't know, but anyway, I stopped doing it for a while, and I
       graduated from high school and I went to college, and I totally
       forgot about being attracted to women for two years.

Q: How'd you do that?

A: I decided to fall in love with this guy I met who used to smoke
       pot and walk around with a paper bag over his head.

Q: How did you do that?

A: I became obsessed with him ... but I was real funny about it ... I
       used to come on to him and beg him to sleep with me and stuff
       and then if he ever tried anything I'd go *nuts* with morality and I
       also absolutely did not want to get pregnant.

Q: You were ambivalent.

A: Mmm. Then, one day—I must have known him for a year, he
       says, "My roommate isn't coming home tonight and I haven't
       had a chance to masturbate all weekend, want to sleep with
       me?" I was stoned and I said sure, and it was very much fun.
       Until I had to go to sleep in his roommate's bed because there
       was sperm all over his. Then he came over to the bed I was
       sleeping in and we did it again, so then I had to go home
       because there was sperm all over everywhere. When I got back
       to the dorm I lived in I didn't stop smiling for a week. But

basically, he liked tripping much more than he liked me, and he also liked a friend of mine from high school better than he liked me, and so we stopped sleeping together. *It drove me nuts!* I went very crazy and to the University Mental Health where my shrink told me I was *intense.* I felt paralyzed. All I wanted to do was blow the guy who dropped me's cock off with a pop gun, you know...okay, so I moved out of the dorm...into a women's dorm...I kept going over to the guy's room and begging him to love me, but love was never really an issue for him. So I lived in this women's dorm and I smoked pot a lot and wrote plays and I met some very neat women who lived in the dorm I lived in...and one of them was a large, soft, smart woman named Debra, and I guess that was when I really knew I was into women.

III. Deb ra
Deb ra
Deb Deb Deb ra

Debra was a woman who played games

Debra was a Leo
who played games with names
initials
initials was the game with names
I was short
she was lovely
and big

And lovely
and she was warm
her earlobes made my nipples jump
her earlobes made my nipples buzz
her earlobes were exquisite
little gold hoops
hung from her earlobes
and the gold hoops
slipped through her soft hair
and my nipples went la-la-la-la

("Do I look like a lover?" I ask you
"Do I look like a lover?")

Klangklangklangklangklangklang...
Sirens sound the sirens sirens sound the sirens

We're having (ta dah!)
homosexual panic!

IV. An Interlude/An Insight
(Personal But Not Confidential)

When I knew what all of this meant was one night when I was a sophomore in college. After the guy with paper bag on his head, during my buzzy breasts and Debra's earlobes. One night, see, five of us perky co-eds was sittin in my room smoking joints... joints and joints and joints and joints... nine joints. I was very very very high, and so was everyone else. Before I knew it there was Annie R. curled into me, and both of us was crooning a soft little solo into the other's ear.

We were in the middle of three other people so we were fairly discreet. Ra Ra Deb was visiting her mother. La La Jude was having fun getting silly with Annie R.... Ooh everything tickled and ooh everything was high, and ooh, what a good giggle we all had ... and who would have thought you could have this much fun with your clothes on??????

The next day, I went into total hysteria. I called up everyone I knew and asked them if I was gay after I told them I thought I was gay.

Annie told me in the vending machine room that she was glad I didn't ask her to sleep with me because she would have said yes.

Rumor has it that Ms. R. is currently a Gemini studying law at MIT and that we may have lost a good one. Rumor correctly has it that I am an Aquarian studying everyone at a discreet women's college somewhere in the mid-west, although I am not, as it might appear, with the emotional CIA.

V. Siren Siren Siren Siren Siren Siren

Back at University Mental Health:

"Intense! Very intense.
It's a phase. Choo choo.
It's adolescent menopause!"

VI.

Do I look like a lover?
Do I look like a lover?

We sat in her white
cinderblock room

Do I look like a lover?

We played initials and smoked pot...

Tension
In a white room
Panic
On a single bed
with creaky springs

I watched the earlobes
the earlobes watched me
I smoked the pot
the pot smoked me
nobody was really sure
that there was such a thing
as lesbian
then...

Everything I had forgotten about came flooding back in a waterfall of
women's names... *Janie K.* (Here!) *Mrs. Y.* (Here) *Ms. C.* (Yes!) ooh, it
was all happening as thick as layers in a German Chocolate cake *Holly J.*
Lynne F. Bayla Betsy...

Deb Deb Deb Deb Deb ra
Deb Deb Deb Deb Deb ra!

Gimme a little kiss
will ya huh
gimme a little squeeze
will ya huh?

(insanely heavy breathing
insanely insanely heavy breathing)

I can still hear her screaming
silent
all the way down the hall
she disappears/hands over ears
into concrete mazes/hands over ears
mirrored halls/mazes/hands over ears
fun house dorm/hands to stomach
not yet
co-ed

good bye Debra (I wave a feeble wave)
come back Debra
I just want a little snuggle
Debra just want a little kiss
Debra
Debra
I will ignore
this throb in my cunt
Debra
I will ignore
this buzz in my breasts
Debra
it's okay, Debra
I was only kidding, Debra
Please come back, Debra
this is like a movie
of a bad LSD trip
Debra
all I said was
I love you Debra
all I wanted to do was
hold you Debra
under a blanket in one of these crummy
university dormitory
beds
Debra...
no one would get pregnant
Debra
everything would tickle
Debra
we could have a good time
being in love,
Debra...
in secret, Debra—

"Sorry Judith
I'm busy reading Lawrence
so sorry Judith
he says love is intense
he says love is a gothic thing
he says love is a cold thing

sorry Judith, I'm busy being cold
sorry Judith
I'm busy playing Laura Nyro
so sorry Judith her passion is intense
she says love is a pure thing
she says love is a gothic thing
sorry Judith
I'm busy getting hot
sorry Judith
my mother wouldn't like it
sorry Judith she says dykes don't
exist
I'm busy being Catholic
though I was raised a Protestant
orgasms
aren't shared
and I'm very scared."

good-bye, Debra
come-back, Debra!

fat chance, Judith
fat
chance.

VII. Epilogue

Judith got over it and into someone else and then someone else and
someone else after that and a lot of someone elses later, she is happy to
announce that she has been having a swell time these past few years. She
just saw the first woman she ever slept with in the Saints in Boston and
they still liked looking at each other even though it's been a *long time*
since they last saw each other. I have no idea where most of the other
people in this story are, except for B.W. who in one sentence helped me
to put everything in perspective. Debra, we think, is busy being a Leo
somewhere on Massachusetts' North Shore.

How I Spent at Least One Summer Vacation

39

Susan Leigh Star

Does it count when you're seven?
Does it count when you're eleven?
Does it count when you're just "messing around"?
Does it count when you're "practicing for the boys when you grow up
so you'll know what to do and won't be embarrassed (giggle)"?
Does it count at Girl Scout Camp and there aren't any boys around?
Does it count in high school and you don't care about the boys anyway?
Does it count before one reaches the hormonal stage of puberty, before
latency, before the onset, ahem, of genital sexuality?
Does it count before you have pubic hair?
Does it count if you have one pubic hair?
  Two?
  Three?
  At what point does pubic hair constitute genuine Lesbianism?
Does it count if one of you pretends to be a boy?
If both of you accidentally pretend to be boys at once, does that make
you both faggots?
Does it count if you stay outside?
Does it count if you never even kiss?
Does it count if a boy watches?
Does it count if you're drunk?
  Stoned?
  Unhappy?
  Never got enough mothering?
  Got too much mothering?
  Can't have children?

Have children already?
Like men?
Hate men?
Does it count if you're best friends anyway?
    If you don't have an orgasm?
    If it's a schoolgirl crush?
    If it's not reciprocated?
If you close your eyes?

Debbie Castalucci was the second smartest girl in fifth grade, next to me, and we were best friends. One day we decided to make a bottle of the most deadly poison in the world—one drop could kill a person, a whole bottle devastate the planet. This would give us power over the whole world.

Debbie had a chemistry set from Christmas and so did I. We put a bit of every chemical from the set in a small bottle—including the brine shrimp embryos that grow in a saline solution, so they'd wiggle around inside the person and increase the agony. We added alcohol to diatomaceous earth, combined it with potassium and NaCl.

The contents of the bottle turned from white to a sickly brown. After the chemicals came the secret ingredients: mushrooms. In my front yard grew a peculiar mushroom which was bright yellow and which bruised green when you rubbed the underside. These were the most poisonous mushrooms in the world, I informed Debbie. We carefully diced up half a large one, quickly wiping our hands on our jeans afterwards.

I hid the bottle under my shirt and ran with Debbie to the stone wall near the front yard. Moving aside a stone, we put the bottle in a tiny crevice far in back where it could only be found by rummaging about with our hands in the damp leaves and moss.

The responsibility of knowing that we had in that tiny bottle the power to destroy the whole word was immense. Before sleep each night I would contemplate what I had done in creating such a poison. There was always the chance that someone would accidentally drink from the bottle, or that some innocent chipmunk or squirrel would die from the fumes filling their den in the stone wall. While I felt that it would be a genuine service to humanity to give a little to Mr. Ryan, my social studies teacher, if they caught me I'd probably be forced to drink all of the poison to atone, and die a horrible death.

Eventually the responsibility weighed too heavily, and Debbie and I disposed of the bottle's content in a solemn ceremony behind the stone wall. We buried the poison in a deep hole and dragged large flat rocks over the place. But the terrible knowledge remained. My career as a Lesbian guerrilla terrorist had begun.

You understand this has to be a kaleidoscope: Layered, multiple, alternately foggy and clear. Coming out. And going back in. And peeking through the keyhole. Different parts bubble up from time to time. There's no such thing as a linear Lesbian.

Vignette:

I have just become lovers with Ms. A. M. On Christmas morning, out of a benighted sense of guilt, I tumble out of her bed and drive to Rhode Island to celebrate the yuletide with my genetic family. Because my VW bug has been smashed up by queer-hating neighborhood "youngsters" I drive her Ford van.

The whole family comes out into the snowy driveway as I maneuver the truck into the front yard.

FATHER: "Where did you get the truck? How did you learn to drive something like that?"

DAUGHTER: "Oh, it's my roommate's. She lent it to me so I didn't have to take the Greyhound bus."

F.:   "Oh." Pause.

MOTHER: (in a hesitant tone of voice) "Is she a *big* girl?"

The gynecologist was an efficient, tired-looking woman. She wore horn-rimmed glasses and her hair swept in frizzy curves from her face. She sees twenty or thirty students a day in the clinic. This is my semi-yearly checkup.

"Last period?"

"Two weeks ago."

"Regular?"

"No, it varies a lot."

"Cramps, headache, unusual discomfort?"

"No."

"Let me take your blood pressure."

She snaps the black belt around my arm, patting the velcro closing and pumping the rubber bulb.

"110/70."

"General health?"

"Fine. I get some tension headaches."

"Had a Pap Test lately?"

"Yes, in June."

"What method of birth control do you use?"

"I'm a Lesbian."

I see the woman's lips tighten slightly and there is a pause as she swallows. She is mustering all of her liberal tendencies. She writes something down in my file.

I wonder what she has written: some medical code for queer? Outside the pale of heterosexual norm?

"Uh, Miss Star...how long have you been a, ah, bisexual?"

We are sitting in a circle listening to Robin Morgan read "The Network of the Imaginary Mother" on tape. Risa is trying to explain to Ilene how parthenogenesis is the natural completion of her Lesbianism: the three aspects of the goddess in one female—mother, daughter, and crone.

I come out of the bathroom smoking a tampax cigar: "Now see here, tomatoes, every one of you just needs to meet the right gentleman, and this horrible affliction can be cured."

"Hey, they want me to give a talk at Foothill College next week. Does anybody want to talk next week to a women's studies class?"

"On what?"

"Lesbianism."

We howl. "Yes before I was a Lesbian I had no natural rhythm, my acne was terrible, I was constipated. And now..."

"...you see before you..."

"...the natural wonder of the earth..."

"...the bliss of being queer..."

"...the glory of sisterhood fulfilled..."

Lesbianism and magic. What my story really means to me deepest down is my blood struggle to vindicate the fairies.

Part of my story is being a believer. I believed it when they said that there were little winged females who could fly, who visited little girls at night and gave them what they wanted. I used to see them beside my bed and talk with them, all in different colors of light.

I believed it when mother said boys were awful and didn't I want to play with little girls who were gentler and smarter anyway? I believed that there were princesses: I was a princess, held captive by my parents, who were educating me in the ways of the mundane working class so that I would understand my people better when it came time for me to rule as queen. I believed that god was my ready and willing companion.

I had trouble when it came time not to believe. I knew there had to be a way to straighten it out. The world of magic was all that made sense to me. I followed every clue: buddha, angels, church, indians, nuns, judaism. Girls. Women. Witches.

Them. Their world was antimagic. The only way I survived was through books, where the magic still happened. I had trouble realizing that what happened in the books "wasn't real." Bookworm. My brain, the words became survival skills. I sharpened the words, learned to use them in Their ways. Won scholarships, freedom. Went to college to escape antimagic.

Coming out? I said it was a miracle. Each of us a miracle. But it wasn't courage, I just never could learn to stop believing in magic, in feeling, in women, in myself. That I would have my wish come true. That the first star of the evening would make me happy.

I held on to my outrage that their world excluded magic. That stayed when everything else left. No, I didn't always call it women. The part the boys got hold of: mysticism, transcendence—I fell for. Buddhism, meditation, denying the earth, denying the body. But all to find the magic again, to find out the secret of the fairies.

In Rhode Island, near my house, was a lake. In a secluded spot lived a tree that I found out was my mother. I don't know how I knew. I was ten, twelve. It had a long limb that stretched out towards the water, but low enough so I could climb onto it with ease. Each week I went there to kiss her. I rubbed my cheek against her bark and knew that it was her skin and she could feel me rubbing her. The crook in her arm would hold me for a long time. It was a secret from everyone but my sister. She had her own tree.

The most painful part is when it was silent. Being 14, 15, 16, and loving a woman 27, 28, 29. She loved back, but there were no words. I was a prisoner—immobile, tortured by high school and being very conscious of what they were trying to do to me.

We danced around each other as "friends" and as student and teacher. There were unwritten rules that we obeyed without knowing that we were obeying them, certain separations of language. It was all right, for example, to write love letters to each other, speaking of commitment and depth of feeling, as long as the word "friend" appeared also. We could look into each other's eyes for long periods of time as long as we didn't touch.

To be in that situation was to be flattened, two dimensions, suffocating. The fact of our different ages slammed before us every time we moved. I had no money, no job, no car; I had to be home at 5:00 p.m. every day and in bed by 10. After a while, my parents began to be suspicious of our relationship...my mother would ask oblique questions about whether she had ever been married. Eventually I was forbidden to see her, and had to invent absurdly complicated strategies for getting out of the house and over to her place. In order to be together I had to leave my house at 7:00 a.m. and pretend to walk to the schoolbus, where she would come by in her car in time for coffee and a chat. For two years.

She had been a nun; I was her precocious student. We wrote letters every day—between classes, on the bus; if we couldn't see each other on the weekend we wrote more often.

The first time I saw her breasts as she changed into a bathing suit is charred on my mind, and bleeds still. The rare touches, the rare glimpses we were allowed.

When I left for college we had plans to be together, free and alone for the first time...weekends, evenings. Just before I left she told me that she was getting married to another teacher, someone she'd always described in contemptuous terms. I was stunned—I don't remember thinking anything consciously, but it was another two years before I got close to a woman and began, finally, to say to myself that I was a Lesbian.

I always feel puzzled when someone asks me, did you come out through the movement? When I started finding my way back was when I found the word Lesbian—and that was because of the movement. In the times when I didn't even know there was a word for what I was, I was so weak, able to be swayed; to be annihilated and no one would ever know it. When Mary told me she was getting married, there were no words for my outrage—I just took it in. To protest would have been to unlock the silence that protected us, to create something new and possibly to have destroyed even the silent space we had.

But in writing this, I found that all of the above *count*. When I count the Lesbian in me at age seven, or ten, or fifteen, I count the part of me that was free, self-loving, identifying (however unconsciously) with femaleness. I begin to see my life as a whole: the places I held out, refused to settle; what they did and tried to do to me/us; and the reclaiming, the creating of my woman strength.

Since getting heavily involved in the movement I have been trying to find words for my experience, to politicize and name different kinds of things that have been unnamed. All the shades of communication and love between women or girls, all the ways that we can be for each other need validating, again and again. I want the silent spaces that we have to be of our choosing, not the prison boundaries of our imaginations, of our lives.

The Garden Variety Lesbian

40

Barbara Grier

My name is Barbara Grier. I was born on November 4, 1933 in Cincinnati, Ohio. I am the daughter of Dorothy Vernon Black Grier and Philip Strang Grier. It was a first marriage for my mother and my father's second marriage. He had two sons, William and Brewster, by the prior marriage. My parents were not young to have a family. My father was 34 and my mother was 32 when I was born. Five years later my next youngest sister Diane was born, and five years after that my youngest sister Penny (Penelope) was born.

While I was very young my parents traveled a great deal. Consequently, before I was five I was in every state in the Union, Canada and Mexico. Outside of the basic facts that I have outlined, my parents being somewhat older and the fact that we traveled a great deal, I can think of no particular circumstance about my earlier years that would be considered unusual or different. I did get a great deal of attention, of course, having been an only child for five years and seven months. I have no indication in my memory of any kind of emotional attachment with any person before age eight and this portion of my life is entirely hindsight. I say that carefully, because when I went back later as a teenager and started reconstructing the years of my life before I came out, which means before I was twelve years old, I had to do some conscious thinking about what had taken place before in order to find instances of behavior that would indicate that I would grow up and become a Lesbian. I recreated my childhood while I was a teenager, going back in my head and figuring out at what point I first actually was "manifesting" Lesbian tendencies. I was able to go back and realize that when I was eight years old, I was madly in love with my babysitter, whose name was Susan Stevens, who lived in Chicago, Illinois. Now she was less my babysitter than she was the babysitter for my five-years-younger, almost six-years-younger, sister, Diane. And I can remember clearly being in love with her and then perhaps two other young women, before I was twelve, and of an age when the symptoms of the lovesick syndrome occur that I was curious enough to go to the library and obtain enough information to make it possible for me to go home and announce my homosexuality to my mother. I came out at age twelve, when I discovered reasonably, for myself, that I was a Lesbian. I did not know that word, of course; I didn't know the word homosexual, either. But when I discovered behavior patterns in myself that I could tell were different from behavior patterns that my friends or other young women around me had, I investigated it in a quite sensible way for a fairly bright child: I went to the library and started looking.

I soon found the multi-syllabic word "homosexual," and while I didn't feel that I fit any of the descriptions given in the textbook-type things that I was finding, I could tell that there was enough similarity so that there was no question in my mind, that it did describe me—except of course, even instantly, even as I first made this discovery, I had the conviction that the attitude on the part of the writers in the books was entirely wrong. I was a superior being, and I immediately felt that the Lesbianism, or the discovery that I was homosexual, explained everything in my life. I had always felt superior, and I had always thought that there must be some particular reason, some particular thing that made me superior to the people around me; and I believe that almost immediately on discovering that I was homosexual, I began to believe that this was the explanation for the superior functioning, for the superior intelligence I possessed, among other things. And I had something happen immediately to reinforce this.

I was very close to my mother. (My parents separated when I was ten and divorced when I was thirteen. I don't actually believe that this has a great deal to do with the story except that my next step was to go home and tell my mother. Remembering how I behaved with my family, growing up, if my father had happened to be physically present, I would have gone home and told both of them. There is no question about this in my mind.) As it was, I went home and told my mother and my mother treated it moderately lightly—that is, she said that since I was very young, that I was much too young for such an announcement, that I should probably wait a few months at least before deciding that this was an absolute fact. But if it turned out, indeed, that I was a Lesbian, then that was fine. The same things would be expected of me that I knew would always be expected of me; in other words, I was to be an honorable person in every way all of my life, and if I were honorable all of my life nothing but good would come to me. It was sort of a modified and less melodramatic version of Polonius' advice to Laertes. My mother supplied the name Lesbian to me in automatic, I think unthinking, conversation the first time I told her that I was a homosexual. She simply started using the term "Lesbian" and I automatically adopted it and have used it ever since. We talked about this particular event—that is, my mother and I talked about it in later years—several times. At some point along the way she wrote a nice long letter for the magazine *The Ladder*, back before I was editor of it, some time in the middle 60's when there was a program, more on less, going on in the pages of the magazine, comments by parents, and so on. My mother's comment was very positive, very upbeat. She was in many ways a very unusual person.

This is supposed to be about coming out, and actually in a sense, that is all that there is to my coming out. I came out. I knew at age twelve that I was in love with my best friend. Her name was Barbara Shier. I also knew that it was unusual or different. I investigated it, I found a name or a handle for it. I went home and told my mother about it, and received, in effect a parental blessing. And from that time on, I've lived as a Lesbian, openly. I am positive that it is the reason that I have been extremely happy all of my life. In other words, I did have the required miserable teen years that we all live though. (When I say "all" I do not mean "all we Lesbians" I mean "all we people.") Everyone seems to be unhappy to some extent during their teen years. I fell in love bunches of times during my teen years. I slept with perhaps ten to fifteen women between age twelve and seventeen. At age eighteen, I married for the first time. Another woman, of course.

I had some humorous things happen to me through the years. I had a counselor in Colorado Springs High School, whose name I can't remember—she became very upset, not by the fact that I was a Lesbian, but by the fact that I refused to keep it a secret. And I did upset her, to some extent. She would talk with me, then become so unnerved in talking with me that she would cry and wring her hands and say, "Whatever will we do with you?" So I probably had some mildly traumatic experiences—that was, certainly. And in the same city (Colorado Springs), one young woman, who was at least eight years older than I, started a conversation wtih me at a bus stop near my home. In the course of the conversation, after we had seen each other perhaps a half a dozen times at the same bus stop, she learned that I was a Lesbian and went home and told her mother. I would have been fifteen or sixteen years old then, fifteen probably. She was at least eight years my senior, so she would have been 23-24. She went home and told her mother that I was a Lesbian and of course I have no way of knowing what kind of conversation they had—but I do know that about three days later, or four days later, I was called to the counselor's office (the same counselor in Colorado Springs High School) and confronted by, of all things, two Police Officers from the Colorado Springs Police Department, and they literally took me out of the school in the daytime, took me to the police station and badgered me, for an hour or so with questions. Some of the ordinary, usual questions that we learn to accept and expect. Things like "What do you do with your girl friends?" in reference to genitals and so on, and even some things I hadn't heard of, and some suggestions that hadn't occurred to me, which I remember thinking about with curiosity. I realize now, of course, that this was all highly illegal. My parents were never notified. I was under age. I was threatened, coerced, and then dumped back in school with instructions never to speak to this particular woman again, and never to go near the place where she worked, which happened to be one of the downtown theaters. Now, I had no interest in this young woman, which is kind of remarkable, because I was interested in so many young women, but I was really put out by the prohibition about the Peak Theater because I enjoyed that theater a whole lot and I resented having to give up one of the five available theaters in the downtown Colorado Springs area.

My mother and I both discussed this police event that took place in Colorado Springs when I was fifteen. But even though she was horrified by this, her horror had nothing to do with the gay aspects of it... what she was horrified about was that her daughter could even be taken to a police station. (Now remember, this is prior to anything resembling Civil Rights activity in the south where the Black Civil Rights movement began, and in those days, at least in my family, it was taken for granted that respectable people never had anything to do with the police... except if you lived to be old enough, you might be helped across the street by one sometime, or if you were very young you might have one standing guard at the crossing by your school. But certainly one was never arrested, one was never in any kind of intimate situation with a policeman—it was unheard of—and the idea also that there were threats and coercion, upset her, but she did not articulate it in the Civil Rights sense because, even though she was very well-educated, and very sophisticated, that concept simply didn't exist. The police were a law to themselves. There are people who will probably question that, but I assure you that that was the way it was when I was fifteen years old, which was in 1948.)

Outside of that incident, I had some humorous and embarrassing things happen. The fact that I insisted on telling everyone I was a Lesbian, everywhere I went, of course did create some social problems at times, but they were funny. Primarily, because after a certain point, shock actually has value, within the realms that the person is able to deal with shock. And, in those days, telling people you were a Lesbian—I can't think of anything comparable today that would have the same effect. I did sort of create temporary catatonic states in people occasionally. But I enjoyed that. I mean that was like a weapon in the hands of a teenager. I was no different from any other teenager—that is to say, obnoxious, overbearing, arrogant, positive that I knew everything about everything. And my being a Lesbian colored my teen years to some extent. I had one or two parents voice objections to me; rather sophisticated parents of one of the women I was interested in going to bed with when I was about sixteen objected to me to the extent of taking to walking her daughter back and forth to ice-skating practice at the ice-skating arena at Broadmoor Hotel in Colorado Springs. Everything questionable certainly did happen to me in Colorado Springs. But nothing really eventful.

I went from Colorado Springs into Dodge City, Kansas and then into Kansas City, Kansas, and graduated from high school in 1951. By that time, I had to help support my mother and my two younger sisters, so I went immediately from high school to work; and within a year of that time I had met and married Helen Bennett and that was a very happy event. And I went from a very promiscuous teenager to an absolutely monogamous and faithful, upright, uptight middle-class-type lover. Helen went to library school in Denver, and we came back to the Kansas City area because we both had parents in the area (that is, I had my mother and two younger sisters, and Helen had elderly parents). For the next twenty years we very happily resided in the Middle West, in the general Greater Kansas City area, either in the Kansas City, Kansas area or across the river in Kansas City, Missouri.

My public life, I guess, is pretty well-known. I became an editor and a writer, and I became an editor of *The Ladder*. Before that I worked for *The Ladder* in various capacities. I went about still telling everybody in each clerical job that I had through the years that I was a Lesbian and I never had any difficulty whatsoever with it.

I am absolutely convinced that if everyone would come out and come out at once and stay out in every sense that we could put an end to most of our problems in the area, and I mean coming out in every sense that is, everyone should come out and admit to themselves that they're a Lesbian; everyone should come out and admit to everyone else they're a Lesbian. I do feel that there are areas of discretion: one does not attack elderly people and force the idea on them because in some cases you're dealing with people who simply cannot comprehend what you're talking about. Now those things, of course, shouldn't happen because that's just a matter of bad taste, poor judgment. Other than that, I don't really think there is any excuse for not coming out. There might have been a few excuses when I was doing it in the early days. There were still, after all, some things that could happen to you, but now that there isn't anything in the way of job security to worry about or anything like that, I think we could end all of our oppressions virtually immediately if we would just simply come out and stay out.

I certainly have been happy all of my life. Helen and I separated after twenty years of marriage and I have remarried. I am married to Donna McBride. Incidentally, you will note that I have talked about my family, I have named my family, the women I have had something to do with. I feel it is very important that we talk very candidly and openly about where we are, what we're doing, where we live, how we live. Not as if we're divorced from the world. In other words, I did have a mother and father, I have two younger sisters, I do have two older half brothers, I do live—physically—on this earth, in a particular place. I do specific things. I'm real. I'm not an article in a book. I am a real person, with a real valid life. I have relatives, some of them are gay, some of them are not gay. I'm out with my relatives and I don't worry about it. And if they worry about it, they haven't let me know they do. I think I can also show, to some extent, my argument for being out in every sense. My next youngest sister, Diane, is also a Lesbian. And she is a closet Lesbian. She's been married for a great many years to another woman, and she lives with this woman, has a good job—they both have good jobs. And they are in positions that are untouchable; that is, there is no way they can be fired for being Lesbians, and they both know it and acknowledge this. But they haven't come out, and they don't come out where they work because they don't want their co-workers to know they are gay. So somehow, even though there was this positive home atmosphere (my sister Diane certainly did receive the same kind of treatment I had from my mother), she managed somehow to grow up carrying some of the conventional prejudices. I don't know how or why. I don't deal with her on an intimate basis. She's the only member of my family I have nothing to do with, by choice, by decision, because I disapprove of her being in the closet. Now, I can't do anything about friends of mine who are not out, but I do have the option when it comes to my own flesh-and-blood sister to decide that what she is doing is morally reprehensible to me, unconscionable, and cannot be stood. And that, therefore, I have the right to decide that I will have nothing to do with her, and, therefore, I *have* nothing to do with her.

I don't know that I have solutions to any problems beyond that. I do think that is not the main solution to Lesbians' problems, if there is a "problem" in being a Lesbian. I have always thought of it as some kind of heaven-sent blessing. I am aware of course that there is some sort of dramatic effect obtained in any kind of movement when you can show the forms of oppression. And I am sure that is simply a personal attitude on my part that chooses to see less oppression and more blessing. I know that there are many areas where Lesbians still suffer prejudice, but I do feel that, by forcing the world to accept the millions of women who are Lesbians, by the act of those Lesbians themselves, coming out would solve most of these problems automatically.

41 Sacred Vow 1

Susan Leigh Star

smiting myself against myself
over and over

and i rip your skin
from your body that i have adored. our weapons are scars
our reasons are half-remembered hopes forged from our blood
in complete ice
all we have ever known is aloneness
and all i have ever wanted was to be
a monster adored

we thread our ways through our own nightmares
losing and finding
the mutual dream.
this light shall cost everything.

my life before you was a throat before it cries
my recurrent dream at night was of being captured and held, screaming,
with no sound coming out.

seeking to be vulnerable to you
in as many ways as i could
i sought to repair us both
to hear the scream
to own the dream

if we are to survive
it will be together

we who have never known mercy
cradling our own pain
against the cold
against each other
must learn love

i do not seek to reduce you
a million times in the course of our love
we will create beasts knives death

i am throwing my lot in with you
i will not betray the hope
even when i lose the dream.

Epilogue: Coming Around

Susan J. Wolfe

To speak of my emergence as a Lesbian and a feminist as a "coming out" process is probably a misnomer for two reasons. First, in looking back over my life, it seems to me that my primary identifications have always been with wimmin, although it certainly took me long enough to realize that and/or to admit it. Second, I was perfectly sure that I was a Lesbian at the age of sixteen (although I would not have used that term to designate myself), but I managed conveniently albeit nervously to forget that fact until I was twenty-nine. It also feels somewhat arrogant to speak of my coming out when, by my own standards, I'm only just accomplishing that now, as I respond to the sense of love and community awakened in me through this anthology and by the wimmin who've contributed to it.

As one of our writers has said, in retrospect it appears that "everything counts" as you move toward a recognition of your Lesbianism. Nevertheless, I managed to remain ignorant of mine, ignoring all the obvious signs. Yes, like so many of us, I was a "tomboy": I scorned dolls, had male playmates, owned a baseball glove and basketball. My earliest childhood fantasies were of civilizations composed of wimmin with superhuman powers, and I fantasized that I had come from some other planet whose people would one day reclaim me. My dreams, too, were populated only with girls and wimmin. Flashing back, I now realize that I experienced my first "crush" in second grade, falling in love with a classmate whose amiability and honey-brown ponytail attracted me. But all of this was a normal part of growing up, of course; I was "going through a phase."

I remained safe throughout my childhood. My feelings remained uncategorized by hateful labels; I had, after all, no vocabulary with which to name my emotions. If I continued to have "crushes" on classmates, girls who lived downstairs, and girls I met on summer vacation, I had the good sense not to discuss them with anyone, and so I never suffered the rejection or mockery experienced by so many of my sisters. My tenuous security rested on ignorance, though, and I was too bright to remain unaware forever.

At the age of eleven, I began to vacillate between a strong desire to be normal (that is, a girl who liked boys) and an equally strong desire to love girls. I spent a summer evening sitting at the bedside of a friend, stroking her hair until she finally fell asleep, and left feeling remarkably alive but puzzled: I seemed to feel "love," if the symptoms described in the popular music of the late 1950's could be ascribed to lovers, but that feeling was reserved for boys. Or was it? Back in the city, I listened in agony while my best friend told me how much trouble she was having courting some unworthy male snake. My patience was rewarded with a kiss on the cheek. My friend Linda fled back into her apartment, but I flushed with joy and felt triumphant all day. If I could not compete with males sexually, I could at least be a better friend, and that was nobler somehow.

I had just entered puberty. As I became more aware of my body, I felt as though I was the victim of some horrible misunderstanding. Believing that only boys could win the love of girls, I grew unhappier daily. My discontent grew in direct proportion to the size of my breasts. I used to imagine that I could acquire the power of transsexualism at will; I would miraculously turn into a handsome boy, and Linda would fall in love with me without realizing that it was my mind inside a male form.

Naturally, our love was destined not to be; I did not turn into a boy; instead, I went away to Hunter Junior High School, an all-girl's school in midtown Manhattan. There I avoided young wimmin I found attractive, and instead became the constant companion of a womyn who, like me, enjoyed basketball, knock-hockey, and lemon cokes after school. One night, though, during a sleep-over at her house, she suggested we neck so that she could "get some practice" for a boy she was interested in. We did, for some time, but the experience was so traumatizing in the cold light of day that both of us cut classes the following morning. I was literally nauseated, and consoled myself by reading Biblical passages for hours, hoping that a merciful deity would construe this act as repentance.

After this experience, I shied away from any physical contact with wimmin and even went to the extent of avoiding close friendships. By means of this subterfuge and my new-found normalcy, I managed to delude myself that I was still safe—until the age of sixteen, anyway. I was dating an older man (twenty-one) whose family I'd met one summer at some resort cottages; I met big brother the following summer, and I suppose he found me attractive. I found him attractive because he impressed my wimmin friends and because, being in the Navy, he was away most of the time. In 1962 teenage monogamy flourished, and going steady was a convenient excuse for avoiding other young men. I was normal; I was accepted by my peer group; I wore a man's ring on a silver chain around my neck, which greatly enhanced my prestige among my classmates. His absence only lent an air of romance to my solitude.

I had to assume I was heterosexual; I was behaving heterosexually, wasn't I? Well, there was one exception, though... and her name was Sally. I still feel a kind of weakness for Sally, my first love, but I honestly can't remember how we became lovers. I know we were introduced by a mutual friend, and that we spent a great deal of time together at her house, a large, rambling, ramshackle house which contained five children, one dog, a loving mother, and little in the way of material luxury. And we drifted into friendship and closeness, so that the lovemaking seemed so natural, I can't remember how it progressed— but I remember how it started.

We were sitting on her darkened front porch on an old maroon davenport, and she lay her head on my lap. Her father's incessant bullying had given her a migraine. Then I was massaging her scalp, lost in the fragrance of her hair, which felt thick and soft in my hands... and I moved one hand. I knew why. Her breast felt warm and surprisingly firm, and lightning did not strike. No irate parent or curious sibling charged onto the porch. We were not discovered.

In fact, we were never discovered. We made love in my parents' apartment, in the bedroom, on the living room floor listening to classical music on the stereo. But we did have the sense, or the fear, to avoid touching in public. We knew that our love must remain covert. Society had conditioned us well; so effective was my training that I never told anyone at all about Sally until I re-emerged as a Lesbian, twelve years later.

Even if I'd thought to "get help," I probably would not have called myself a Lesbian. Since I was simultaneously fucking Donald, I was obviously a bisexual, and, in any case, I didn't know either word. Mother had carefully indicated a womyn cab-driver who lived in our apartment complex, who wore men's trousers and Arrow shirts and a d.a. cut, but she called her "a queer." If I had for a moment thought I was like that womyn, I would have called myself "a queer."

During this period of my life, I managed to enact both "masculine" and "feminine" roles. I always took the initiative in making love with Sally; she never touched me, although she would allow me to lie on top of her and kiss and touch her anywhere that it felt good. Donald always seduced me, assuming the missionary position when we had intercourse. I didn't feel the rush of pleasure that I got merely from kissing Sally, but the foreplay felt good, anyway. Since I didn't know about vaginal orgasms or clitoral orgasms or orgasms in general, I didn't worry because I experienced contractions lying on top of Sally that were absent from my sexual contact with Donald.

Nature and the rhythm method did me in. Donald was a good Catholic; I have been endowed with a high degree of fertility. We usually had vaginal intercourse except when I was fertile or menstruating, in which case I indulged him by performing fellatio, a practice which disgusted me but which prevented his balls from falling off (an eventuality which, I was assured, was bound to come to pass if his sexual urges were not satisfied). Donald did not use contraceptives; I was too naive to know I could. And where could I have obtained and concealed them? I was sixteen, living at home with my parents. He "reasoned" that unpremeditated intercourse was merely a sin of the flesh; it might have become a sin of the spirit if he had taken precautions.

When I missed my period, I had no illusions. I knew I was pregnant. Ironically, the only time I ever came close to achieving an orgasm through "normal" sexual relations brought the end to my medical virginity and got me pregnant. The notion of marrying was appalling. I wanted to go to college, to study, to learn what books had to offer. Abortions were illegal. I would have my baby, and then give it away.

Harder than it sounds. My parents were enraged, then crushed, but they rallied. I spent four months in a home for unwed mothers and had an eight-pound, fifteen-ounce son. I held him and I fed him and I gave him away—and went back home and to school to tell the lies. Only my parents and Donald and Sally ever knew—except for the wonderful wimmin who made my stay in the home bearable.

I returned to discover that Sally was dating Donald. I was stunned, since she had listened intently to my bitter account of the fellatio and the fucking. In fact, she and I had remained lovers until I left for the home. We had lost contact only because outside contact with friends was not permitted, to preserve secrecy.

1963 taught me a great deal. I learned that wimmin can give each other support in a painful, impossible environment—and then disappear, never to be heard from again. From Sally I learned of betrayal. For years, I never trusted a womyn again. I was too stupid to learn anything from my experience with Donald—I guess I never expected much from him anyway. I never saw him again.

I did see Sally once, though, after her marriage to him. She was living on the top floor of a one-family house turned duplex, and her apartment was sparsely furnished. The sink in her living-dining-kitchen area was full of dirty breakfast dishes, and they were covered with coffee grounds. I was clutching the notification of my college scholarship in order to show her that I hadn't needed either of them. I don't know why I confronted her, but I know what I gained and lost from the encounter. As I left, I remember straightening my shoulders and walking in great strides. I never looked back, but I never forgot.

Today I see the whole episode in a different perspective. We were not even individuated characters, Sally, Donald, and I—we were simply acting out a drama that is as old as patriarchal civilization. The eternal triangle: two wimmin and the man who separates them. She had betrayed me for the man I rejected... but, in a deeper sense, she had taught me a lesson I was to recall later. Straight wimmin, or gay wimmin who identify primarily with men, will betray you in the end. I no longer have delusions about who my sisters are.

But in 1964 I set about becoming a "happy heterosexual." Wimmin touched me deeply, and a womyn had wounded me more than she or I knew; very well then, I would turn to men. I would be safe because I was normal, and safe emotionally because I was impervious. I found a steady boyfriend, whom I dated for three years and, yes, reader, I married him. If I continued to have dreams, waking and sleeping, in which wimmin touched me and held me, I ignored them, and in time they decreased in frequency. I had seduced George and become pregnant again, this time terminating the pregnancy via an illegal abortion, which was much less painful than my experiences as an unwed mother. With the use of the birth-control pill, I then embarked on an active premarital sex life.

I now realize I have really run the gamut by which patriarchal culture punishes us for having the capacity to bear its sons and our daughters. I have borne an illegitimate child and lied to everyone about it to avoid stigmatizing my brother and family; I endured an abortion and the hemorrhaging that followed, which, I suspect, came quite close to killing me. Finally, in order to "get back" the child I felt I had surrendered due to societal pressures (and because, in our one family-one house culture, it's impossible to raise children without incredible self-sacrifice on the part of the mother), I bore my husband a son and heir. I was even told by George that I need only have the one child, provided I "did it right the first time," i.e., had a male child.

I enjoyed mothering for its own sake, and, if my sex life diminished, that was normal, wasn't it? After all, people just got used to each other, the magic wore off, we were busy with our respective careers (I was in graduate school, he was in sales), and busy with our child and our house in the suburbs. I forced myself to study for my doctoral exams at night, after my son went to sleep. I never thought of asking for assistance; my feminist consciousness was nil. And if it rankled when people asked why I needed all that education to raise a baby, I swallowed my pride and smiled. I won acceptance from the heterosexual, heterosexist, middle-class, middle-brow society around me.

Gradually, I forgot I had ever been alive. Evenings were spent around the television set; afternoons were spent in class or in housecleaning. In 1973 we moved to South Dakota at the urging of my husband; George didn't want me to "waste" my education—he wanted me to "have the opportunity to try working." I went perfunctorily from college professor to housewife, switching roles as I commuted back and forth between South Dakota and Sioux City, Iowa. I took my turn teaching Sunday school for a year. I became increasingly miserable despite my new "independence," and I knew why.

With our move from New York to Iowa, with my new status as a professional and the self-confidence that came with it, I began to resent my role as "little woman" to a salesman who read one book a year. Furthermore, the feelings for wimmin that I'd repressed so carefully for years began to get stronger and stronger. I almost drove off the Interstate one day because of the intensity of a sexual fantasy involving myself and a teaching assistant. I remember saying to myself, "God, I know what this *is!*" The worst part of it was that as George was becoming repugnant to me, gaining over a hundred pounds and becoming more and more immersed in salesmanship and consumerism, I was meeting intelligent, attractive, aware wimmin—and falling in love with them at the rate of about one a week.

I tried prayer. I went to religious services once a week and prayed to a Jewish patriarchal God to "make me normal" or to find me someone to end the miserable isolation and frustration I was feeling. Nothing happened. I even tried taking the initiative. One young womyn in one of my classes really attracted me: she seemed strong, intelligent, self-sufficient, proud. I invited her to accompany me to a linguistics conference four hundred miles away; I had the excuse of being a poor night driver, and the precedent of a student having accompanied me the year before. She was going deer-hunting with this male professor, she said; the echoes of the past were too strong, and this time I succumbed to male supremacy without a fight. Or almost without a fight. Having no notion of how to approach a womyn, I tried heterosexual courtship techniques. I brought her a rose in a bud vase and a bottle of champagne for her birthday. She recalls thinking that I was very considerate, but my disguise was so effective that neither she nor I suspected what I was really up to.

I really didn't. I hadn't the slightest idea of what I'd do in order to get her to fall in love with me, or what I'd do if she did. I wondered why it had seemed so easy years before. In the meantime, I relinquished my futile attempts to attract her, and took up drinking in earnest. I became an alcoholic. From the moment I arrived home at about five or six at night until the moment I went to bed, I drank until I was falling-down, stupified drunk—about a pint of liquor a night. Eventually, the only way I could fuck my husband was in this condition. It is a tribute to the true state of heterosexual matrimony that he didn't seem to care or even to notice.

For three years my dissertation went untouched while I loved wimmin and clung to my marriage and security because I was afraid, and because I loved my son. I could not write, I could not create or even think very well—but I was respectable, and, in the eyes of the society around me, heterosexual. But I had the labels now; I knew I was a homosexual.

I was scheduled to go on leave to write my dissertation. My department was threatening to fire me, my dissertation director was leaving for Africa in six months, George was urging me to finish my degree so he wouldn't "have to feel guilty for bringing me out here." It was December, there was snow on the ground, and Cathy (the womyn I'd been secretly in love with for over a year) and Beth and I were going out drinking. George had been told not to expect me home. He thought my little jaunt was an excellent idea; I'd never done anything like it before, even in college. I always dated him.

I had every intention of getting Cathy drunk. Of course, in order to accomplish this, I had to get roaring drunk, too, and I succeeded brilliantly at both of these. She confided in me, telling me about things that had happened in her childhood that she'd been repressing, and suddenly collapsed, weeping, as I held her in the bathroom in the sleazy bar. Quite as suddenly, she looked up and kissed me, and just as easily, I kissed her back. I remember thinking again, "I know what this *is*!" Later, when I was half-sober, I spent hours in a sleeping-bag on the floor with her, just running my hand along her back and sides, too incredibly shy and excited to conceive of doing anything else. Much later, when I sobered up completely, I became enraged; I had to convince myself that this was all *her* fault, if it hadn't been for her I'd still be acting like a straight womyn, she'd attacked me, etc. I managed to forget for a week that I'd deliberately gotten us both drunk... and that I certainly could have attributed the entire night to drunkenness.

Over the next few months, George had surgery and I sprained my ankle severely. Cathy took care of us both. She and I listened to music I hadn't heard for years, discussed teaching and literature, made love, shared time and thoughts and life. I began to get my energy back in loving her and being loved by her. I came to understand, by contrast, what it is men do to wimmin. They drain us of everything vital and prop up the empty husk, all in the name of what they call "love." Every ounce of life I'd had in me had gone towards pleasing George, and he was never satisfied. I began to hear myself apologizing to him for everything,

something I'd done for years and never noticed. As my resentment
grew, he began to notice my coldness and comment upon it. He also
began to drink, and told me that was "a bad sign." I couldn't help
wondering why he'd never noticed *my* drinking or considered it a bad
sign.

I might have knuckled under, I might have capitulated to the
arguments and blandishments and male reasoning, I might have
repudiated the one great love I'd ever felt. I might have rationalized my
growing feminist consciousness, my increasing love and respect for
wimmin and what we can give one another. I did turn over the idea of
moving away from Cathy and resuming a "normal" life in order to
preserve my family, my income, my security and my place in society. But
there was Julia.

Cathy and I had been on the screening committee that hired Julia,
a controversial action in a state like South Dakota, because Julia was (and
is) an out-front, outspoken (some might say rude) Lesbian feminist
separatist. Julia was my replacement for the six months I spent writing
my dissertation. In order to be sociable, she stopped by my house one
day while I (and Cathy) was nursing my sprain. It was obvious that she
knew that Cathy and I were lovers the moment she looked at us. But
then, she was not blinded by homophobia and was not about to assume
that marriage to a man rendered a womyn immune to her natural
Lesbian tendencies. I showed her some poetry I had written.
(Miraculously, I'd become able to write poetry again, after having been
unable to for twelve years... a period which coincided with my frantic
attempts to attain a heterosexual orientation.) Over the next six months,
Julia and I exchanged ideas about linguistic theory, and energy, and she
began to familiarize me with the exciting wimmin's culture that was
emerging—with music, journals, poetry, novels.

And when I finished my dissertation, she did the only possible
thing: she forced me to choose. George had been insufferable to her
while she visited me, doing male superiority trips, asserting his rights to
do what he wished in "his" house, flaunting his inflated salesman's salary
(which says a great deal about what is valued in patriarchal society). She
had tolerated him in order that I might finish my degree, but she would
no longer allow me to drain off her energy to give to him.

I realized that I was betraying wimmin—the two wimmin who had,
in different ways, done so much for me—exactly as Sally had betrayed
me thirteen years earlier. My situation grew less and less bearable.

Julia and I were doing research together...in her house, in Lincoln,
Nebraska. Finally, George forced me to choose. He insisted that I was
withholding my energy; he *actually* said, "You have no energy left to
give me anymore," and then I knew that the men have always known
what it is they do to wimmin. He insisted that I give up either my research

or my job; that I give up either my independent, creative thought or my economic independence... I thought long and hard, and I refused. I chose. I chose my sisters. I chose my work.

I felt, and still do feel, fortunate to have come out to come into a growing body of Lesbian art and literature, grateful to emerge into Lesbian identity as a part of Lesbian culture. I am also fortunate to have found a lover who has been a feminist for as long as she can remember, and a friend who would introduce us to feminism and Lesbianism in theory and in practice. Out of the debt that I feel to Julia for her support and her sharing, out of the love that I feel for Cathy, for Julia, and for the many wimmin I am just beginning to know, I began to feel as though I ought somehow to contribute something of myself to the wimmin who are and who will be my sisters.

The past year has not been easy. I have gotten my divorce; I have relinquished most of my belongings and, worst of all, the custody of my son. George caught Cathy and me love-making twice; at least, he saw the tell-tale signs. He has since made reference to my "lifestyle" in an effort to dissuade me from bringing Cathy along when I see "his" son, presumably to frighten me with the possible loss of my visitation rights. Despite my convictions that I was doing the right thing, pursuing the only course that would enable me to survive, it was still a wrench to resettle and start again. However, it has also been a very rewarding year, a year in which I have finally begun to get in touch with myself, my spirit, my mind, and my body. Cathy and I are living together now, and Julia and I continue to work on projects that satisfy us: papers on Lesbian humor, papers establishing Indo-European as a matriarchal culture, and, most important for both of us at this moment, this book.

When I began to think about writing my coming out story, I realized that I had not considered myself "out" until I committed myself publicly to the production of this book (which also impelled me to announce myself as a Lesbian feminist in other public contexts), and to the wimmin who have helped to write it and who will read it and who ought to read it. I now consider myself a womyn-identified-womyn and, more important than that, a womyn-committed-womyn. There are still some who do not know that I am a Lesbian feminist, and proud of it. I know that coming out, in the sense of identifying myself or labeling myself for others, is a life-long process which has just begun. I realize, with the benefit of hindsight, that I spent thirty years of my life wavering between the false security of marriage promised to me by the patriarchy and my own identity as a womyn. The path has not been smooth. Nor will the path I have now chosen be an easy one—but I have chosen. I have found myself in finding wimmin who love me, and for me that is "coming out" in the best sense of the term.